PREVENTING
VIOLENT
CONFLICTS

A Strategy for Preventive Diplomacy

MICHAEL S. LUND

UNITED STATES INSTITUTE OF PEACE PRESS

Washington, D.C.

United States Institute of Peace
1550 M Street, N.W.
Washington, D.C. 20005

First published 1996
Second printing 1997

Printed in the United States of America

The paper used in this publication meets the minimum requirements of American National Standard for Information Sciences—Permanence of Paper for Printed Library Materials, ANSI Z39.48-1984.

Library of Congress Cataloging-in-Publication Data
Lund, Michael S., 1941–
    Preventing violent conflicts: a strategy for preventive diplomacy / Michael Lund.
      p. cm.
    Includes bibliographical references.
    ISBN 1-878379-52-6 (pbk.)
    1. Diplomatic negotiations in international disputes. 2. Pacific settlement of international disputes. 3. Conflict management. I. Title.
    JX4473.L86 1996
    327.1'7—dc20

           96-4786
           CIP

Dedicated to my father,
Malcolm Gerhardt Lund,
1913–1995

CONTENTS

FOREWORD

CAN WE ACT TO PREVENT VIOLENT INTERNATIONAL CONFLICTS? AND SHOULD WE?

Hopeful declarations in the early 1990s that the Cold War's end would make possible a "new world order" have, to widespread disappointment and concern, been disproved by new and persisting patterns of international conflict. While great power confrontations have eased, international stability has in fact eroded since the 1991 collapse of the Soviet Union. Not only have long-running regional conflicts persisted, as in Korea, Angola, and Afghanistan, but substantial bloodshed and chaos have erupted in such places as Somalia, Rwanda, Chechnya, and the former Yugoslavia.

THE COSTS OF INACTION

In countries far from the fields of battle, these conflicts of the post–Cold War world are seen by many observers as posing little harm to their own nation's interests, and there is significant public resistance to taking on the costs and burdens of international peacekeeping to maintain stability. Yet, undeniably, the endurance of violent conflicts in many regions of the world has widening impacts and accumulating costs. Hundreds of thousands of lives have been lost in Bosnia and Rwanda, and millions of displaced persons are swelling the ranks of the world's refugees. The price tag for a growing number of peacekeeping and humanitarian assistance missions has increased dramatically. Scarce funds for stimulating economic development are being diverted into short-term relief operations and costly reconstruction efforts. A less tangible, but no less real, cost has been the erosion of political support for collective security operations. The impact of Somalia and Bosnia has been to discredit the idea that international cooperation can help solve common problems, and limited funding and political opposition have damaged the stature of the United Nations and other international bodies.

For the United States, while many of today's conflicts may not directly threaten our national security, they do disrupt trade and investment, gnaw at our sense of responsibility to prevent human suffering, undermine fledgling democracies, and strain our partnerships with key countries. Uncertainties about whether, and how, to respond to these conflicts have accentuated rancor in our domestic debate about America's role in world affairs and fueled efforts to reduce appropriations for a U.S. presence abroad. They have threatened the bipartisan political consensus that traditionally has supported U.S. foreign policy and world leadership in pursuit of our national interests abroad. Even though both the Bush and Clinton administrations can legitimately claim successes in peacekeeping operations in the Middle East and Gulf, and in matters of nuclear nonproliferation and fair trade, such achievements of high diplomacy have been overshadowed in the public mind by the practical difficulties and costs associated with responding to violence and turmoil in the former Yugoslavia and a number of African countries.

THE SEARCH FOR SOLUTIONS

Recognizing the costs of inaction and the political uncertainties associated with American interventions in such regional and local conflicts, the Policy Planning Staff of the Department of State in 1993 asked the United States Institute of Peace to assess prospects for a policy of "preventive diplomacy." The presumption of such an approach was that relatively modest political or economic interventions in pre-violent conflict situations would prevent disputes from getting out of control and subsequently becoming more disruptive as well as more costly and difficult to resolve.

A prime stimulus for this high level of interest in conflict prevention was the call for preventive diplomacy issued by UN Secretary-General Boutros Boutros-Ghali in his 1992 report, *Agenda for Peace*. Other world leaders echoed the secretary-general's call, including Presidents Bush and Clinton, Russian president Boris Yeltsin, and leaders from Britain, France, and Germany. "Preventive diplomacy" was discussed in the UN General Assembly and in a variety of international conferences, multilateral organizations began exploring new conflict prevention mechanisms, the U.S. and other governments launched preventive initiatives, and nongovernmental organizations initiated research and action projects on the same theme. Perhaps not since the founding of the United Nations was so much international attention focused explicitly on how to prevent *future* conflicts from developing as opposed to alleviating *current* crises.

In this context, the Institute of Peace, under the leadership of Michael Lund, assembled an eminent group of diplomats, policy analysts, and representatives of nongovernmental humanitarian assistance organizations with firsthand experience in international operations to explore whether and how the United States could most effectively conduct a strategy of early warning and preventive action, unilaterally or multilaterally. The assessments and proposals of this study group, which met on four occasions in late 1993 and early 1994, were woven by Dr. Lund into a draft report, which was widely circulated among interested policymakers, practitioners in conflict resolution and development assistance, and scholars of international affairs and foreign policy.

Largely in response to the Rwanda crisis of spring 1994, the subject of conflict prevention acquired even higher priority on the foreign policy agenda of the U.S. government. With the Lund draft report being one of the few studies available on this relatively new subject, *Preventing Violent Conflicts* was used in international seminars, media discussions, training sessions for international professionals, and university classrooms to shape exploration of the topic.

OUTLINING A PRACTICAL STRATEGY

Despite the recent currency of the concept of preventive diplomacy, the operational meaning of the term has not been easy to specify.

While some advocates contend that preventive action should come into play only in cases of imminent or even hot war, others insist that it is no less relevant to humanitarian disasters or instances of political repression. Still others believe that it should address such issues as overpopulation and poverty. Likewise, issues of *who* should act preventively, and *how* and *when* they should do so, have also been subjects of disagreement. Reflecting this diversity of opinion, the very name given to the idea varies widely, with terms such as "preventive diplomacy," "preventive action," and "crisis prevention" vying for acceptance.

As Michael Lund remarks in his introduction, "A less ambiguous, more precise definition is needed if the heightened interest in preventing conflicts is to produce any policy guidance and a meaningful assessment made of its promise and limitations." *Preventing Violent Conflicts* goes a considerable distance toward meeting such a need. This book is the most comprehensive, in-depth, and balanced analysis to date of the present practice and future potential of preventive diplomacy. It not only provides a workable definition but also develops useful lessons from concrete cases of recent preventive efforts, addresses the operational and organizational issues entailed in applying preventive diplomacy, and outlines a systematic international strategy for proactive initiatives. The book also seeks to provoke further discussion among those who may know something of the idea but have yet to wrestle with the concrete implications of an interventionist policy as a guide to applied diplomacy.

CONDITIONS FOR SUCCESSFUL PREVENTIVE ACTION

Michael Lund reminds us that the notion of preventing conflicts is not new, at least not in its essentials. History, especially that of the nineteenth and twentieth centuries, offers many examples of proposals and even practical achievements in discouraging the use of armed force as a means of dealing with international disputes. Even since the end of the Cold War, various methods and forms of preventive action have been applied with varying measures of success in dealing with previolent conflict situations in Macedonia, the Baltic states, Ukraine, the Korean peninsula, and the South China Sea. Lund argues therefore that the central issue is not so much *whether* preventive diplomacy can work, but rather *under what conditions can it be effective.*

Not all conflicts can be prevented from escalating into violence, especially when highly organized parties are bent on provoking crises or projecting armed force. But the author seeks to show that well-timed, carefully measured, and appropriately tailored political interventions by a range of third parties—including governments, multilateral bodies, and nongovernmental organizations—in many instances have defused rising tensions and enabled the disputants to resolve their disagreements peacefully. In so acting, third parties have served their own interests as well as those of the contending states or factions.

Preventing Violent Conflicts is published at a time of growing debate in the United States over the country's post–Cold War international role. Public discussion has yet to generate specific policy alternatives to either of two unsatisfactory options: indifference toward all international conflicts, or dangerous and costly interventions into already inflamed hot spots. This book explores a third alternative: U.S. support for multilateral action, using proven measures to anticipate and respond to potentially explosive conflicts, before they erupt into unmanageable violence. In an era when resources for international programs of all kinds are in sharp decline, such an approach offers a cost-effective way to protect U.S. interests abroad, save lives, sustain American international leadership, and preserve our values in a world still ridden by conflict.

Richard H. Solomon, President
United States Institute of Peace

ACKNOWLEDGMENTS

L ike a river, this book flows from many streams.

The members of the United States Institute of Peace's Study Group on Preventive Diplomacy first marked out key issues and facets of this subject and provided insightful leads. Chapters 3 and 4 draw heavily from the stimulating presentations of Luigi Einaudi, Robert Frowick, James Goodby, Brandon Grove, Mohamed Sahnoun, and William Zartman.

Samuel Lewis suggested the study group and has provided continuing inspiration and support for this work. I benefited greatly from the detailed comments and suggestions on earlier drafts provided by the following individuals: Howard Adelman, David Biggs, Lincoln Bloomfield, Douglas Bond, Kevin Clements, Hank Cohen, Jurgen Dedring, George DiAngelo, Don Gross, Fen Hampson, Bruce Jentlesen, Donald Krumm, David Little, Jack Maresca, Connie Peck, Don Rothchild, David Shorr, Louis Sohn, Astri Suhrke, and Saadia Touval. Alex George gave feedback and much more in furthering my pursuit of this subject.

Susan Allen's initial research assistance helped get the Preventive Diplomacy initiative off to a good start. Special mention should be made of Craig Kauffman, whose painstaking chronologies provided much case-study data, and whose willing help, insights, and enthusiasm were key to the project's research and outreach success. I also thank the hundreds of participants in the training sessions, seminars, delegations, conference panels, and classroom discussions of the past two years, whose curiosity and good questions about this new subject made it exciting to be an explorer. Many others in the network of staffers in U.S. and international agencies and NGOs who are becoming engaged in the subject provided much useful information and insight in many conversations.

Two people especially helped expedite the rewriting of the manuscript. Nigel Quinney's wordsmithing smoothed and brightened my initial prose, and his patience undertaking other tasks far beyond an editor's role greatly expedited the book's production. Harriet Hentges combined professionalism and warmth in her oversight of the process. I will greatly miss the interest and camaraderie of Pamela Aall, Eileen Babbitt, Ken Jensen, Joe Klaits, David Little, Lewis Rasmussen, Tim Sisk, David Smock, and Mark Soley.

Finally, I thank my wife, Judith Bailey, my daughter Ingrid, and my son Peter, who cleared the way for a summer writing marathon and cheered me on.

PREVENTING
VIOLENT
CONFLICTS

1

BETWEEN IDEA
AND POLICY

We tend to study how wars are caused and fought rather than how they are prevented. Yet, many times in history world and national leaders have sought to avoid wars by taking steps to discourage the use of armed force as an option for settling disputes. For example, the Concert of Europe formed in 1815 set rules of behavior among the great powers and helped maintain peace among them for almost forty years. Despite its reputation as a failure, the League of Nations negotiated several disputes that otherwise could have led to war. A central purpose of the United Nations, established in the wake of World War II, was to "save succeeding generations from the scourge of war" by "effective collective measures for the prevention and removal of threats to peace."[1] It was not only through the Security Council and other political mechanisms, but also through its functional agencies, development programs, and associated economic agreements that the UN system was expected to play this role. As Secretary-General Dag Hammarskjöld stated in 1960, "The responsibilities and possibilities of . . . the exercise of preventive diplomacy also apply to the economic sphere. Far less drastic in their impact as the economic activities must be, they are of decisive long-term significance for the welfare of the international community."[2]

Although the Cold War circumscribed the United Nation's ability to control conflicts, other multilateral and unilateral initiatives in the post–World War II period had conflict prevention as a goal. The Marshall Plan, for example, aimed at stemming the rise of radical antidemocratic forces in war-ravaged Europe. NATO was created as both a defense alliance and a commitment ultimately to expand the circle of peaceful democracies. The doctrine of containment and the West's deterrence strategies were designed to avoid a third world war with an expansionist Soviet Union. Subsequently, arms control treaties greatly reduced the risks of nuclear or conventional war between the West and the Soviet bloc, and global nonproliferation treaties were negotiated to control the military uses of nuclear power and other dangerous materials. What is now the European Union was inspired by the dream of ending the historic antagonisms on continental Europe, starting with joint French and German control over coal and steel—the raw materials of armaments—and then widening the issues and increasing the number of countries involved in economic cooperation. The notion that war would be less likely with intercultural understanding has animated such people-to-people programs as the U.S. Peace Corps and the Dartmouth Conference.

But while efforts at conflict prevention thus are not new, the end of the Cold War has elicited more interest than ever before in the idea of addressing conflicts at an early stage through specific preventive procedures. The heavily publicized difficulties encountered by the United Nations, the United States, and other third parties in coping with recent military and political quagmires in Somalia, Rwanda, and Bosnia have overshadowed the fact that much attention has been given to preventing such crises from occurring in the first place. In fact, in the past five years preventive diplomacy not only has enjoyed considerable vocal support but also has been practiced to a significant extent. To give a few notable examples:

• In January 1992 the first-ever meeting of heads of state and government of the UN Security Council concluded with a request from the council for "analysis and recommendations on ways of strengthening . . . the capacity of the United Nations for preventive diplomacy, for peacemaking and for peace-keeping."[3] The ensuing report by Secretary-General Boutros Boutros-Ghali, *Agenda for Peace*, devoted a chapter to preventive diplomacy and received positive endorsements from the UN General Assembly in October 1992. Since then, the UN Secretariat has been restructured to encourage ongoing monitoring of potential humanitarian crises in particular regions, and its three main units—those dealing with humanitarian affairs, political affairs, and peacekeeping—are instituting a joint procedure for earlier warnings of these crises so that preparations for relief and peacekeeping can be readied and preventive actions tried. Observing the continuing bloodshed in Bosnia and the eruption of other crises in Rwanda and elsewhere, world leaders such as British foreign minister Douglas Hurd, German foreign minister Klaus Kinkel, and President Boris Yeltsin of Russia have joined the secretary-general in calling for the development of ways to prevent these conflicts from occurring in the first place.

• Among the most vocal supporters of preventive measures have been high-level U.S. officials. Addressing the UN General Assembly in September 1992, President Bush stated that "monitoring and preventive peacekeeping, putting people on the ground before the fighting starts, may become especially critical in volatile regions."[4] The Bush administration's 1993 statement of U.S. national security policy followed with the affirmation that "the most desirable and efficient security strategy is to address the root causes of instability and to ease tensions before they result in conflict." It saw the United Nations emerging as a central instrument for the prevention and resolution of conflicts and advocated increased U.S. support for such efforts because they "contribute to the early attenuation of conflict, rather than allowing it to expand into a serious national threat."[5] U.S. troops were subsequently dispatched to Macedonia as part of a UN preventive military deployment.

• Foreign policy statements by the Clinton administration have put even more emphasis on preventing conflicts and humanitarian crises. In his 1993 confirmation hearings, Secretary of State–designate Warren Christopher declared: "We cannot careen from crisis to crisis. We must have a new diplomacy that can anticipate and prevent crises . . . rather than simply manage them."[6] Subsequently, National Security Council Director Anthony Lake affirmed that "in addition to helping solve disputes, we must also help prevent disputes . . . [and] place greater emphasis on such tools as mediation and preventive diplomacy."[7] In a mid-1994 speech on Africa, President Clinton declared that his administration would develop programs that "help African nations identify and solve problems before they erupt";

and at the summit of the leaders of the member nations of the Conference on Security and Cooperation in Europe in December 1994, he urged that "we must work to prevent future Bosnias."[8] The administration has adopted "crisis prevention" as a major theme of its foreign policy.[9]

Clinton administration policy statements have continued the Bush administration's linkage of preventive diplomacy with national security. Thus, in the 1994 *National Security Strategy of Engagement and Enlargement*, unilateral and multilateral efforts to address the roots of conflicts and reduce growing tensions are seen as a necessary complement to the reduction of U.S. military forces in the more cost-conscious post–Cold War U.S. security strategy. The administration stresses "preventive diplomacy—through such means as support for democracy, economic assistance, overseas military presence, military-to-military contacts and involvement in multilateral negotiations in the Middle East and elsewhere—in order to help resolve problems, reduce tensions, and defuse conflicts before they become crises."[10] The document also recommends retooling intelligence capabilities to enhance early warning of impending conflicts and emphasizes peace operations as an important means of containing local conflicts.

These administration pronouncements have been followed by U.S. government projects to anticipate potential crises and respond to them, sooner rather than later, in a more systematic, institutionalized way—at least with regard to certain subregions and issues. These projects include a recently completed experiment in the State Department to pinpoint on a monthly basis a potential crisis and to recommend government-wide efforts to address it. The Greater Horn of Africa Initiative in the Agency for International Development (AID) is endeavoring to mobilize ten governments in that region, along with a subregional organization and nongovernmental organizations, in a concerted effort to prevent future conflicts and improve food security. These activities appear to have been prompted in part by the Rwandan crisis in spring 1994, followed by President Clinton's tasking of AID's director to head an interagency process to create an early warning system for the U.S. government.

● Regional multilateral organizations have not merely voiced their support for preventive diplomacy and created mechanisms such as special envoys and observer missions for doing it. They have actually applied these instruments to areas of tension—such as Estonia and Guatemala—with some success. Members of what is now the Organization of Security and Cooperation in Europe (OSCE; known as the Conference on Security and Cooperation in Europe [CSCE] until January 1995) committed in their 1990 Charter of Paris for a New Europe to "seek effective ways of preventing, through political means, conflicts which may yet emerge." The OSCE has since dispatched missions to at least nine areas in Central Europe and states of the former Soviet Union, such as Estonia, Macedonia, Moldova, Hungary, and Kazakhstan, threatened by incipient or escalating crises.[11] The Organization of African Unity (OAU) in 1993 established a new mechanism that has "as a primary objective, the anticipation and prevention of conflicts,"[12] and activated it in Congo (Brazzaville) in 1993 and Rwanda in 1993–94.

Since 1990 other such preventive procedures have been formulated, adopted, or actually employed by the Organization of American States (OAS), the Economic Community of Central African States (ECCAS), and the Association of Southeast Asian Nations (ASEAN) through its Regional Forum. Some of these organizations have also created units (now active) to help build democratic institutions: examples include the OSCE's Office of Democratic Institutions and Human Rights (ODIHR; originally established as the Office of Free Elections in 1990) and the OAS's Unit for the Promotion of Democracy (established in 1990). Although, as we shall see, democratization per se does not necessarily prevent violent conflicts in the short run, it is essential to creating conditions for peace in the long run.

• Mention must also be made of nongovernmental organizations (NGOs), whose low-profile but increasing contributions to conflict prevention and management in areas of tension such as Macedonia and Burundi too often are overlooked. NGOs encompass such varied groups as development organizations; humanitarian relief and refugee organizations; conflict resolution groups engaged in "track-two" diplomacy; private foundations and organizations promoting democracy building; watchdog groups advocating human rights; and universities, institutes, and international professional associations engaged in conflict research and training. Able to play many roles that governments are unable or unwilling to perform, NGOs are becoming (explicitly or tacitly) more significant partners for governments and international organizations in preventing conflict.

To sum up: although a great deal of pessimism currently prevails regarding the efficacy of international involvement in regional conflicts, the post–Cold War era has also seen an unprecedented burst of interest and activity devoted to addressing such conflicts before they become crises.

Four trends have converged to prompt this recent interest in preventive action: the emergence of a new, more cooperative international milieu; the sobering experience of international intervention in already advanced conflicts; the prospect of more threats to international stability; and the growing economic and political constraints on governments' exercise of foreign policy. Let us review each of these trends in turn.

A NEW CLIMATE

Relations between the two global rivals of the post–World War II era have shifted from confrontation to greater cooperation on a range of major issues such as nuclear arms control and the Middle East peace process. Indeed, more than at any previous time this century, none of the major centers of power (the United States, Russia, Western Europe, China, and Japan) perceives other major powers as currently posing a serious military threat or as being fundamentally antagonistic to its interests. Total global military spending was about $1,000 billion in 1986–87 but has declined ever since, and military and arms expenditures by most of the major powers have been greatly reduced.[13] In such a world, the international agenda can be less driven by crises. This new era is by no means conflict- or crisis-proof, but we no longer teeter on the brink of strategic nuclear war or face regional conflicts that might escalate into direct confrontation between the military forces of hostile blocs. With no dominant threats making constant, often overwhelming claims on policy attention and resources, many people believe the cycle could be broken whereby current hot spots preclude efforts to address those areas of rising tension that threaten tomorrow's peace.

Whatever the international community's shortcomings regarding the breakup of Yugoslavia, the Balkan imbroglio so far has not led major powers or neighboring countries to enter the fray militarily on one side or another, as they did in 1914. In what was formerly called the "Third World," the end of global confrontation has led to forbearance by major powers from intervention in internal conflicts and removed the ideological fervor that animated regional and domestic politics in many developing countries. Former barriers to communication between governments have been removed, and more pragmatic and collaborative solutions to grievances and policy differences are more possible. All states continue to be wary of infringement on their sovereignty, but many nations have opened their doors more widely to outside assistance in coping with security, economic, and political problems.

The effects can be seen throughout the world: In sub-Saharan Africa, where the breakup of the Soviet Union cut off external financing of Marxist regimes, and where international and domestic pressures have encouraged the winding down of old civil wars and the opening up of repressive postcolonial and one-party regimes to wider political participation. In Latin America, as well as Africa, where the end of world ideological competition has undercut strident anti-American and anti-Western Marxist rhetoric about neocolonialism and neoimperialism. In the Middle East, where the Madrid peace process was made possible in part by the ending of Soviet support of militant Arab regimes and the further erosion of Arab solidarity following the Iraqi invasion of Kuwait. And in the region of the former Soviet Union itself, where Ukraine, Belarus, and Kazakhstan are dismantling the nuclear arsenals left from the Cold War.

Even more positively, the global ideological conflict has been replaced by wider and deeper agreement around certain normative principles through which states and political groups are increasingly expected to pursue solutions to their political disputes. Values such as democracy, human rights, and market-based economics, along with the peaceful resolution of differences, are now more explicitly accepted as leading principles for managing not only international but also national affairs. Although by no means embraced by all nations, democratic ideals and practices are more common than ever before; respect for human and minority rights is more widely accepted as a norm for judging nations; and the inclination to eschew the use of force to resolve conflicts is more in vogue. This sense of a value congruence was reflected in the 1992 UN Security Council summit, which showed "an unprecedented recommitment, at the highest political levels, to the Purposes and Principles of the [UN] Charter."[14] The spreading values are now written more firmly into recent statements by several regional organizations: the 1990 Paris Charter of the OSCE, the 1990 Santiago declaration of the OAS, and the 1993 Cairo summit document of the OAU. In Latin America, where all but one government has been elected democratically in the past decade, a hemisphere-wide consensus now exists around the legitimacy of democratic institutions.

The end of the Cold War has also liberalized national and international economic relations by basing them more on market forces. Such hallmarks of market economics as privatization of industries, the reduction of government subsidies, and increasing international investment and trade can help in the long run to depoliticize conflicts of interest between states and internal political factions and to transform them into peaceful forms of competition. If market-based economics leads to wider prosperity, it can absorb otherwise destabilizing social discontent. More and more nations, from both the "East" and "South," are restructuring their state-dominated economies and integrating themselves into the international economic system, as evidenced by the recent surge in membership in the General Agreement on Tariffs and Trade (GATT), the approval of the Uruguay Round of GATT, the measures taken to create the Asian Pacific Economic Community (APEC), and the creation of the new World Trade Organization. Even where highly statist regimes remain in place, such as in China and Cuba, the material benefits of market-oriented policies and economic incentives are persuading more leaders that their futures may lie with increasing their countries' economic growth and prosperity, rather than with waging nationalistic campaigns at home or abroad.

To be sure, the governments and political groups that increasingly voice these principles do not always behave according to them. And how they are interpreted and implemented, and on whose timetable, is still subject to much dispute. Some of these principles have wider support than others. Many countries in the Middle East and Asia in particular still balk at endorsing democratization and human rights, and emphasize instead the longer-established norm of noninterference in a state's domestic affairs. But it is highly significant that many more states are willing to go on record as accepting these principles as appropriate standards for judging both their treatment of one another and the policies they adopt within their respective borders.

As these values become embodied in procedures of the United Nations and other international organizations and in treaties, the international system also gains a greater institutional capacity to actualize the new spirit of political cooperation by addressing conflicts as they emerge. This capability encompasses a wide range of international mechanisms and actors, with varying roles to be played individually and collectively.

Although during the Cold War UN secretary-generals sometimes used good offices and special envoys to help mediate interstate conflicts, and occasional UN peacekeeping missions sought to maintain local settlements, the superpower rivalry largely impeded the capacity of the United Nations and its Security Council to fulfill the role envisioned by its creators. Now, however, there is wide acceptance of the use of the UN Security Council, Secretariat, and other UN and related agencies, as well as other multilateral institutions, in major and proactive roles in conflict prevention as well as management and resolution. Evidence of this shift in opinion includes not only the Security Council–backed peace enforcement action in 1990 against Iraq, but also the dramatic rise since the late 1980s in the cases brought to the International Court of Justice, the increased activity of the International Atomic Energy Authority, and the recent initiatives within the UN Secretariat to set up early warning and preventive response procedures. No vetoes have been cast by Security Council members since May 1990. More new UN peacekeeping missions were deployed in the period between 1988 and 1993 than in the years between 1948 and 1987 (an indication, it is true, not only of greater cooperation but also of the frailty of many states). And, as we have seen, several regional organizations have gone beyond espousing shared principles to operationalize specific conflict prevention and management mechanisms.

In sum, notwithstanding the sobering realities of recent years, the international community is now more inclined to see international and national conflicts and related problems as solvable and to act on them using a variety of commonly agreed-upon peaceful methods.

RECENT QUAGMIRES, GROWING FRUSTRATION

To speak of opportunities with the end of the Cold War is not to ignore the conflicts and instabilities that have characterized this new era. All too clearly, new crises and threats to national, regional, and global security have emerged. Although the end of the Cold War fostered the winding down of old conflicts in such places as Namibia, Nicaragua, Lebanon, Mozambique, and South Africa, other conflicts continued in Angola, Sri Lanka, and Sudan, and new conflicts emerged in such places as Georgia, India, Rwanda, Tajikistan, Turkey, and Yugoslavia. Overall, as one study shows, the net total of active armed conflicts around the globe remained about the same from 1989 through 1993—averaging about fifty every year.[15] Thus, the continued spread of democracy, market economics, and a readiness to resolve disputes peacefully is hardly assured. Indeed, the initial expectation of a smooth transition to a "new world order" has given way to widespread disillusionment and serious doubts that the international system can respond adequately to rising new violence and disorders.

As the international community exercised its newfound sense of cooperative endeavor by intervening through diplomacy and peace-keeping in several emerging conflicts, it encountered immense obstacles. The record of the United Nations and international community in mediating, alleviating, and terminating national and regional wars and other conflicts has not been wholly disappointing. Considerable success has been achieved in Cambodia, Namibia, El Salvador, and Haiti, for example; even the mission to Somalia accomplished its stated humanitarian objectives. Nevertheless, even where some progress eventually has been made, it has been purchased at a high price, requiring considerable international political resolve, multilateral coordination, financial resources, and military clout. Moreover, where international conflict interventions have failed, the serious limitations of traditional instruments of international peacemaking—peacekeeping, sanctions, and mediation—in coping with virile new conflicts have become painfully apparent.

In the former Yugoslavia, for example, notwithstanding the eventual achievement of an uncertain Bosnia peace agreement, most of the time UN and European Union mediators had to demonstrate heroic perseverance and patience merely to eke out occasional and short-lived cease-fires. International diplomacy unaccompanied by the credible threat of military force or powerful immediate sanctions had little effect in inducing combatants to desist from fighting. Even though UN economic sanctions have been imposed, they have not worked well or been easy to implement, at least not until a great deal of harm has been caused to innocent civilians in the targeted countries as well as to countries cooperating in the imposition of sanctions. The limits of peacekeeping as an international instrument have also been revealed. Whereas previous peacekeeping missions had traditionally been deployed only after warring parties had agreed to peace, the recent, typically undermanned missions have been thrust instead into situations of active war and frequently have found their mandates impossible to fulfill. In Bosnia, as elsewhere, peacekeeping has even been criticized for perpetuating the conflict by reducing the incentives of the parties to negotiate a settlement.[16] Some argue that even where peacekeeping forces have achieved a cessation of violence, as in Cyprus, they have rarely been able to withdraw without conflict reigniting.[17]

Understandably, then, recent experiences in places such as Angola, Liberia, Somalia (in the latter stages of the mission), and Bosnia have fostered a deep skepticism about the merits of such interventions and widespread reluctance to become involved in other political and military quagmires. The setbacks experienced in Somalia, for example, contributed to the U.S. refusal to commit ground troops to peacekeeping forces in Bosnia and ruled out U.S. direct military intervention to stop the mass killings in Rwanda. Pictures of an American soldier being dragged through the streets of Mogadishu and the dismal spectacle of UN peacekeepers being stymied by Serb forces in Bosnia fueled a major backlash—in the U.S. Congress in particular—against U.S. participation in UN peacekeeping missions, especially in places perceived to be of little vital interest to the United States. This has led to cutbacks in U.S. funding for these operations and for the United Nations in general.

The impression has grown in many U.S. circles that, as the lone superpower, the United States has been under inordinate pressure to play world policeman and clean-up crew and too often is dragged into local or regional wars and political crises by default, because other nations and the United Nations have failed to act decisively. Understandably, many people worry that the United States may overextend itself and weaken its global preparedness to deal with higher-priority international problems. A pointed response to this concern was the issuing in May 1994 of a U.S. presidential directive on peace operations, PDD-25, which spelled out tough feasibility criteria to be met before U.S. forces will be committed to UN peacekeeping missions.

Yet all these disappointments and cautions also brought to the fore a second argument on behalf of preventive diplomacy. While the frustrations and complexities of the recent interventions have led many to conclude that *all* actions in strife-torn places such as the former Yugoslavia are imprudent, an increasing number of analysts, practitioners, and statesmen are asking how the quagmires came to develop and whether they could have been avoided. A large portion of the problems of the recent interventions, they argue, is the lack of early and effective international action: the longer that crises are allowed to fester, they harder they are to resolve. As the spiral of violence and destruction intensifies, polarization deepens, the number of divisive issues increases, societal institutions crumble, the prospects for settling conflicts decrease, and the risks of conflict spreading increase. As the dangers, difficulties, and costs of intervention then mount, nations are more inclined to stay out or pull out of apparent quagmires. After several such enervating crises, donors tire of contributing aid and other resources. The whole idea of international involvement becomes ever more discredited.

This growing view that earlier intervention might avoid the lost lives, wasted treasure, and political headaches experienced with later interventions is based on more than wishful thinking and old adages about ounces of prevention. Behavioral theory in conflict resolution and a few empirical studies suggest that mediations and other third-party conflict interventions are likely to be more effective when many of the conditions of advanced conflicts are absent: the issues in dispute are fewer and less complex;[18] conflicting parties are not highly mobilized, polarized, and armed; significant bloodshed has not occurred, and thus a sense of victimization and a desire for vengeance are not intense; the parties have not begun to demonize and stereotype each other; moderate leaders still maintain control over extremist tendencies; and the parties are not so committed that compromise involves massive loss of face. This and emerging case-study research provide strong prima facie evidence that previolent conflict conditions may be fundamentally more tractable than situations of sustained violence or ongoing force.

In addition, prima facie evidence from places where preventive initiatives were taken and incipient conflict did not escalate (such as in Macedonia, Congo, and Guatemala—described in chapter 3) suggests that the prevention efforts had at least something to do with the result. A further source of support for the merits of preventive action comes from diplomats and peacekeeping officials who have been directly involved in managing recent conflicts and have judged that if more adequate countervailing actions had been taken promptly at crucial points, the conflicts might not have escalated as far as they did.[19]

From this perspective, the current debate over whether or not the United States should play an active role abroad too often misleadingly frames the issue narrowly—as a simple choice between, on the one hand, embarking on military intervention into the most difficult of conflict situations (where U.S. troops are expected to separate or defeat aggressive forces or restore civil order to ravaged societies) and, on the other hand, abstaining from international involvement of any kind. But serious consideration should be given to a third policy option: preventive involvement. In fact, the more typical choice seems to be between early involvement of various kinds or belated military intervention. Diplomatic, economic, and military policy tools, if deployed early, might head off disastrous outcomes. In the process, they could enhance rather than undermine the reputations and credibility of the United Nations, the United States, and other major players and elicit the approval of domestic constituencies concerned, rightly, that intervention be cost-effective.

In sum, the argument has increasingly been made that preventive diplomacy presents a proactive yet prudent middle course between an unrealistically overreaching interventionism and a blanket isolationism. This argument surely deserves a wider public airing.

FUTURE CONFLICTS AND THREATS

If the recent wars and their attendant humanitarian crises were merely passing miseries unlikely to be widely repeated, then a general stance of noninvolvement toward post–Cold War conflicts—though extremely unfortunate for their victims—might at least be defensible in terms of the national interests of those nations not directly party to the conflicts. However, a third factor that has spurred the recent rise in interest in preventing conflicts before they escalate is the likelihood that in the years ahead crises and threats will grow more numerous, not less, and will pose significant threats to international peace and security and to the interests of many nations.

The end of the Cold War may have removed a singular and obvious threat to the security of the major powers and, indeed, the globe—that of nuclear holocaust—but in its place have arisen a variety of other potential threats and crises. In an effort to characterize the basic nature of the post–Cold War world, some analysts contend that one or another single trend or factor—be it, for example, widespread "chaos" caused by the collapse of many nation-states, or a global "clash of civilizations"—will decisively shape the nature of future conflict throughout the world. However, the threats and crises in the years ahead seem much more likely to be diverse in source, nature, and scale. A formidable list of the main forms of future conflicts and associated humanitarian disasters could plausibly comprise the following: expansionist regimes, some with nuclear weapons, seeking regional dominance through intimidation; nuclear or conventional wars between states over territory and natural resources; the collapse of national economies and states; efforts to overthrow newly established constitutional democracies; secessionist conflicts over the domain of states; civil wars driven by competing ideologies (e.g., secularism vs. Islamism); and conflicts involving indigenous, ethnic, or regional minorities and likely to feature gross human rights violations, "ethnic cleansing," or genocide. Only the first two on this list might pose imminent threats to the international security of large areas. Most of the rest, if infrequent, would be relatively slow to develop, relatively small in scale, and highly dispersed. In their cumulative effect, however, they would seriously erode the hard-won achievement of basic international order. All these threats, then, if left unattended, have the potential to deepen and widen until they directly impinge on the interests of many nations. In short, acting on the new opportunities for conflict prevention may be not a luxury but a necessity.

While the nature and intensity of tensions and conflicts vary from region to region, no area is free of these potential threats to peace and security: Not Europe, where further tensions in the Balkan region, Central Europe, and the new states carved out of the former Soviet Union could erupt. Not Asia, and particularly not its Northeast (Korean peninsula) and South (India-Pakistan) subregions, where regional security and the nuclear nonproliferation regime are being seriously tested. Indeed—notwithstanding the positive impact of economic ties fostered by ASEAN, for example—with many East Asian regimes increasing their military spending and arms imports while ignoring international criticism of their treatment of political opposition and minority groups, Asia poses many of the possible exceptions to the notion that values like democracy, human rights, and peaceful settlement of disputes are taking hold worldwide. Not the highly armed Middle East, where, even with the historic breakthroughs of the early 1990s, the road to enduring regional peace remains long and uncertain. Not Africa, where the near-starvation of the Somali people, the horrible massacres in Rwanda, and debilitating confrontations over issues of popular rule such as in Zaire and Nigeria could be repeated in other divided nations. Not Latin America and the Caribbean, where governance issues remain unresolved and Haiti demonstrates the trials of democratization.

Some possible future threats are rooted in conditions that emerged during, or even before, the Cold War but were obscured or repressed by the ideological or geostrategic dictates of superpower rivalry. For example, forces arising within many Arab countries since the 1970s—modernization, rising popular participation in politics, economic decline due to falling oil prices, and the effects of the Gulf War—are increasing the insecurities of long-established regimes. In countries such as Egypt, economic discontent and resentment at Western influence are helping to fuel the rise of militant Islamic movements, which threaten both the long-term prospects for democratization and inter-Arab regional stability.

Rapid population growth, environmental degradation, and competition for scarce natural resources also continue to encourage and sustain conflict. Disputes over the Middle East's scarce water could worsen, and Africa's chronic poverty, low agricultural productivity, and environmental degradation persist as the breeding grounds for violence. The most serious problems of proliferating nuclear arms and chemical and biological weapons may have abated somewhat in the past decade in places such as South Africa, Argentina, Brazil, Ukraine, and even Iraq and North Korea. Nevertheless, more small conflicts could increase the demand for such weapons, the supply of which is facilitated by wider access to the know-how and materiel to develop and launch them. In addition, the proliferation of conventional and small arms continues to fuel local wars and regional tensions, thus keeping alive the use of intimidation and force as the options of choice in many national and interstate disputes.

But other emerging conflicts and tensions can be called post–Cold War in their impetus, because they have arisen out of relatively new forces unleashed with the end of the Cold War. The demise of the largely bipolar balance of global power and the superpower ideological rivalry in developing regions has eroded or eliminated the discipline, cohesion, and predictability that characterized not only bloc politics but also the national political life of many small nations. However confrontational it was at the level of international relations, the Cold War served to create or bolster systems that ordered domestic politics and restrained social discontent: rigidly disciplined and militarized societies and economies on the communist side and, on the other side, often highly autocratic Third World regimes propped up by an array of military and economic supports from the West. But with the Gorbachev reforms of the late 1980s and the removal of the worldwide Soviet threat in the early 1990s, both these forms of maintaining domestic social order were dismantled. Yet, viable, legitimate governmental and private institutions based on the new rules of democracy and market economics have been slow to replace the old. Meanwhile, the tasks of adjusting to the new pressures for more open politics and economics have placed tremendous strains on many nations and their governments, strains that have sometimes led to significant violence.

The areas most immediately vulnerable to upheaval seem to be those with the least historical experience in handling the complexities of multiethnic identities, pluralistic politics, market economics, and so forth. In the prime cases of the former Soviet Union and Yugoslavia, for example, the unchecked and bloody play of ethnic and religious hatreds, separatist ambitions, and political and economic turmoil is to some degree the consequence of the nationalities policies of the Soviet era. The breakup of the Soviet Eurasian empire, while granting freedom to millions from totalitarianism, has yet to be replaced everywhere by a viable alternative framework for maintaining political order and security. In Croatia, Bosnia, Belarus, Georgia, Nagorno-Karabakh, and Tajikistan, for instance, the vacuum too often has been filled by demagogic nationalism, devastating separatist or civil wars, and local autocrats. More pluralistic but fragile newly independent states such as Ukraine and Macedonia could be threatened by similar turmoil. Such tensions still confront the biggest country in the world, Russia. Several disputes over the autonomy of particular regions within the Russian Federation remain unresolved, and quarrels have erupted between Russia and nearby new states over the status of ethnic Russians in those areas. In Moscow, xenophobic rhetoric has been heard from extreme nationalists who vie with more moderate and reformist parties for the support of the Russian electorate. As this entire region seeks to compete in the capitalist marketplace, the pressures are strong to maintain arms production as a source of jobs and hard currency, such as in Eastern Europe, or to tolerate trade in illicit drugs as an income source for budding entrepreneurs, such as in Central Asia.

No less familiar than the problems of the former Soviet Union are the unemployment, destitution, inflation, rapid urbanization, rising populations, and other potentially volatile social conditions in Africa that are sometimes exacerbated by the removal of state controls and subsidies, devaluation of currencies, and privatization of state enterprises. In Latin America, as elsewhere, raised expectations of material progress combined with impatience over new, often clumsy democratic institutions has invited executive or military usurpations of constitutional authority in the name of progress.

Simultaneously, other disintegrating forces—among them, increases in the numbers of refugees and economically motivated immigrants, the growth of transnational corporations and of multilateral economic institutions, and the wider reach of communications technologies—have eroded national borders and generated new expectations, insecurities, and social tensions that many existing political structures and their leaderships have yet to accommodate. In fact, in some countries, such as Sierra Leone, and in large portions of others, such as Pakistan, the combination of collapsed Cold War supports and new transnational forces has almost destroyed the effective exercise of government authority. Governance has been effectively ceded to a variety of warlords, drug lords, mafioso, and criminal syndicates, who rule relatively unfettered over quasi-private domains that cut across recognized state borders. The destabilizing societal consequences of these new trends are felt not only in relatively impoverished parts of the world that may face increasing marginalization (as reflected, for example, in the Chiapas peasant rebellion and the industrial violence in Mexico since the adoption of NAFTA). They are also manifested in some of the wealthiest countries. Witness not only the drug trafficking in the West but also how the absorption of large numbers of refugees from Eastern Europe and the economic burdens of reunification helped to fuel the rise in xenophobic neofascism in Germany, and how the fear of further immigration from North Africa swelled the ranks of voters for the National Front Party in France. The loss of jobs to foreign countries and other economic insecurities have led in the United States to the emergence of local militia groups, the members of which see international conspiracies at work—a belief that for some justifies violence directed at government officials and other symbols of the global forces seen to be usurping control of the militia members' lives.

Even where one-party, communist, military, and otherwise authoritarian regimes hold on, such as in the Middle East, Cuba, and in

China, Vietnam, and Burma and other regimes in Southeast and East Asia, the spread of the democratic spirit and the empowerment of minorities could well inspire further popular protests against these entrenched regimes. If followed by crackdowns by unyielding and brittle regimes, the pursuit of popular democracy and human rights could plunge these countries into destructive intrastate conflicts. Within rapidly developing Asian states, such as Indonesia and Thailand, increased democratization might eventually unsettle the political bargain whereby economic prosperity has substituted for more open, genuinely multiparty, and pluralistic politics.

These wide-ranging examples suggest that, paradoxically, the same liberalizing post–Cold War values and structural changes that offer new opportunities and methods for consensus, cooperation, and peace are also generating, at least in the short run, widespread societal and interstate tensions that can result in violence, repression, or the total breakdown of societies and states. Which course will be followed seems to depend greatly on whether the contention over political control that arises receives effective political management and is channeled into procedures and institutions able to resolve disputes at an early stage.

If the old and new instabilities are allowed to grow into violent conflicts, they may not simply block but actually reverse the limited progress made in many regions of the post–Cold War world toward international cooperation, democracy, open economies, trade and investment, human rights, material improvement, and increased interstate security. Still, should those people living in the relatively wealthy and peaceful West be greatly concerned if such progress is indeed thwarted? After all, except where and when their vital national interests may become immediately imperiled, what reason do they have to take proactive measures abroad?

In fact, the United States and other major Western powers have several compelling reasons to be concerned with what happens elsewhere in the world. Leaving aside the question of whether there exists any moral obligation to help one's fellow human beings, a variety of pragmatic considerations add up to a powerful argument for rejecting the superficial appeal of noninvolvement.

In the first place, noninvolvement seems to be something that the West, and the United States in particular, is unable to abide by. U.S.

public opinion may react against the frustrations and costs of interventions in Somalia and Bosnia by supporting calls for no further involvement in distant trouble spots. But that same public opinion, fueled by graphic reports of atrocities in Rwanda or Somalia or Sarajevo, can be equally insistent that its government act to help reduce the suffering portrayed in the media. In short, despite the debate, the United States seems prone to get involved eventually in most emerging crises.

In the second place, the costs of nonintervention are by no means insignificant. In certain recent conflicts, such as Chechnya, Chiapas, and the Turkish-Kurdish struggle, direct U.S. military involvement was ruled out because established governments party to those conflicts are in some fashion allies or partners of the United States. Indeed, these conflicts were regarded at first as being of minor importance and the other nation's affair. Nevertheless, nasty little wars subsequently exacted extremely high indirect financial and political costs on U.S. interests: bilateral relations with the responsible governments were strained and alliances weakened; those governments' scarce budgetary resources that otherwise could have gone into needed development and economic reform (for which stretched donor assistance dollars already had been expended) were siphoned off to military purposes; the stature of national political leaders, such as Russian president Yeltsin, with whom the U.S. wishes to work on other important issues, was diminished; and politically exposed U.S. leaders had to strain to justify continued close relations and further assistance.

Even in war-torn countries with which the United States has hostile relations, local conflicts affect U.S. interests, largely in terms of opportunity costs. In Sudan, for example, U.S. direct involvement may be politically, militarily, or logistically infeasible, difficult, or ineffective. The political costs of allowing such wars to go on is not significant, at least not yet. Nevertheless, these conflicts have had significant impacts in other ways that, though largely hidden, are substantial, such as in foregone trade and business opportunities for the United States. For instance, between 1982, when the civil war in Sudan began to escalate, and 1992, U.S. annual exports to that country fell from $192 million to $51.5 million. During the same period in Sudan's less troubled neighbors Kenya and Uganda, U.S. exports doubled.[20]

Nor can one neglect the financial costs of humanitarian aid and eventual reconstruction of war-torn societies when the United States does get involved, but in a belated and thus only remedial fashion. The United States pays these costs through bilateral aid or through the United Nations or international financial institutions. For example, the United States paid $97.6 million in humanitarian relief for Sudan in 1993 alone.[21] In Mozambique, the costs since 1992 of refugee repatriation, military demobilization, infrastructure repair, government budget support, and new elections—excluding the UNOMOZ peacekeeping observers—have been between $1 and $2 billion.[22] Peacekeeping, too, is an expensive business. The annual price tag for the eighteen UN missions around the world in 1993 was expected to be $3.6 billion;[23] the United States pays about 30 percent of the costs of peacekeeping. Overall, the amount the United States has paid in recent years simply to repair a few war-ravaged sub-Saharan countries through peacekeeping, relief aid, and reconstruction has far exceeded the amounts it would otherwise likely have contributed to peacetime development assistance for all the sub-Saharan countries.

A third reason why abjuring involvement is self-defeating is that it brings loss of status and influence. For how long will the United States want to remain on the sidelines when other major powers (such as Russia and China) or aspiring powers (such as India, Indonesia, and Brazil) increasingly wield preponderant influence in managing conflicts in their regions on their own terms? One of the strongest incentives in the coming years for the United States to take a major role in conflict prevention and management—at least in those areas and instances where it can make a difference—may simply be that it will not want to be left out when its peers or rivals acquire ever more influence.

Further arguments could be cited against the United States acting only when its vital interests are perceived to be endangered. For example, a basic problem with drawing a priori distinctions between "major" threats to U.S. "vital" interests, such as those posed by nuclear states, and potential conflicts that are presumed to be of lesser importance, is that you cannot always tell ahead of time how great their impacts and costs will be.

The rationale for looking more seriously at more vigorous Western participation in preventive action seems clear enough: Given that

Western noninvolvement is in many instances chimerical; that few conflicts fail to affect the interests of the West in some significant fashion; and that belated or nominal involvement is usually ineffective, costly, and frustrating; it therefore follows that the political and economic advantages of early action wherever feasible to prevent disputes from spiraling into violent conflict outweigh the advantages of noninvolvement, especially if modest preventive actions are found to go a long way.

NEW CONSTRAINTS

A fourth impetus behind the new interest in conflict prevention is the growing realization that the ability of hitherto powerful individual states to influence world events through their traditional foreign policy tools is diminishing. In theory, the more cooperative atmosphere should make states more willing to act to address common problems, but in practice states are severely constrained from doing so because of their limited financial, material, military, and political resources. If the new threats are to be met, therefore, they must be dealt with through methods that stretch available resources as far as possible. Preventive diplomacy appears to offer just such a cost-effective approach.

During the Cold War the leaders of the rival blocs were able to exert very substantial political influence over the members of their respective blocs. With the end of Cold War confrontation, that leverage has either disappeared entirely—as in the case of the now defunct Soviet Union—or has been significantly reduced. Although the United States possesses more diplomatic, political, military, and economic power than any other nation, its ability and that of its allies to influence affairs abroad through extended deterrence, regional alliances, sanctions, and a host of other policies formerly relied on has been reduced by defense cutbacks, domestic policy concerns, and the emergence of more autonomous regional political and economic groupings.

Defense spending and military forces are being drastically reduced by the United States and European powers such as Great Britain and France, which historically have been involved in regional operations around the world. Between 1990 and 1994, the U.S. defense budget, adjusted for inflation, was reduced by 24 percent. By 1997, it is likely to have fallen by 40 percent from the 1990 figure.[24] The cumulative decline in spending over the past ten years was 35 percent. In 1987, defense and related tasks accounted for 6.5 percent of U.S. gross domestic product, but by the end of 1995 they are estimated to take no more than 4.1 percent, a decline of 27 percent. U.S. conventional forces have been cut by one-third since 1990.[25] U.S. allies have made cuts of a similar, though somewhat less dramatic, magnitude. Little of this reduction in the strength of Western allied forces can be countered by Japan and Germany until those countries comprehensively overhaul post–World War II doctrines and attitudes that limit foreign involvement and the size of their militaries. The use of first-strike nuclear weapons by the West to compensate for conventional force reductions may be virtually ruled out politically and morally, except perhaps against threats of truly global proportions.

Economic tools are similarly weakened. With many more developing economies becoming export oriented and globally competitive, the Western share of the world's total production of goods and services is likely to decline. Consequently, the economic instruments available to Western nations for pursuing foreign as well as domestic goals have less impact. The enforcement of economic sanctions and the bestowal of Most Favored Nation status both carry less weight than once they did, for example, now that nations with increasingly diversified economies can buy or sell goods in so many other markets. And with global economic competition intensifying, Western countries are less inclined to hurt their own domestic industries through such strategies.

Another constraint on international involvement is largely domestic: economic recessions, budget deficits, politically weak coalitions and governments, and the preoccupation of U.S. and other electorates with their own nations' problems. Slower economic growth rates, rising taxes, unemployment, immigration, crime, and other domestic problems have garnered public attention, and the portion of national budgets that relatively well-off democracies are investing in overseas foreign aid and security assistance is diminishing. In the United States, for example, the cutbacks in foreign assistance begun by the Bush administration were continued by the Clinton administration, which put its highest priority on its domestic policy agenda. The November 1994 congressional elections that gave the Republican Party control of both houses for the first time in decades resulted in drastic proposals to limit the infrastructure and tools of U.S. foreign policy. If implemented, these proposals would reduce appropriations for foreign assistance and other nonmilitary international programs that are widely extended across the globe and reduce the budgets of the aid, arms control, and information agencies and consolidate them within the State Department. At the same time, the development of high-tech defense systems to guard against nuclear missile attack would receive increased funding.

At first glance, these domestic constraints on traditional foreign policies might seem only to make preventive diplomacy more difficult. Perhaps they will. But assuming that utter indifference toward growing global and regional threats is an unrealistic policy option, these constraints actually provide a further impetus to explore a preventive strategy, especially if carried out multilaterally by pooling resources. As we have seen, many of the usual policies for managing escalated conflicts abroad—such as military assistance, peacekeeping missions, military intervention, and development and reconstruction aid—are increasingly expensive, dangerous to implement, and/or politically unpopular. Conflict prevention policies would be much less demanding on each participating country's material resources and political energies. Peacekeeping may be more cost-effective than fighting wars, but preventing wars and thus the need for peacekeeping is more cost-effective still, and less risky.

FURTHER STEPS

In sum, four post–Cold War trends suggest that deliberate efforts to avert conflicts are 1) *more widely supported and frequently made* because of a generally more propitious international climate; 2) *more cost-effective* than recent belated mediations and interventions have shown themselves to be; 3) *more advisable*, given the possibility of numerous future threats to peace and stability; and 4) *more politically attractive*, in light of global and domestic constraints on military and economic policies and the lack of popular support for military action in distant countries.

However, though preventive diplomacy is becoming more widely used and discussed—at least within many policymaking and academic circles, though clearly not yet among the public at large—only limited progress has been made in translating this emerging approach into workable operating strategies and ongoing practice. As we have seen, post–Cold War preventive diplomacy clearly has progressed beyond academic discussion and is now being undertaken in several institutional settings. Even so, standard operating procedures for early warning and preventive response have yet to be widely instituted and regularly applied by the United Nations, the U.S. government, and regional organizations, and preventive diplomacy has yet to be elevated to the status of accepted official governmental or international policy.

In the U.S. government, for example, despite the fact that virtually the entire top echelon of U.S. policy officials subscribes to the preventive idea, the record of progress toward the institutionalization of methodical preventive strategies is uneven. Individual agencies and units look at particular regions and types of potential crises. To be crisis preventers, most U.S. officials and policymakers have to depart from established job descriptions, policy agendas, and bureaucratic routines. Still absent are authorized government-wide mechanisms for regularly monitoring a wide range of incipient post–Cold War conflicts using systematic indicators; contingency procedures that require explicit assessments of national and subregional political disputes; and a clear sense of what is at stake, what objectives are feasible to pursue, and which policies might best accomplish those objectives.

In short, the state of the art of preventive diplomacy is somewhat more than an idea but somewhat less than a policy strategy. Thus the question today is not whether preventive diplomacy will come into being; it already operates in various ways in many settings. The issue is whether it will be extended, and if so where and in what forms.

LACK OF WILL OR LACK OF A WAY?

Why are proactive procedures toward potential conflicts still generally the exception in the U.S. government, the United Nations, and elsewhere, rather than the norm? A widely invoked explanation is the lack of "political will" to get involved early. This does have an impact. Lack of will exists not only because threats are neither imminent nor pressing, and are sometimes so remote in time as to seem hypothetical. It also exists because potential post–Cold War threats vary greatly in terms of the level of danger and risk they pose to individual countries and regions. The world lacks a strong sense of common dangers. And even for major powers such as the United States, which have a great deal at stake economically, politically, and financially in conflicts around the world, the conflicts typical of recent years do not directly threaten those powers' survival, but rather constitute more gradually corrosive factors that eat away at national interests without being detected.

Nevertheless, the explanation of lack of political will is ultimately too diffuse to pin down the specific reasons why more is not being done to prepare for the emerging threats. It also cannot explain why the United States and other third parties sometimes *do* get involved in disputes preventively, such as through the OSCE and OAS, even though there has not always been an immediate, compelling threat to national or organizational interests.

Thus, one has to look for more specific reasons. An obvious one is the press of daily business on policymakers and administrators to attend to current crises and ongoing program operations. Certain conventional mind-sets also obstruct the pursuit of preventive diplomatic action—for example, misplaced fears of infringing on national sovereignty (most such diplomacy is, in fact, voluntary on the object nation's part). Because of the frequent but undifferentiated usage of the term "intervention," preventive efforts and their requirements are often confused with more intensive, risky, and costly interventions, such as recent peacekeeping missions, even though these typically come into play at later, more dangerous stages of conflicts.

But this book assumes that a fundamental reason for the lack of progress is not so much the lack of will or of time as it is the lack of a way—namely, the lack of understanding and knowledge, particularly at the high and middle policymaking levels of the U.S. government and other key entities, of the range of potential risks posed by post–Cold War trends and of their real costs, of the various policy methods and entities that can in fact be used to reduce them, of the particular strategies that appear to work the best, and of how to implement those strategies.

Policymakers may lack sufficient confidence to sanction further steps toward more regular preventive procedures in large part because they know little about the initial efforts already under way within their own governments and within international organizations. In view of the relative obscurity of OSCE local missions and NGO track-two work, for instance, many policy-level U.S. officials are understandably unaware that preventive diplomacy has been practiced in a number of places recently and that prima facie evidence suggests it has sometimes worked. Policymakers are also unsure about how to institute preventive diplomacy. Few if any concrete proposals have been presented to U.S. policymakers that lay out in specific, practical terms how processes of preventive diplomacy or crisis prevention might work regularly and widely within or across various agencies of the U.S. government or other entities, especially how such processes would modify existing program objectives, regulations, staffing, budgets, and so on. In short, mid- and high-level policymakers have not considered adopting concrete preventive strategies because nobody has detailed how they might do so.

Developing such detailed plans for undertaking preventive diplomacy would be aided by having better answers to a number of difficult conceptual and empirical questions, among them: In today's world, what specific kinds of interstate and internal conflicts and crises and related man-made problems are most likely to occur in different regions in the coming years, what are their likely costs and implications for U.S. and other nations' global interests, and which of them can and should one try to prevent? What exactly is preventive diplomacy? How do preventive policies work? What policies, programs, and methods are most effective in preventing conflicts? At what points in an incipient conflict, for instance, is it most promising for third parties to get involved? What is the relationship between the negative goal of avoiding violent conflicts and such positive goals as promoting democracy, economic growth and development, and human rights? Is preventive diplomacy the responsibility of the United States, the United Nations, regional organizations, or individual states? What is the role, if any, of other actors? How can one secure more political and bureaucratic support for devoting resources to incipient problems and not just the pressing crises? In short, who should warn whom about what problems, and who should do what in response?

The purpose of this study is to make headway in answering some of these questions and to suggest how the United States might move closer toward operating a feasible international strategy of preventive diplomacy. Thus:

- Chapter 2 develops a working definition of preventive diplomacy by distinguishing it from other forms of diplomacy and foreign policy and differentiating among its subtypes. It answers the question: *What is preventive diplomacy and how does it differ from other forms of conflict intervention and international policy?*

- Chapter 3 looks at recent efforts in preventive diplomacy and draws together these experiences and other cases to address the question: *What methods and entities seem to work when applied "on the ground" to preventing specific conflicts, and why?*

- Chapter 4 explores the main policy and implementation tasks and issues that are being faced by preventive diplomacy initiatives and offers preliminary recommendations for overcoming these problems. It tackles the question: *What operational challenges must be overcome in undertaking effective preventive diplomacy more regularly, and how might existing policies and operations of the U.S. government and other national and international organizations be affected?*

- On the basis of the preceding analysis, chapter 5 suggests how a more comprehensive, ongoing multilateral strategy or system for post–Cold War preventive diplomacy led by the United States and other nations might be organized and how it could gain political backing. It responds to the question: *What would a more systematic, deliberate multilateral strategy of preventive diplomacy look like?*

2

CONCEPT, TOOLS, AND TARGETS

The term *preventive diplomacy* suggests different things to different people; as yet, it has no agreed-upon meaning among practitioners and scholars. To some, it conjures up efforts by a high-level official such as a UN secretary-general or U.S. secretary of state to contain an erupting international crisis or stop a war. To others, it suggests unofficial, track-two diplomacy—informal contacts and dialogue among disputing parties, often conducted behind the scenes by NGOs. Some consider the word *diplomacy* to refer only to peaceful methods of discussion, such as negotiation and bargaining, but others do not exclude use of armed force or other forms of coercion as a method for preventive diplomacy.

Because preventive diplomacy does not specify what is to be prevented, some assume it deals primarily or solely with wars—that is, open, armed hostilities by two or more antagonists. But others believe it also should address one-sided conflicts such as genocide, less overt coercion such as the repression of human rights and "ethnic cleansing," and humanitarian disasters such as a massive exodus of refugees. Some associate the term with the amelioration of basic conditions that can breed violence, such as poverty, overpopulation, and ignorance. Indeed, as preventive diplomacy has come into vogue recently, it is being waved like a banner over almost any attempt to remedy one or another post–Cold War problem.

To confuse matters further, policy discourse has recently embraced a host of similar terms: *preventive action, preventive engagement, preventive deployment, conflict prevention,* and *crisis prevention.* Often, these terms are used very loosely and even interchangeably with other current phrases such as *peacemaking, conflict management, conflict resolution, democracy building,* and *peacekeeping.* Not surprisingly, the welter of new slogans now associated with preventive diplomacy has sparked skepticism that there is little substance behind them.[1]

The most expansive definition of preventive diplomacy would encompass everything that modern states do to conduct their relations, including consular relations, trade, commerce, scientific and cultural exchange, travel, and so on, because all these policies and activities could have some effect on the long-term prospects for peace, conflict, and related issues. The same reasoning would include a wide range of a state's domestic programs. But equating preventive diplomacy with large portions of international relations and national policy is to dismiss the concept, for a definition that embraces everything means nothing.

Clearly, a less ambiguous, more precise definition is needed if the heightened interest in preventing conflict is to produce any policy guidance and a meaningful assessment is to be made of its promise and limitations. A more rigorous definition should pinpoint the essence of the concept and distinguish it from other forms of diplomacy, foreign policy, and conflict intervention. It should be generic and flexible enough to be applicable to different contexts and yet specific enough to be operationalized. It should also indicate *when* during the emergence of a situation preventive action is taken; *who* principally takes such action; *how* they pursue it, in terms of instruments and techniques; and *what* problems it targets.

ORIGINS AND EVOLUTION

In developing a workable concept of preventive diplomacy appropriate to the post–Cold War era, it is instructive to consider notable previous efforts at explicit definition. Although the basic idea of preventing conflicts is not of course new, the term *preventive diplomacy* was only first coined by Secretary-General Dag Hammarskjöld in 1960.[2] Reflecting the Cold War context in which he worked, Hammarskjöld attached this label to UN efforts undertaken in cases of localized disputes and wars that might provoke wider confrontations between the two superpowers. Among other instances, he mentioned the Suez crisis of 1956; the Lebanon crisis of 1958; minor disputes around that time, such as that between Thailand and Cambodia; and the Congo UN peacekeeping mission begun the year he wrote. Hammarskjöld believed these relatively low-level conflicts created a political vacuum into which East-West rivalries could intrude, thus risking World War III. He urged more support and recognition of the important role that the United Nations was playing in sealing these conflicts off from the larger global maelstrom.

Hammarskjöld's definition is important not only as historical precedent but also for its ingredients. According to Hammarskjöld, the United Nations through its secretary-generals or their representatives and the Security Council was the agent of preventive diplomacy, and the mediation, good offices, fact-finding missions, earmarked economic assistance, and peacekeeping operations it undertook were the instruments. Thus, from the first, preventive diplomacy embraced not just those activities of peaceful discussion, such as negotiations, that are traditionally carried out by the emissaries of governments or multilateral organizations. Preventive diplomacy also included the use of military forces and other tools such as peacekeeping. For Hammarskjöld, whether the level of violence of a conflict was low or high, or even whether a dispute was intrastate or interstate in nature, did not determine its suitability as a target of preventive diplomacy. The warrant for triggering preventive action was whether a situation posed a threat of a wider East-West crisis or war.

Because Hammarskjöld's notion of preventive diplomacy operated by definition at the margins of global power politics, it received relatively little attention as a distinct concept, even though several places where it was used were in the headlines. The idea of preventive diplomacy has received much more explicit attention since the Cold War ended, however, in part because of the way in which Secretary-General Boutros Boutros-Ghali broadened and publicized it in his widely circulated report *Agenda for Peace*.[3] Boutros-Ghali envisioned preventive diplomacy serving as one of four key elements in a UN-led effort, supported by the major powers, to address both long-standing and newly arising interstate, civil, and ethnic wars.

In the report, Boutros-Ghali describes preventive diplomacy as "action to prevent disputes from arising between parties, to prevent existing disputes from escalating into conflicts and to limit the spread of the latter when they occur."[4] Here, *disputes* implies conflicts that have not become violent, whereas *conflicts* implies violence. Conceptually, then, preventive diplomacy means action to address almost any instance of potential or actual violence, whether or not it is interstate or intercommunal, and whether or not it might pull major powers or other countries into a larger war. Boutros-Ghali includes regional organizations as well as the United Nations as possible agents of preventive diplomacy, and the instruments he lists include early warning, fact-finding missions, confidence-building measures, demilitarized zones, and preventive deployment of peacekeeping forces.

Whereas Hammarskjöld's concept sought to strengthen the Cold War role of the UN secretary-general and Security Council and the tools at their disposal, Boutros-Ghali's more ambitious approach is rooted not in particular agents, tools of prevention, or kinds of conflicts addressed, but in the notion of responding to violent conflicts as they emerge and spread. In fact, he sees preventive diplomacy acting to limit such conflicts at not one, but several points—or "thresholds"—in their development: very early on, when preventive diplomacy focuses on the basic sources of disputes; later, when it tries to prevent disputes from becoming violent; and much later, when it seeks to contain the expansion of escalated violence.

GETTING TO THE ESSENCE

Defining preventive diplomacy to include all these possible entry points into a conflict appeals to many constituencies and some conflict analysts, for the definition embraces an extremely broad range of forms of intervention. But from an analytical point of view, associating preventive diplomacy with interventions throughout virtually the entire life span of a conflict—from the causes of a dispute through many possible levels of escalated, sustained violence— makes the concept too broad to be useful and has serious pitfalls.

If preventive diplomacy is conceived as alleviating those fundamental conditions that fuel disputes between governments or groups, for example, it would tackle such pervasive phenomena as resource maldistribution, the drive for power, poverty, social inequality, and ethnic and cultural identities. This would entail policies as vast and varied as income redistribution, psychotherapy, family planning, economic development, and progressive education. Indeed, current officials of the U.S. government argue in support of programs that improve economies abroad, democratize governments, tackle overpopulation and environmental degradation, and establish the rule of law, on the grounds that they function as crisis prevention (*crisis prevention* being the preferred term to *preventive diplomacy*).[5] Not surprisingly, some governments and spokespersons from the developing world tend to think of preventive diplomacy as primarily economic development.[6]

There are several reasons to question the wisdom of equating preventive diplomacy with the job of correcting often pervasive and deeply rooted social ills. To begin with, such an equation would risk dispersing the energies of preventive diplomacy and diminish its chances of securing substantial political support. In the second place, although basic socioeconomic, political, or psychological conditions may lay the groundwork for violence, they do not necessarily produce it. A number of recent wars have raged in areas that are far from being among the world's most impoverished. Conversely, some poor countries, such as Rwanda, have received high per capita amounts of economic aid and yet still witnessed terrible violence. Defining preventive diplomacy as the amelioration of poverty might indeed increase the material welfare of the areas targeted for preventive action, and this might in turn reduce their chances of violence in the relatively remote future. But the causal links are uncertain. In the meantime, such a broad focus for preventive diplomacy risks overlooking the more proximate behavioral sources of violent conflicts, which, in rich as well as poor areas, are political in nature.

In the third place, many societal conditions giving rise to disputes should not necessarily be eliminated from human experience, even if they could be. The clash of interests arising from economic competition, cultural and religious diversity, and nationalist sentiments, for example, is not necessarily undesirable and is often constructive. What can be prevented and what should be prevented are not the underlying sources of conflict that arise naturally but rather the pursuit of divergent interests through armed force or some other form of coercion. Fourth, policies aimed at transforming basic social and political conditions can themselves foster violent conflicts rather than prevent them. Rapid democratization or socioeconomic development, for example, can destabilize societies and increase the chances of violence. Thus, while preventive diplomacy may share the aims and instruments of economic development, democratization, educational reform, and human rights, these causes per se are not preventive diplomacy.

The definition in *Agenda for Peace* also encompasses actions to limit the spread of violent conflicts, even after they have escalated. Preventive diplomacy might thus include measures such as hot lines, ultimatums that threaten armed force at the height of a tense international crisis, deployments of armed forces in the early days of an active war, and even the negotiation of cease-fires and the subsequent deployment of peacekeeping forces. Sometimes called "late" preventive diplomacy,[7] this approach is reminiscent of Hammarskjöld's notion of preventive diplomacy as containment of regional crises. It seems to be accepted by at least some within the current U.S. administration: U.S. policy in Bosnia in support of the United Nations, for example, has been justified in terms of preventing a wider Balkans war.

But this tack confuses preventive diplomacy with crisis management and ending wars. Certainly, in a very loose sense, anything intended to keep a conflict from worsening might be described as *preventive*. But it strains the bounds of meaningful terminology to call confrontational tactics or efforts to curtail a full-blown war—say, the bombing of Hiroshima—preventive diplomacy! To collapse all these stages of intervention together is to abandon distinctions that might have crucial implications for policy and operations.

THE CORE OF PREVENTIVE DIPLOMACY

The concept of preventive diplomacy requires a narrower focus than is given in *Agenda for Peace*. Fortunately, in seeking to construct a more useful and precise definition we can build on the core notion expressed in the recent burst of interest in preventive diplomacy—

namely, that proaction is better than reaction, that crises can be better addressed as they emerge rather than when they have already deepened and widened. As chapter 1 noted, this emphasis on proaction can be explained by several factors, among them the immense difficulties faced by the international community in trying to mediate cease-fires and reduce the bloodshed in conflicts both small and large; increased expectations that the international community can, and thus should, do better in managing conflicts; and empirical observations and theoretical conclusions to the effect that conflicts are easier and cheaper to prevent than they are to manage, contain, or terminate. In sum, the conceptual core of preventive diplomacy has to do with keeping peaceable disputes from escalating unmanageably into sustained levels of violence and significant armed force—in Boutros-Ghali's terms, to "prevent existing disputes from escalating into conflicts." This essential core could easily be lost if the concept incorporates a host of actions—related and important but different— that are taken both at very early and at very advanced stages of conflicts.

Given the current milieu, preventive diplomacy is thus here defined as follows:

> Action taken in vulnerable places and times to avoid the threat or use of armed force and related forms of coercion by states or groups to settle the political disputes that can arise from the destabilizing effects of economic, social, political, and international change.

Such action can involve the use of a variety of "diplomatic" (in the narrow sense), political, military, economic, and other instruments and can be carried out by governments, multilateral organizations, NGOs, individuals, or the disputants themselves.[8]

PREVENTIVE DIPLOMACY IN THE SPECTRUM OF CONFLICT

This definition thus helps clear up much of the confusion between preventive diplomacy and other terms now commonly used for other forms of diplomacy, foreign policy, and conflict intervention. Figure 2.1 depicts the place or stage in the full life history of a typical conflict (whether civil or interstate) that preventive diplomacy occupies in relation to actions taken at other points in a conflict.

Figure 2.1. Life History of a Conflict

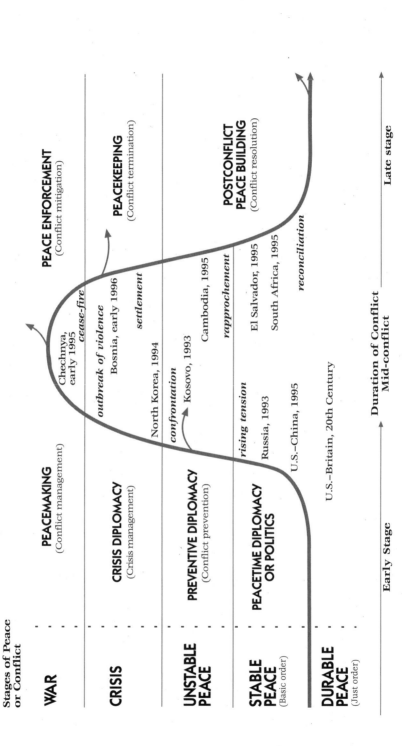

Stages of Peace or Conflict

WAR

PEACEMAKING
(Conflict management)

PEACE ENFORCEMENT
(Conflict mitigation)

CRISIS

CRISIS DIPLOMACY
(Crisis management)

PEACEKEEPING
(Conflict termination)

cease-fire

outbreak of violence
Chechnya, early 1995
Bosnia, early 1996

settlement

UNSTABLE PEACE

PREVENTIVE DIPLOMACY
(Conflict prevention)

POSTCONFLICT PEACE BUILDING
(Conflict resolution)

North Korea, 1994

confrontation
Kosovo, 1993

Cambodia, 1995

rapprochement

El Salvador, 1995
South Africa, 1995

reconciliation

STABLE PEACE
(Basic order)

PEACETIME DIPLOMACY OR POLITICS

rising tension
Russia, 1993

U.S.–China, 1995

DURABLE PEACE
(Just order)

U.S.–Britain, 20th Century

Duration of Conflict

Early Stage   Mid-conflict   Late stage

LEGEND

Stages of Peace or Conflict

War is sustained fighting between organized armed forces. It may vary from low-intensity but continuing conflict or civil anarchy (e.g., Somalia, early 1992; Algeria, 1995) to all-out "hot" war (e.g., World War II, Vietnam).

Crisis is tense confrontation between armed forces that are mobilized and ready to fight and may engage in threats and occasional low-level skirmishes but have not exerted any significant amount of force. The probability of the outbreak of war is high (e.g., Cuban missile crisis of 1962). In national contexts, this condition might involve continuing political violence (e.g., Colombia, 1990s).

Unstable Peace is a situation in which tension and suspicion among parties run high but violence is either absent or only sporadic. A "negative peace" prevails because although armed force is not deployed, the parties perceive one another as enemies and maintain deterrent military capabilities (e.g., United States–Iran, 1995). A balance of power may discourage aggression, but crisis and war are still possible. Government repression of groups is one domestic variety of this level of conflict (e.g., Myanmar [Burma], 1995).

Stable (or Cold) Peace is a relationship of wary communication and limited cooperation (e.g., trade) within an overall context of basic order or national stability. Value or goal differences exist and no military cooperation is established, but disputes are generally worked out in nonviolent, more or less predictable ways. The prospect of confrontation or war is low (e.g., U.S.-Soviet détente, late 1960s; Israel-PLO accommodation, 1994; U.S.–Chinese relations, 1995). Domestic equivalents of this involve national political compacts among competing, sometimes hostile political factions (e.g., South Africa, 1994–95).

Durable (or Warm) Peace involves a high level of reciprocity and cooperation, and the virtual absence of self-defense measures among parties, although it may include their military alliance against a common threat. A "positive peace" prevails based on shared values, goals, and institutions (e.g., democratic political systems and the rule of law), economic interdependence, and a sense of international community. Peaceful, institutionalized settlement of disputes prevails. The domestic form of this stage ranges from processes of national reconciliation to a legitimate constitutional democracy, within which there are shifting political allegiances and a sense of social justice. The possibility of conflict or repression is virtually nil (e.g., United States–Canada; the European Union's goal of common economic institutions and foreign policies; unified Germany).

In figure 2.1 the course of disputes that become violent conflicts is
traced in relation to two dimensions: the intensity of conflict (the vertical axis) and the duration of the conflict over time (the horizontal
axis). The line that forms an arc from left to right across the diagram
portrays the course of a conflict as it rises and falls in intensity over
time. Its smoothly curving bell shape is oversimplified to characterize an "ideal type" life history. As suggested by the arrows that deviate from the line, the course of actual conflicts can exhibit many
different long and short life-history trajectories, thresholds, reversals,
and durations. Even conflicts that have abated can re-escalate.
Nevertheless, the model has heuristic value in allowing us to make
certain useful distinctions among the conflict interventions that re-
late to different levels of intensity.

The far left column of the diagram displays five levels or stages of
amicability or animosity (labeled "Stages of Peace or Conflict") that
can exist among two or more parties. As explained in the legend to
figure 2.1, these five levels delineate gradations in various aspects of
the parties' relationships, such as their awareness of differences and
separate identities, political polarization, value congruence, mutual
trust, and hostile behavior. All the levels involve some degree of conflict but of significantly different intensity and forms of expression.
Examples of current conflicts at these levels are given in italics inside
the arc.

Placed around the outside of the arcing line are widely used terms
for various kinds of interventions into conflicts. These terms are
arranged in two roughly parallel series: the "P" series (preventive
diplomacy, peacemaking, peace enforcement, peacekeeping, and
peace building), which is generally employed in discussions associated with the United Nations; and the "C" series (conflict prevention, crisis management, conflict management, conflict
mitigation, conflict termination, and conflict resolution), which is
generally preferred in the academic literature on conflict. Either series may be used provided that it is understood that the terms form
sequences of related but different conflict interventions, each applicable to differing stages of a conflict.

As seen in the figure, preventive diplomacy would typically begin
to come into play when tensions in the relationships between parties

are in danger of shifting from stable peace to unstable peace or worse. It applies then not only to situations that have seen no recent conflict but also to postconflict situations where violence or coercion have been largely terminated but the efforts of postconflict peace building are apparently insufficient to move the conflict into stable peace and away from the danger of re-escalation. Its aim is to keep actual or potential disputes from taking the form of confrontation or all-out violence and to return them to processes of regular diplomacy or national politics or, even better, a durable peace. But if it fails, and such situations deteriorate into crisis, preventive diplomacy ceases to apply as a concept. In short, *preventive diplomacy is especially operative at the level of unstable peace.*

Located as such, preventive diplomacy can be distinguished more sharply from two neighboring, more familiar forms of diplomacy and conflict intervention with which it is frequently confused: peacetime diplomacy, or peacetime politics; and crisis diplomacy, or crisis management.

Peacetime diplomacy is the mode of diplomacy conducted by states that enjoy more or less stable relations—the stuff of ordinary, peacetime international relations and national foreign and defense policies. On the national level, peacetime politics constitutes the governing processes or national politics of more or less stable countries. While such countries may not be fully democratic, they are not in turmoil. The realm of peacetime diplomacy and national politics is not necessarily one of total harmony and tranquility; vigorous, even bitter political disputes and debates may take place, and if exacerbated by certain conditions (resource scarcity, economic decline, or demographic change, for example), international relations and national politics may generate serious tensions. By and large, however, a basic order prevails because the parties value preserving this order and their relationship more highly than they value the objectives pursued in specific disputes. Thus, the chances are low that these tensions will rise to a level where parties threaten or use arms, violence, or repression as the means for settling emerging disputes.

Peacetime diplomacy may involve considerable joint effort to promote the material well-being of the states or groups involved (such as education and science cooperation; commerce, trade, and investment; and protection of the environment). States may also engage in military cooperation to strengthen their security. These efforts may not always ensure that future conflicts will not arise between them; in fact, sometimes they increase the chances of conflicts. However, to the extent such ties are increased between the parties, the ingredients of an even more stable peace, or a durable peace, are established and the probability of conflict between them decreases to nil.

Crisis diplomacy, or crisis management as it is more commonly called, lies on the other side of preventive diplomacy conceptually and involves efforts to manage tensions and disputes that are so intense as to have reached the level of confrontation. The threat of force by one or more party is common, and the actual outbreak of hostilities is highly likely.

Operating between peacetime and crisis diplomacy is preventive diplomacy. Focused on neither routine foreign relations and general development nor crisis and war, it concentrates specifically on troubled, unstable places and at times where the potential is high or rising that regimes or peoples will take up arms or use other forms of coercion to "resolve" emerging political differences. Such disputes are especially likely to occur where and when rapid or disruptive basic changes are occurring, such as shifts in political, economic, or military power, which severely strain the existing institutions and other means normally relied upon to handle disputes peacefully. But preventive diplomacy per se does not, therefore, take up every dispute or conflict of interest, or seek to solve every social or economic problem and fulfill every potential human need. It comes into play only when policies, institutions, and procedures between states and groups at the local, national, or regional levels that could handle disagreements and maintain a process of orderly resolution either do not exist, are breaking down, or fail to regulate political disputes and conflicts of interests, thus creating considerable risk of the threat or use of armed force and other forms of coercion or the outbreak of widespread violence.[9]

Table 2.1 summarizes the differences between peacetime and crisis interventions toward conflict, compared to preventive diplomacy. These differences are seen in the stage of conflict and peace, the time

Table 2.1. Typology of Actions toward Conflicts

	Peacetime Relations	Preventive Diplomacy	Crisis Management and War Diplomacy
Intensity of Conflict	Low; chances of violence low to remote (e.g., Quebec self-determination)	Moderate; chances of violence possible to probable (e.g., Crimea secession)	High; violence actual or imminent (e.g., southern Sudan War)
Time Frame	Long term	Medium term to short term	Immediate
Objectives	Conduct normal negotiations and ongoing affairs of state. Maintain, strengthen stable relations and institutions. Over time, improve national and global welfare.	Carry out policies and create processes to reduce tensions, resolve disputes, defuse conflicts, head off crises	Contain crises, stop violent or coercive behavior, end wars, enforce cease-fires
Examples	G-7 summits U.S.-China dialogue NAFTA 1992 Rio agreements	Quadripartite (Berlin) agreement OSCE High Commissioner on National Minorities Counterproliferation programs Macedonia preventive peacekeeping deployment	Suez crisis Cuban missile crisis UN mediation in Iran-Iraq War Bosnia war peacekeeping UN peace enforcement in Gulf War

frame in which decision makers have to operate, their primary objectives or tasks, and examples of instruments and agents.

VARIETIES OF PREVENTIVE DIPLOMACY

Even when distinguished from peacetime diplomacy, on the one hand, and crisis diplomacy, on the other, preventive diplomacy still includes great variety in terms of types, instruments (or "tools"), and implementers of intervention (here also referred to as "actors" or "preventers").

Table 2-1 reflects the fact that the key to preventive diplomacy is the timing of its activation in relation to evolving conditions in a given place on the ground. Accordingly, preventive diplomacy is not confined to any particular instrument or agent. In principle, it might involve several types of "functional" activity: diplomatic (in the narrow sense), military, economic and social, political-institutional, judicial-legal, and normative-ethical. Many of its tools—such as mediation, military forces, human rights monitors, democracy-building projects, economic aid or sanctions, and even military assistance—are used for mid-conflict and other stages of conflict as well. The key to whether a tool is used for preventive diplomacy, however, is whether it is being specifically targeted and oriented to places and times where violence or armed force are threatening in the medium term. Implementers might be similarly varied, including not only the United Nations and regional organizations, but also individual states, NGOs, and the parties to disputes themselves. The range of tools and their agents that might make up the full "toolbox" of preventive diplomacy is listed in appendix A.

Many tools and agents may be involved because several tasks may have to be performed to keep tense, vulnerable situations from erupting. These tasks could range from avoiding the negative (for instance, diverting parties from potential confrontations) to strengthening the positive (establishing international regimes or buttressing national institutions for addressing disputes peacefully). Such tasks include:

- suppressing violence;
- removing the weapons through which violence may be carried out;

- addressing the issues in dispute by engaging the parties in dialogue or negotiations;
- creating or strengthening the procedures and institutions through which such negotiations can be regularized in permanent institutions such as governments;
- alleviating the egregious socioeconomic conditions that provide tempting occasions for incitement to violence; and
- modifying perceptions and feelings of mistrust and suspicion among the parties.

Although many situations will call for the performance of all of these tasks, specific circumstances will dictate which tasks have the highest priority. One of the most important factors that determines which tasks are of greatest importance, and thus which instruments and agents are likely to be most needed, is how remote or close at hand the threat of violence is—in other words, the degree of hostility that exists between potential parties to a conflict.[10]

To illustrate: If an outbreak of violence is possible but not imminent, there is still time to reduce, restrain, or regulate the weaponry available to the parties in dispute through such measures as disarmament, arms control, and nonproliferation enforced by international agreements, or through security guarantees provided by a defense alliance. This breathing space also makes it possible to channel future disputes into peaceful modes of resolution by strengthening local, national, and/or international political institutions and procedures such as power-sharing arrangements, special commissions, legislatures, and multilateral forums, or by assisting in the creation of these institutions where they do not exist. Misunderstandings and distrust among the disputing parties might be addressed through low-profile, track-two diplomacy. To resolve specific substantive issues, preventive diplomacy could use arbitration and other judicial or quasi-judicial procedures such as offered by multilateral commissions or the International Court of Justice, or the good offices, mediation, and negotiations offered by a third-party government, the United Nations, regional organizations, or a prominent individual. To alleviate egregious inequities and resource shortages that tempt violence, preventive diplomacy might provide economic assistance to highly vulnerable places.

However, if violence appears imminent, preventive diplomacy does not have the luxury of concentrating on these tasks. Instead, attention must be focused on blocking or deterring violence through such means as sanctions or threats of force from the UN Security Council or a powerful state.

Table 2-2 thus distinguishes three varieties or subtypes of preventive diplomacy: preconflict peace building, preemptive engagement, and crisis prevention. These differ in terms of the conditions for which they are suited, their tasks, their time frames, and their instruments and agents.

TARGET PROBLEMS FOR PREVENTIVE DIPLOMACY

The definitions of Hammarskjöld and Boutros-Ghali tend to state the target of prevention as "conflicts" in the sense of open, mutually violent encounters between two or more parties of more or less equal power, such as in a civil war or an interstate war over territory. In practice, however, both during and since the Cold War the international community has acted through mediation, sanctions, peacekeeping, and other means to prevent or manage not only these kinds of conflicts but also a wider range of man-made problems that involve violence or coercion and result in massive suffering. These target problems have included genocide (as in Rwanda in April 1994); "ethnic cleansing" (as in Bosnia); humanitarian calamities such as massive famine and disease or huge refugee flows brought about by civil anarchy (as in Somalia in 1991–92 and Goma, Zaire, in 1994); the collapse of societies and states and resultant widespread violence (as in Congo in 1960); gross human rights violations and political repression (as in the case of the apartheid regime in South Africa); and the takeover by force of established democratic procedures and institutions (as was attempted in recent years in Haiti, Guatemala, and Peru).

In light of this record of international action, preventive diplomacy needs to include the full range of *prospective* problems that the international community has shown itself concerned to avoid or ameliorate. These encompass not only possible open, bloody conflicts, but also "one-way" conflicts where a government or group dominates a weaker party through armed force or coercive methods (e.g., Kosovo,

Table 2-2. Subtypes within Preventive Diplomacy

	Crisis Prevention	Preemptive Engagement	Preconflict Peace Building
Primary Objectives	Block violent acts, reduce tensions	Address specific disputes, channel grievances into negotiations, engage parties	Create channels for dispute resolution, build political institutions, define norms, change attitudes, reduce sources of conflict
Techniques	Economic sanctions, coercive diplomacy, deterrence	Special envoys, mediation, arbitration	Problem-solving workshops, arms control regimes, CBMs, conflict resolution training, human rights standards, collective security
Examples	North Korea negotiations Macedonia peacekeeping	OSCE High Commisioner on National Minorities Observers	NGO Balkans Peace project NPT CSCE standards
Intensity of Conflict	*Near crisis*, low-level violent acts, taking up of arms, threats, violence probable	*Low-level conflict* over particular issues, tensions, polarization, violence possible	*Unstable peace*, diffuse political instability, uncertainty, distrust, anomie, violence possible
Time Frame	Short term	Short to medium term	Short to medium term

Nigeria, and Myanmar [Burma] today), or where the sudden demise of effective government authority leaves basic human needs unfulfilled. At the same time, however, if preventive diplomacy is to remain a feasible and operational concept, its definition cannot target all conceivable underlying sources of these problems (such as social, economic, and political inequality or material deprivation).

The definition offered above does accommodate both overt, two-party conflicts and political repression because of its stipulation that preventive diplomacy is directed at "the threat or use of armed force and related forms of coercion by states or groups to settle political disputes." Thus targets for preventive diplomacy can include the use of armed force or other forms of coercion to settle political disputes over such issues as territorial control, the composition and form of governments, and the political status of groups within a state. Many of the tools and agents listed in appendix A—for instance, human rights monitors, democracy-building projects, sanctions, and conflict resolution training—are more appropriate for addressing such situations than they are for dealing with violent, open warfare. Such preventive actions are seen as warranted and necessary both because the coercion is in itself a violation of international norms and because it can provoke violent reactions that can engender (as in Somalia from 1988 to 1992) civil wars or other major crises that compel an international response.

To summarize, the following kinds of prospective situations fall within the definition adopted here:

- interstate conventional or nuclear war, such as over control of territory;
- violent conflicts between communal groups or between groups and states, occurring either within states or across state boundaries, such as civil wars, ethnic secessionist conflicts, revolutions, and genocide;
- state-sponsored terrorist campaigns or insurgencies against particular groups or states;
- gross human rights violations, such as "ethnic cleansing" and political repression;

- irregular coercive interruptions of democratic or democratizing governments, such as through military or executive coups; and
- the collapse of an economy or society and effective government.

Whether each and every occurrence of these problems should or can be addressed by the international community is a separate, practical question, not a conceptual issue. These matters are dealt with in chapter 4. Another distinguishable issue is which specific combinations of instruments and agents are likely to be effective in preventing these problems from occurring in given places and times. What kinds of interventions fit which situations best, and how they are most effectively carried out, are the focus of chapter 3.

3

──────────────●──────────────

LESSONS FROM
EXPERIENCE

We have now defined preventive diplomacy, but we are still a long way from knowing how it is actually practiced. Who gets involved, why, and what do they do? What kinds of efforts succeed and what fail? Does effectiveness depend on who is involved, when they take action, the instruments they use, the issues and other circumstances they face?

As interest in preventive diplomacy has grown, the need for answers to such practical questions has produced a great deal of descriptive information and a host of policy and action recommendations. The advice ranges from vague truisms such as "Collect accurate and timely information!" and "Encourage communication between parties!" to specific proposals for establishing professorships of preventive diplomacy in African universities and a global commission on self-determination. But the scarce time and resources of governments and other entities do not allow all promising ideas to be realized.

If policymakers and other practitioners are going to feel confident that they can take cost-effective actions to prevent possible future conflicts, they need more than wish lists and untested admonitions. Policy guidelines are required that derive from systematic assessment of those ingredients that have helped prevent conflicts in the past and of those approaches that have failed.

EXISTING LITERATURE

Curiously, by and large the extant literature provides relatively little specific help in developing such guidelines. Very few articles or books have investigated what kinds of policies or actions prevent conflicts and under what conditions. Descriptive materials tell about prevention programs and projects being carried out, by whom, and in which countries or regions. But they are sketchy and often promotional in nature and do not evaluate the results of these activities. The numerous histories of past wars rarely focus on how those wars might have been avoided. As one author notes, "For every thousand pages published on the causes of wars there is less than a page directly on the causes of peace."[1] These studies deal almost entirely with wars between states, moreover, not the internal wars typical of the post–Cold War era so far.

In the social sciences, almost all empirical research on conflicts deals with their advanced violent stages, their basic causes, and the problems of managing, containing, and terminating them. It has little to say about how manifest conflicts develop out of their latent sources, and how they might be nipped in the bud. Not many years ago, social psychological and other research took up the topic of preventing nuclear war, but the findings are only indirectly applicable to the lower-level, more gradual conflicts typical of the Cold War and post–Cold War periods. Although some post–Cold War conflicts, especially the violent breakup of Yugoslavia, have been extensively analyzed, these studies are case specific, thus producing few generalizable conclusions, and they leave untreated many other recent conflicts.

True, the type of conflict referred to as "ethnic" is receiving growing attention, but this research is often overly generic rather than grounded in cases. When it does take up individual conflicts, it usually enumerates their sociological and cultural sources and describes their politics, but as static factors; it does not trace the dynamics of their emergence or solution. Some of these studies deal with institutional solutions such as federalism that, once in place, might ameliorate such conflicts, but little empirical analysis has looked closely at specific processes through which these conflicts grow and the types of early interventions that might avert their escalation. Although some scholars are starting to look closely at the incipient stages of ethnic conflicts and related crises such as genocide in order to develop early warning indicators and conflict models, these analyses so far have more to say about the origins of potential conflicts than what to do to avert them. Some more policy-oriented studies of recent conflicts are becoming available, but these focus mainly on tools of intervention such as economic sanctions and peacekeeping, which, again, are used typically only after war is in full swing.

One might expect systematic policy advice on how to prevent incipient conflicts to emerge from the self-described field of "conflict management" or "conflict resolution." Pertinent theoretical works provide promising hypotheses about conflict escalation, but these theories have not been rigorously tested in real-world instances of post–Cold War conflicts. Useful empirical studies look at particular mediations and negotiations conducted at advanced conflict stages and examine the tactics, styles, and cultural factors involved. But one is left unsure about the effect these individual episodes actually have on the overall course of conflicts and whether the conclusions reached are applicable to preconfrontation or previolent stages of conflict.[2]

Fortunately, a few studies are directly relevant to the subject of effective conflict prevention. Some have examined a large number of cases of past conflicts to see what correlation exists between the nature of the issues in dispute, the level of fatalities, and the duration of hostilities, on the one hand, and whether conflicts were settled peacefully, on the other. Although their large samples include few conflicts that have arisen since 1989, these studies provide strong quantitative evidence that factors such as past antagonisms, the timing of third-party efforts at resolution, and the behavior of the disputants themselves have a significant effect on whether or not conflicts are amenable to peaceful resolution. As summarized in table 3.1, the quantitative studies and behavioral conflict theory suggest phenomena such as "group-think," "entrapment," and victimization that help to explain why already escalated conflicts are more difficult to resolve than low-level conflicts. But neither this theory nor the quantitative studies provide much detail on interactions between the various forces behind the growth of conflicts or on specific processes through which peaceful outcomes are achieved. One study taking a process approach to specific post–Cold War conflict prevention efforts is available and it is extremely useful, but it is limited to four European conflicts.[3]

Following the definition of preventive diplomacy developed in chapter 2, this chapter seeks to identify key generic factors that appear to be conducive to the peaceful settlement of emerging political disputes that might otherwise become crises or violent conflicts.

It seeks to advance further the work that has just begun to search systematically for factors that may explain whether emerging disputes are settled peacefully or turn into violence. The post–Cold War period has seen a number of new conflicts toward which preventive actions were taken in varying degrees and forms and with widely varying degrees of success. By seeking to codify policy lessons from these experiences, this analysis hopes to provide some preliminary guidelines of the kind needed by diplomats or other practitioners on the ground and by policymakers at headquarters.

Based on a review of a range of recent cases of preventive diplomacy, this chapter begins with illustrative accounts of three characteristic types of post–Cold War political disputes. Some of the disputes reviewed ended peacefully, others in violence. These accounts briefly describe the historical context, issues, participants, and outcomes of the conflicts. They point out those moments when political disputes heated up and when preventive action was taken to cool them down. Drawing on these and other cases, the next section of the chapter characterizes who has been engaged in these preventive efforts, explains why they became involved, and describes the preventive policies and methods of intervention they employed.

The third section turns to the critical evaluative issue: What factors account for effective prevention? In view of the fact that specific efforts at conflict prevention were made in all the cases reviewed, it seems likely that their differing outcomes can be explained, at least in part, by characteristics of the actions as well as their contexts. To explore this intriguing possibility, those factors associated with the cases of failure in the political management of these disputes are compared with those factors appearing in the cases of success. The result of the analysis is presented in the form of five salient factors that appear to have differed fairly consistently between the violent and peaceful cases, and thus to be among the most important determinants of violent or nonviolent resolutions of emerging post–Cold War political disputes.[4]

CASE STUDIES: SIMILAR CHALLENGES, DIFFERENT OUTCOMES

The decline of state socialist ideology, increased political pluralism, the transfer of authority over economic policy decisions and state

Table 3.1. Factors Affecting Groups in Conflict and Third-Party Interveners: Before and After Escalated Violence*

	Factors Affecting the Parties to a Dispute	
	Pre- or Low-Violence Stage	Violent Stage
Positions on issues	Malleable, less formed	Crystallized, rigid, zero-sum thinking
Nature of issues	Objective, discrete number of specific issues	Subjective, proliferation of issues, generalized and diffuse
Goals	Improve own situation, do well	Hurt other regardless of effect on self
Extent mobilized, unified	Low "groupness," complexity and ambiguity tolerated, cross-cutting relationships	Sides taken, polarization, "enemies" defined, shrinking middle ground
Number of parties	Limited	Expanded, allies recruited and outside commitments made
Sense of hurt, injustice	Moderate, incipient	Feel victimized, legacy of bitterness, reciprocal violence
Degree of trust	Potential to be high, easier to build	Low, difficult to rebuild
Communications between sides, chances for mutual empathy	Open or potentially open	Noncommunication (except through violence), "group-think," distorted information

continued on next page

Table 3.1. *continued*

Factors Affecting the Parties to a Dispute

	Pre- or Low-Violence Stage	Violent Stage
Perception of other	Complex, individuation, moderation, relatively objective perception of information	Simplistic, dehumanization, stereo-typing, extremism, distortion of information, "mirror-image" phenomenon of each party seeing own motivations and behavior as rational and "right" while seeing other's as inexplicable and "wrong"
Extent of institutional, social ties between sides	May still exist	Destroyed networks, political institutions
Extent of leaders' flexibility vis-à-vis constituents	Some maneuverability	Under pressure to win on battlefield, entrapment, "out-macho" alternate leaders
Conflict behaviors	Primarily forms of negotiation	Reciprocal violence
What is required to get parties to come to the negotiating table	Chance of obtaining some demands	Mutual hurting stalemate

Factors Affecting Third Parties

	Pre- or Low-Violence Stage	Violent Stage
Leverage over, access to disputants	Parties may seek or accept help	Each party convinced of winning
Physical risks of involvement	Low	High
Costs of carrots, sticks required to stop the fighting	Low (parties less committed to positions)	High (parties more committed to positions)

Need to use force, coercion to stop the fighting	Low (less desire for revenge and punishment)	High (more desire for revenge and punishment)
Difficulty getting third-party domestic support for involvement	Low	High
Risks, stakes in multilateral involvements	Relatively low	High (e.g., command and control issues)
Likelihood and extent conflict affects own interests	Low	Moderate to high
Tendency to take a partisan position toward the conflict	Small impacts and moral ambiguity of issues less likely to spark one-sided interventions	Effects and moral symbolism of conflict more likely to evoke support for one side or the other

* Based on author's synthesis of the following sources: Stephen Ryan, "Grass-Roots Peacebuilding in Violent Ethnic Conflict," in *Peaceful Settlement of Conflict: A Task for Civil Society*, ed. Jörg Callie and Christine Merkel (Rehburg-Loccum: Evangelische Akademie Loccum, 1993), 313–342; Dean Pruitt and Jeffrey Rubin, *Social Conflict: Escalation, Stalemate, and Settlement* (New York: McGraw-Hill, 1986); Ronald Fisher and Loraleigh Keashly, "The Potential Complementarity of Mediation and Consultation within a Contingency Model of Third-Party Intervention," *Journal of Peace Research* 28, no. 1 (1991): 29–42; Connie Peck, "Characteristics of Crisis Escalation: Stabilization and De-Escalation: Possible Points for Intervention by the International Community" (paper presented at the International Roundtable Conference on "Preventive Conflict Management," sponsored by the Austrian Federal Ministry for Foreign Affairs and the Austrian Federal Ministry for Defense, 1993), 25–27; Jacob Bercovitch, "International Dispute Mediation: A Comparative Empirical Analysis," in *Mediation Research: The Process and Effectiveness of Third-Party Intervention*, ed. Kenneth Kressel and Dean Pruitt (San Francisco: Jossey-Bass, 1989), 284–299; Jacob Bercovitch and Jim Lamare, "Correlates of Effective Mediation in International Disputes: Theoretical Issues and Empirical Evidence" (paper presented at the annual meeting of the American Political Science Association, Washington, D.C., September 1–4, 1993); Jacob Bercovitch and Jeffrey Langley, "The Nature of Dispute and the Effectiveness of International Mediation," *Journal of Conflict Resolution* 37, no. 4 (December 1993): 670–691; Irving Janis and Leon Mann, *Decision Making: A Psychological Analysis of Conflict, Choice, and Commitment* (New York: Free Press, 1977); Paul Wehr, *Conflict Regulation* (Boulder, Colo.: Westview Press, 1979); Louis Kriesberg, "Preventive Conflict Resolution of Inter-Communal Conflicts," PARC Working Paper no. 29, Maxwell School of Citizenship and Public Affairs, Syracuse University, September 1993; Louis Kriesberg, "Intractable Conflicts," *Peace Review* 5, no. 4 (1993): 417–421; Louis Kriesberg and Stuart Thorsen, eds., *Timing the De-Escalation of International Conflicts* (Syracuse, N.Y.: Syracuse University Press, 1991); and Louis Kriesberg, *Social Conflicts* (Englewood Cliffs, N.J.: Prentice-Hall, 1973).

enterprises to market processes, increased integration of economies, and the spread of information technology: these trends have produced dramatic and powerful changes in the societies, economies, polities, and international relations of all the regions and countries of the world. By changing the rules of the economic and political game and redistributing resources and power, these forces have created new uncertainties and insecurities among masses and political elites alike, and they have led to clashes among competing interests. But the nature of political clashes has varied across regions and countries according to their differing historical, sociological, political, cultural, and institutional legacies and the stages of their political development and state building. Thus, each area presents preventive diplomacy with somewhat different kinds of conflict with which to deal.

To make our policy conclusions more reliable by studying like situations, the conflict cases reviewed here are grouped into three categories of characteristic post–Cold War political disputes. The three varieties of conflict are listed below, along with the examples that are referred to throughout the rest of the chapter. Although aspects of the three kinds of issues in dispute are found in all regions, certain types of conflict tended to be more common in one region than elsewhere. All these conflicts were comparatively small or localized in global terms and arose within or across states but involved opposed interests of ethnic or other political groups; conflicts strictly between states and on a larger scale, such as nuclear crises, are not included. The three conflict categories are as follow.

1. *Ethnopolitical "kin-group" conflicts in Central Europe and the former Soviet Union* (e.g., Croatia, Serbia, and Bosnia; Moldova and the "Dniestr Republic"; Macedonia, Albania, and Serbia; Hungary and Slovakia; Estonia and Russia). Occasional reference will also be made to similar disputes between Russia and Ukraine over Crimea, Russia and Chechnya, and the Czech and Slovak republics.

2. *Democratizing "transition" conflicts in sub-Saharan Africa* (e.g., Zaire, Congo/Brazzaville, Rwanda, Burundi). Occasional reference will be made to Somalia, Zambia, and South Africa.

3. *"New democracy" conflicts in Latin America* (e.g., Haiti, Guatemala, and Peru).

KIN-GROUP ETHNOPOLITICAL DISPUTES IN CENTRAL EUROPE AND THE NEWLY INDEPENDENT STATES

The economic and political reforms initiated by Mikhail Gorbachev led in 1989 to the removal of Soviet political controls and communist management from Eastern Europe as well as from the republics of the Soviet Union, and in 1991 to the breakup of the latter into thirteen newly independent states. This deconstruction of the Soviet empire sparked negotiations among newly mobilized social groups in all the emerging polities not only on economic and social policies but also on such fundamental issues as constitutions; the territorial boundaries of their states vis-à-vis their ethnic communities; the relationship of their administrative units to the center, especially in federal states; and, because the dissolution of the Warsaw Pact required restructuring of military alliances, their international allegiances.

In Yugoslavia, the Baltic states, Hungary and its neighbors, and Moldova in particular, intense disputes arose regarding the loyalties and rights of ethnic groups that became minorities under one government but were majorities under an adjacent or nearby government. Many ethnic majorities that became politically ascendant in parts of the former Soviet Union and Yugoslavia sought to eradicate the signs of their former domination by communist central governments and to codify in legislation and public policies their own position as distinct peoples and masters of their own fate. One consequence of this was discrimination (real, imagined, or likely) against members of other ethnic groups, especially those who had migrated or been sent to their present homes under the old regime. While these minorities feared persecution, the newly dominant ethnic groups often feared that the minorities were planning secession or irredentist movements that would redraw governmental borders and allow the minorities to be embraced by a state in which they would belong to the majority.

Many researchers have concluded that disputes over material resources, territory, interstate security, and sovereignty are generally easier to mediate than those over national identity, values, ideology, and the control of governments.[5] All these latter issues arise in ethnonationalist conflicts such as the kin-group disputes we examine here.

Although arising in the same area at the same time, these similar disputes had different outcomes. Contrary to the conventional wisdom that ethnonationalism in the former Soviet bloc is an irrepressible and inevitably destructive force, some local disputes were settled peacefully. Others, however, did lead to bloody skirmishes or wars, such as those between Croatia, Serbia, and Bosnia; Moldova and the "Dniestr Republic"; and Russia and Chechnya.

Failed Preventive Diplomacy: Croatia, Serbia, and Bosnia

The Yugoslavia Communist Party collapsed with the walkout from its congress of the Slovenian delegation in January 1990, followed by the exit of the Croatian, Macedonian, and Bosnian parties. Multiparty elections in the republics that spring brought noncommunist parties to power in Slovenia, Croatia, Serbia, and Bosnia-Hercegovina. Except in Bosnia, the new leaders were vocal ethnic nationalists, albeit somewhat less extreme in their views than others vying for control of their fledgling governments. Attempts in late 1990 and early 1991 by the federal authorities in Belgrade and the republics to negotiate an alternative constitutional structure to the Yugoslav federation failed and were followed in December 1990 and May 1991 by referendums in Slovenia and Croatia, respectively, that showed substantial support for secession. In June, Slovenia and Croatia declared their independence. Demands for separate status had been made since 1990 by Serb communities outside of Serbia (such as in Krin in Croatia), who wished to remain in the federation, as well as by ethnic communities within Serbia such as the Albanians in the formerly autonomous area of Kosovo, who declared their independence from Serbia after it abolished Kosovo's autonomy in 1990.

By mid-1991 interethnic local tensions and skirmishes were rapidly intensifying in Slovenia and Croatia, and while the local militias continued to arm themselves, the Serbian-dominated federal Yugoslav army (JNA) increasingly intervened on the side of Serbians. Two successive secessionist wars ensued between the Slovenian and Croatian nationalist forces, on the one hand, and local Serbs backed by the rump federal army, on the other. The conflict in Slovenia, which had a very small Serb minority, was brief and ended in victory for the local nationalists. But the Croatian nationalists fared less well, and by late summer 1991 almost one-third of Croatia was under Serbian control.

During this period the aim of the European Community, with U.S. support, was to avoid a violent breakup by mediation efforts and diplomatic pressure on the republics aimed at preserving the federation and resolving the constitutional issues without resort to force. Economic assistance was offered if they stayed together, and breakaway republics were threatened with denial of EC membership. When open fighting erupted in the summer, an EC delegation mediated the Brioni Declaration, which put the two republics' independence on hold for three months, effected a cease-fire, withdrew the Yugoslav army from Slovenia, arranged EC observers, and committed the parties to Yugoslavia-wide negotiations. EC arms sales were banned and economic assistance stopped. Although the Yugoslav army left Slovenia, escalating violence in Croatia spurred talks between delegations of the Republic of Croatia and the Yugoslav army in August. The government of Serbia asked the EC Ministerial Council to intercede with Croatian authorities to stop acts of terror against Serbs in Croatia. On September 1, the EC Ministerial Council agreed to expand the EC monitoring mission to Croatia.

Faced with the takeover by local Serbs of Krajina, a multilateral Conference on Yugoslavia convened in the Hague by the European Community in September finally reached agreement in October, with all parties except Serbia and Montenegro agreeing to a plan proposed by conference chairman Lord Carrington. This plan involved a free confederal association of independent states, special status for regions such as Kosovo with concentrated ethnic populations, the inviolability of internal borders, and international monitors. Republics would receive international recognition of their independence only if they abided by CSCE standards regarding human rights, nonviolent change of borders, and protection of minorities. The development of closer relationships between the republics and the European Community depended on compliance with the agreement; noncompliance would be met with economic sanctions.

However, repeated cease-fire agreements were broken and the fighting continued. The rejection by Serbia of the Carrington plan led again to the termination of EC trade privileges and economic aid, although they were reinstated for all republics except Serbia and Montenegro in December. With Serbian forces suspected of committing major atrocities, Germany (under pressure from its own

Croatian community) threatened to recognize Croatia on its own. An initially divided European Community recognized Slovenia and Croatia in January 1992. An arms embargo had been imposed by the UN Security Council in December, and in January the fifteenth cease-fire arranged by the United Nations finally held. A UN peacekeeping force (UNPROFOR I) created to oversee the cease-fire and a demobilization of forces was deployed to Croatia by March. By mid-1992, however, UNPROFOR I's peace mission was widely acknowledged to be unrealizable, chiefly because of the activities of local Serb irregulars armed by the JNA.

The head of a multiethnic coalition in Bosnia, Alija Izetbegovic, had proposed plans in 1991 to remain in a looser federal Yugoslavia. But the EC decision to recognize the other republics prompted a Bosnian referendum in late February 1992 (boycotted by Bosnian Serbs) and a declaration of independence in March inspired by Muslim and Croatian fears of being left in a Serb-dominated rump Yugoslav state. With Bosnian Serbs gaining control of more and more of the Bosnian republic, and with the discovery of the Serbian practice of "ethnic cleansing," Bosnia was also recognized by the European Community and others as an independent state in April, and, along with Slovenia and Croatia, was admitted to the United Nations. Heavy fighting among Bosnian Serbs, Croats, and Bosnian government forces commenced within Bosnia. Economic sanctions against Serbia and Montenegro were approved by the United Nations in May, and the UN Security Council voted to establish six protected areas for the Bosnian Muslim population. A long process of ultimately fruitless negotiation under the joint authority of the European Community and United Nations was begun in September 1992. By this time, the United Nations, working through UNPROFOR II, had turned its attention primarily to providing humanitarian protection and relief.

Yugoslavia is, then, an example—a well-known example—of failed international preventive action in that several forms of international engagement could not keep the issue of the future political relations of the Yugoslav republics from being settled without armed force. Other recent kin-group disputes, however, have had altogether more peaceable outcomes, even though they were not only similar in nature to the Yugoslavian imbroglio in many respects but also occurred in a similar European setting. It is to these nonviolent disputes that we now turn.

Successful Preventive Diplomacy: Macedonia, Serbia, and Albania

Macedonia presents one of the clearest examples of the international community explicitly taking preventive steps in response to fears of a future conflict. In a September 1991 referendum a massive majority in the Macedonian Republic voted for independence. By mid-1992, many observers were apprehensive that the war between Serbians and the Bosnian government might spill over into Macedonia. The feared scenario was along the following lines: Intensified repression by the Belgrade government of the Albanian majority in Kosovo (the previously autonomous area in Serbia that borders Macedonia) or a Kosovar uprising, would incite nearby Albania to come to the aid of its ethnic kin. This would also destabilize the part-Albanian and shaky coalition government of the independent, multiethnic, and fledgling democracy of Macedonia. Albanians make up about 23 percent of the population in Macedonia, and they harbor many grievances concerning their treatment with respect to educational, language, and cultural rights. The proportion of Serbs in Macedonia is only about 2 percent, so less likely but still possible was a Serbian attack on Macedonia, possibly supported by Greece, which has its own dispute with Macedonia. Either development would precipitate the involvement of any or all of three neighboring countries—Bulgaria, Greece, and Turkey, the latter both members of NATO—thus creating a regionwide Balkans war. Two events in particular led international observers to believe that a violent ethnic conflict was in the making. The first was a riot at an open market in Skopje in November 1992, during which three Albanian men and a Macedonian woman were killed by police. The second was the discovery by the Macedonian authorities in November 1993 that a secret paramilitary organization styling itself the All-Albanian Army was operating within the Army of the Republic of Macedonia and was allegedly in contact with Albanian government officials.

In response, several preventive policies and activities were undertaken and continue to this day. In 1992, President Bush urged the CSCE to place observers in the areas within Serbia of Sandjak,

Vojvodina, and Kosovo, as well as in Macedonia. The missions were established later that year, although those in Serbia were later expelled by Belgrade. A succession of three U.S. foreign service officials has headed the CSCE (now OSCE) Spillover Mission to Skopje that began in September 1992. These diplomats have visited Macedonia's leaders and neighboring capitals, including Belgrade, and ensured that their presence was known to the local and international media. When border incidents have occurred or local controversies over educational and other policies have flared up that could exacerbate the poor relations of the two communities or risk a Macedonian civil war, the diplomats and their staffs have acted to allay tensions. The mission also monitors the country's political, economic, and social development, including elections. The OSCE had also been represented in Macedonia through periodic visits since November 1993 by its high commissioner on national minorities (HCNM), Ambassador Max van der Stoel, who has made several recommendations regarding improvements in the electoral system, the enactment of laws, and the inclusion of Albanians in the armed forces and police.

In addition, first President Bush and then President Clinton have warned Serbian President Slobodan Milosevic that Serbian armed movement in Kosovo would be met by firm retaliatory measures, including possible military force against Serbia proper. In December 1992, at the request of Macedonia's President Kiro Gligorov, the UN Security Council authorized an estimated 700-strong peacekeeping force. Five hundred Canadian troops were quickly dispatched there in January; about 500 Nordic country troops were subsequently brought in and deployed along Macedonia's northern frontier with Serbia and its western boundary with Albania; and 540 U.S. troops, who began to join the force later in 1993, have been deployed in the northeast. The force, which includes civilian monitors, was given the mission of deterring any threats against Macedonia, monitoring the borders with Serbia and Albania, and reporting any developments in the border areas that could undermine confidence and stability in Macedonia or threaten its territory. Through a later authorization, the UN mission also has the civilian mandate of monitoring the social and political situation through the work of a special representative of the UN secretary-general placed there. In carrying out its mission, the

FYROM Command—now known as the United Nations Preventive Deployment Force (UNPREDEP)—has coordinated its efforts closely with the smaller OSCE mission. Of the sixteen UN peacekeeping operations deployed around the world as of mid-1995, it is the only one with a preventive mission—in the sense, that is, of being deployed in an area where conflict might arise but has not recently occurred.

Other measures included the admission in April 1993 of Macedonia into the United Nations, though under the provisional name "Former Yugoslavian Republic of Macedonia" (FYROM) because of the dispute with Greece over Macedonia's name and flag and certain constitutional provisions. More than one hundred nations, including now the United States, have also recognized Macedonia as an independent country. In 1993, special UN envoy Cyrus Vance was assigned to mediate the virulent dispute between FYROM and Greece, which had triggered a punishing economic embargo that denied landlocked Macedonia access to the Aegean Sea. In addition, international NGOs such as Search for Common Ground are sponsoring grass-roots problem-solving dialogues and training activities, university projects, civil society–building programs, and media initiatives to narrow the wide social distance between the Macedonian and Albanian communities, reduce their mutual distrust, and spread understanding of the requirements of a democratic polity, multiethnic society, and nonethnic state.

In September 1995 an agreement was reached through the efforts of UN representatives regarding the dispute between Macedonia and Greece over Macedonia's name, flag, and constitution; Greece has since begun to lift its embargo. In November the provisional signing in Dayton, Ohio, of a Bosnian peace agreement led to the lifting of economic sanctions against Serbia. These developments may mean that the preventive measures taken toward Macedonia have provided sufficient stability for the Macedonian government and sufficient support for the idea of a multiethnic state that these fragile notions were able to weather a period in which they were put under severe strain. But while many practitioners in Macedonia and observers further afield thus credit these measures with contributing significantly to preserving basic stability in Macedonia, there is still no guarantee that they will have sufficed. For one thing, its neighbors have remained ambivalent toward Macedonia's independence, either in fact or in form. How effective UNPREDEP is as a deterrent or would be as a tripwire is not clear. The continuing turmoil in Croatia, Bosnia, and Serbia may still affect Macedonia. Internally, Macedonia's economic condition is still extremely poor due to the impacts of the embargo and sanctions. Most ominous perhaps is the continuing tenuousness of the political compromise that put the coalition in place amid competing nationalist movements. It was put in greater jeopardy when President Gligorov was severely wounded by a car-bomb attack in early October 1995, which has removed him from political life. In sum, it remains to be seen whether this prevention effort will continue to forestall an escalation of tensions.

Successful Preventive Diplomacy:
Hungary and Its Neighbors and Estonia

Like Serbia and Russia, Hungary has taken considerable interest in the interests of its ethnic kin living in neighboring states. Three million ethnic Hungarians live in Serbia, Romania, and Slovakia, where their interests receive little accommodation from governments fearful of irredentism or pressures for political autonomy from these sizable and long-standing Hungarian minorities. Nationalist politicians in these poor countries with communist-led coalition governments have fueled tensions by questioning the loyalties of the Hungarian minorities and largely refusing to acknowledge group rights or adopt measures of educational or cultural autonomy. Hungarian leaders, too, have engaged in nationalist rhetoric. As a consequence, considerable apprehension has developed between, for example, Slovakia and Hungary.

This tension was manifested in the Gabcikovo-Nagymaros hydroelectric project dispute and related controversies between Hungary and Slovakia from 1992 to 1994. In 1989, under pressure from its environmentalists, Hungary canceled its part of the Gabcikovo-Nagymaros hydroelectric project but offered to renegotiate the treaty, pledging to annul it only if negotiations failed. The project then became a symbol of sovereignty in Slovakia's drive for independence, in part because the independence movement was led by Vladimir Meciar, the Slovakian prime minister and federal commissioner in charge of the project before the separation of Czechoslovakia. Hungarian-Czechoslovak talks broke down in early 1992, Hungarian prime minister Jozsef Antall withdrew Hungary from the project in May, and the Czech and Slovak authorities went ahead with a variant of the original project involving a minor diversion of the Danube. Because this action in Hungary's eyes violated the 1920 Treaty of Trianon and the 1947 Paris Peace Conference, which defined the Czechoslovak-Hungarian border, a war of words ensued, and various offers and counteroffers were made and rejected. The Czech and Slovak republics dissolved their union in January 1993.

Believing Slovakia still would not in fact proceed with the project, Antall did not react until a few days after the water diversification began in October. But he then sought the assistance of the Danube Commission, requested the International Court of Justice (ICJ) to take up the matter, and asked for the CSCE emergency mechanism to be used and the UN Security Council to be alerted. Subsequent pressure from and mediation by the European Community led the parties to agree in March 1993 to submit the matter to binding arbitration by the ICJ, by which time expert opinions on the environmental damage the project could cause had become more mixed, helping to defuse the dispute.[6]

The Slovakian record regarding Hungarian minority rights has not been good. For their part, the Slovakians explain their suspicions about their Hungarian minority by pointing to the fact that the Hungarians, who make up about 12 percent of the population in Slovakia, were well represented in the Czechoslovak parliament and had opposed Meciar and Slovak independence. Meciar consistently opposed the demand of the Hungarian minority for increased language and cultural rights, viewing them as precursors to irredentism. Meanwhile, Antall and other Hungarian leaders have made ambiguous statements about the permanence of Hungary's borders and the ultimate unity of all Hungarian peoples. Specifically, Hungary has conditioned its signing of bilateral treaties guaranteeing borders on the granting to Hungarian minorities in neighboring countries of collective rights, including cultural autonomy.

Significantly, both the ethnic Hungarian minority and authorities in Budapest chose to appeal to international forums to seek satisfaction for their grievances. In late 1992, a leader of the Hungarians in Slovakia, Miklós Duray, lobbied the Council of Europe (COE) regarding the situation of ethnic Hungarians in Slovakia, and several ethnic Hungarian parties in Slovakia issued a joint statement to the CSCE describing failures to observe the Helsinki principles that they argued are included in Slovakia's legal system. In response CSCE HCNM van der Stoel mediated an agreement by which a panel of three experts would study the situation between the Slovak and ethnic Hungarian minorities for two years. In May 1993, based on recommendations issued by the COE's Legal and Human Rights Committees to Slovakia, the COE's Parliamentary Assembly Political Committee conditioned Slovakia's admission to the council on ten prerequisites, including the signing of the European Convention on Human Rights and the provision of guarantees for minority rights. Even after Slovakia was criticized by the CSCE and COE for enacting such measures as the removal of Hungarian names from towns and streets, the Slovakian government has been notably slow to implement the recommendations made by the CSCE and council. Still, at the local government level, some accommodations have been reached.

Nevertheless, both Slovakia and Hungary have made a number of bilateral efforts over the last two years to maintain an open dialogue on the question of minority rights and related issues, and have worked to keep major crises from developing. These actions include the establishment in 1992 of a "hot line" between the two prime ministers, proposed bilateral treaties on minorities, joint parliamentary committees on the Danube, a joint bank, an interethnic roundtable, and a military cooperation agreement. Hungary has also passed a comprehensive and liberal law regarding its (admittedly smaller) minorities, in hopes of providing a model for its neighbors.

The chances for continued progress in resolving their minority, governmental, and other issues were greatly enhanced when in May 1994 the European Union inaugurated the Balladier Plan for a stability pact for Baltic and Eastern European countries. The pact engaged these countries in a series of EU-moderated roundtables to discuss their various bilateral disputes—the incentive for the countries to participate being more favorable consideration of their applications to become EU members. In March 1995, on the eve of the final conference of the pact, Hungary and Slovakia signed a bilateral treaty to foster good neighborly relations.

As Estonia moved out from under years of Soviet domination to independence in August 1991, Estonian nationalists sought to reverse the post–World War II Russification of their country by reasserting Estonian prerogatives. Laws passed between 1989 and 1993 regarding language, local elections, citizenship, and the constitution restricted the professional, educational, and cultural opportunities of many among the non-Estonian population (30 percent of the total population) and disenfranchised the majority of them. Russia retaliated in 1992 by slowing down the agreed schedule for the withdrawal of its troops. Tensions reached their zenith when a June 1993 law on aliens was met with demonstrations by the Russian-speaking community, the cutting of gas supplies from Russia, bitter criticism from Russian leaders, and threatening statements from the rising Russian nationalist Vladimir Zhironovsky.

But smooth resolution of the Estonia-Russia dispute had attracted a lot of interest from the U.S. and Western European governments, NGOs, and several multilateral organizations. The nearby Scandinavian states had also taken an interest from the beginning of the dispute in a stable transition to independence for Estonia and the other Baltic countries. In particular, the work of the CSCE HCNM once again appears to have helped avoid escalation of tensions. Over two weeks in June and July 1993, van der Stoel held extensive consultations with government officials and representatives of the ethnic Russians. Earlier in 1993 a CSCE observer mission had been set up in three locations in Estonia. As a result of the wide international interest, the aliens law and a measure to remove Russian from Estonian schools by the year 2000 were submitted to the Council of Europe and the CSCE for comment; Estonia's President Meri sent their comments to the Estonian parliament, which made some modifications to the pertinent legislation. The level of rancor was also reduced by a relaxation of restrictions on local elections, permission to hold a referendum on autonomy for the Russian-speaking areas, and registration of a Russian-speaking party.

DEMOCRATIZATION TRANSITION CONFLICTS IN SUB-SAHARAN AFRICA

The end of the Cold War generated new political currents in regions other than the former Soviet bloc. From the late 1980s onwards, long-standing one-party regimes in sub-Saharan Africa encountered increased domestic opposition to their corrupt and autocratic rule. The collapse of authoritarian governments in Eastern Europe in 1989 added to these pressures. Regimes came under intense pressure from "above" as support from their Cold War patrons declined and from "below" as democratic expectations from their hitherto-suppressed political opposition increased. Incumbent rulers responded to these pressures in varied ways, with some like Mobutu Sese Seko of Zaire and F. W. De Klerk of South Africa recognizing hitherto banned opposition political parties, sanctioning national conferences on the political future of their countries, or holding multiparty elections. In some ethnically divided societies, such as Somalia and Rwanda, peaceful transitions toward full multiparty democracies did not occur, and civil wars, genocide, and massive humanitarian disasters developed instead. In both Rwanda and Burundi, power-sharing political accords arranged in 1993 that promised an end to long legacies of bitter struggles between Hutus and Tutsis collapsed in 1994, resulting in genocide and war in Rwanda and renewed ethnic killings in Burundi. But in other ethnically divided states, such as Congo, South Africa, and Zambia, rather dramatic but relatively peaceful change has taken place. The differing cases of Congo/Brazzaville and Zaire illustrate the political instabilities and potential for ethnic turmoil that can surface when formerly autocratic African regimes begin to democratize; they also provide an opportunity to explore why political systems may respond differently to the stresses of democratization.

Stalemated Democratization: Failed Preventive Diplomacy in Zaire

Thirty-five years ago, UN peacekeeping troops were sent into the Belgian Congo to stabilize Katanga province after a secessionist rebellion against the newly independent postcolonial government. Today, the successor state to the Belgian Congo presents the world with a potential political, social, and economic crisis that many observers believe could involve a complete breakdown of law and order and the outbreak of widespread civil war—a "Somalia writ large," as it has been called—that could oblige the United Nations and other outside parties to intervene once again to restore order.

In response to the domestic and international pressure to democratize and reform the economy that began to build during the 1980s, Zaire's long-time ruler, President Mobutu Sese Seko, declared a one-year transition toward a multiparty system and new constitution in April 1990. The persecuted leaders of two major opposition parties, Etienne Tshisekedi and Faustin Birindwo, were able to come out in the open. Over two hundred new parties sprang up. In the summer of 1991, a widely representative national conference was convened. Despite intimidation by the government, the conference drew up a provisional charter that authorized an elected parliament (the High Council of the Republic) and a prime minister. Subsequently, Tshisekedi was elected interim prime minister.

Soon after the Tshisekedi government began work, however, Mobutu—who had retained a firm grip on the security forces and the central bank—suspended the parliament, dismissed Tshisekedi, and revived a national assembly notable chiefly for its obedience to Mobutu's wishes. When the prime minister refused to leave office, Mobutu brought in new prime ministers in 1992 and again in 1993. He declared a new transitional constitution and promised new elections by 1994. The Sacred Union, a united front formed by the opposition parties, dissolved after two years of persecution, and many supposedly independent parties turned out to be Mobutu supporters.

While Mobutu thus has been able to effectively thwart or take over the democracy movement and retain dominant political power, he is not in complete control of the country. Despite continuing government suppression, the opposition movement has succeeded in paralyzing many of the central government's functions through popular protests. A parallel opposition government has emerged, but it is divided within itself and has not obtained the unequivocal support of the international community.

Years of corruption and the exploitation of Zaire's economic resources by Mobutu and his followers have left the country's economy in ruins. Poverty and hyperinflation are rampant. The government is bankrupt. This economic turmoil had led to military riots late in 1991, when part of the army was not paid, prompting the entry of French and Belgian troops to protect foreign nationals. Military riots broke out again in 1993. As of 1995, there is still no central government effectively in control of the country, and "ethnic cleansing" is occurring in Shaba (the postindependence name of Katanga) and Kasai provinces. Kivu province in the east suffers from unrest caused by the overflow of ethnic tensions from Rwanda and Burundi.

The situation in Zaire has not developed without attracting periodic outside attention. Early warnings of a kind arose as far back as 1965, in the late 1970s with the Shaba invasion, and in the mid-1980s. With the pressures for democracy growing in 1990, human rights organizations turned their spotlights on Zaire, and Mobutu's human rights violations have often been denounced. Outside efforts by the OAU and other third parties to pressure Mobutu to reform the country politically and economically were initiated at crucial moments at the end of 1991, 1992, and the beginning of 1993, but to little effect. A wide array of crisis abatement policies has been tried. Aid has been cut off, the World Bank has declared Zaire uncreditworthy, and the money going in and out of the country has dwindled. The United States has sought to broker agreements between Mobutu and the opposition movement, and recent U.S. presidents have sent personal representatives to meet with Mobutu to persuade him to step down. Mobutu, however, remains unmoved.

In sum, Zaire remains mired in unresolved crisis, yet its political conflict has not escalated to all-out civil violence. Even so, the worst may be yet to come. While a return to full-fledged autocratic rule is unlikely, or at least unlikely to endure, the prospects of Zaire making a smooth transition to democracy are hardly encouraging, especially given Mobutu's talent for coopting domestic politics for his own purposes and the opposition movement's disunity.

Managing the Transfer of Power: Congo

While Zaire became stalled in creating a plural and stable politics, its neighbor to the west, Congo/Brazzaville, was being opened up to multiparty democracy. Although some political and ethnic violence has occurred in Congo/Brazzaville since 1993, it is held up as an example of a relatively smooth transition to pluralist democracy.

Responding to the winds of democracy in Africa and criticism of government corruption, the Congo government, like governments in Zaire and other francophone states, held a broadly based national conference in early 1991. A High Council of the Republic oversaw a one-year transition to a multiparty democracy. A National Assembly was elected in 1992, and the country's first popular presidential elections were held in August 1992. After a new president, Pascal Lissouba, was elected, he failed to honor an agreement with some of his coalition partners to include them in his cabinet. They then formed an alliance with the opposition and won a vote of no confidence in the new government. Lissouba dissolved the assembly, but after violent protests a compromise was worked out to hold new legislative elections in 1993.

Contrary to most expectations, the groups around the former president failed to win a majority of deputies in the election's first round on May 2, 1993. Although these groups disputed the results and threatened to boycott the second round, the government went ahead. Amid an atmosphere of suspicion and hostility, the second round of parliamentary elections was held on June 6. The government's announcement that it had won a parliamentary majority based on the second round led to extensive street demonstrations and gun battles, particularly in Brazzaville, where opposition support was concentrated and arming itself. From mid-June through July violence increased in the capital—leaving at least thirty dead and displacing over one thousand refugees—and spread to the countryside. The killing began to take on an ethnic character because the government and opposition parties tended to draw support from different groups in the north and the south. Curfews and a state of emergency were imposed in Brazzaville.

Publicly committed to preserving the transition to democracy, the High Command of the Congolese Armed Forces (FAC) pressured supporters and opponents of President Lissouba to begin talks to end the political violence. Delegates from both political camps publicly expressed their willingness to negotiate and appealed to their supporters for calm and an end to the use of weapons of war. The appeals, however, were generally not heeded, and barricades continued to be erected and gunfire to be heard.

Eager to try the OAU's new conflict management procedure just adopted at its Cairo summit in June of that year, the OAU Secretary-General Salim Ahmed Salim secured the agreement of the Congo factions to receive a mediator. Their choice was Mohamed Sahnoun, an eminent, experienced Algerian diplomat and former OAU deputy secretary-general. He first sought to draw on the trust he enjoyed among the parties for "listen and learn" consultations with all factions. He invited the president of neighboring Gabon to host the talks in Libreville because of that leader's family links with both Congo presidential candidates. After eight days of negotiations, the factions agreed to cease fire, lift barricades, release prisoners, disarm private militias and gangs, and provide assistance to displaced persons.

The negotiations on the elections proved difficult, but after resistance on both sides, an accord was reached in August whereby the president's party organized a new second round for eleven disputed seats and the opposition accepted the other results of the first round. Contested seats would be reviewed by an OAU-EC arbitration authority, and the agreement would be monitored and implemented under joint OAU-EC supervision. In the second round, the opposition won eight of the disputed seats. When tension arose again in November and December after the government clamped down on remaining opposition militias, Sahnoun returned, and eventually the escalating violence was quelled.

DEFENDING NEW DEMOCRACIES IN LATIN AMERICA: HAITI, PERU, AND GUATEMALA

By the late 1980s, all but two governments in the Western Hemisphere—those in Cuba and Haiti—had achieved power through democratic elections. The ability of new democratic institutions to handle the growing economic problems and political unrest of the period, however, was largely untested.

In June 1991, the thirty-four OAS member states meeting in Santiago sought to protect their recent democratic gains by adopting

Resolution 1080. This short provision simply requires the OAS secretary-general to call a meeting of the OAS Permanent Council immediately upon "any sudden or irregular interruption of the democratic political-institutional process or the legitimate exercise of power by the democratically-elected government in any member state." The aim is for the council to examine the situation, after which a meeting of the foreign ministers of member states or of the organization's General Assembly may be held, all within ten days. Despite strong views still held by many Latin American members regarding the prerogatives of sovereignty and their historic wariness of U.S. domination, by adopting Resolution 1080 the OAS committed itself to common action based on the notion that member states have a valid interest in the democratic integrity of other members. A subsequent proposal now subject to ratification would allow, as a last resort, the suspension of a member government that comes to power by overthrowing a democratically elected government.

When they approved the resolution, OAS members expected it to be activated, if at all, with respect to Suriname, because it alone still allowed military authorities to decide whether the constitution has been violated. But within three years of its passage, Resolution 1080 was put into effect in three unexpected places. Its varying degrees of success in these instances show that the same preventive diplomacy machinery can have diverging outcomes in the same region, depending on the timing of its use and a variety of other factors.

Failed Defense of Democracy: Haiti

Resolution 1080's first test came in September 1991 when military authorities in Haiti abrogated the results of the December 1990 presidential election, won by Jean-Bertrand Aristide. The OAS promptly convened, condemned the action, and asked its member nations to suspend their economic activities with Haiti, freeze Haitian assets, and impose a trade embargo. In December 1991, Prime Minister Brian Mulroney of Canada called for an international naval blockade, which was ultimately implemented by many American states despite the opposition of many European states. An agreement in early 1992 to return Aristide to power was signed but not carried out. Under increasing threats from the United Nations and member states, the

Haitian military agreed to permit a UN observer force composed of five hundred civilians to work in Haiti. (Aristide had requested such a force in part because an OAS human rights observer team in Haiti had been confined to its hotel by the Haitian military.) The military regime soon began to indicate its reluctance to abide by the agreement, however, and in the event only forty observers were allowed to operate in the capital. A UN oil embargo and freeze on the Haitian leaders' assets were was imposed on June 23, 1993. This eventually led to negotiations between the military ruler, General Raoul Cedras, and Aristide, resulting in the Governors' Island agreement of July 1993 by which Aristide was by October to assume his elected office, a new government was to be appointed, the military leaders were to resign, and a UN-mandated military- and police-training mission was to be sent to Haiti.

In October, however, Haiti's military rulers backed down from their commitment. The USS *Harlan County* carrying a military-training mission turned back from landing in Port-au-Prince. Although enforced by a naval blockade in which the U.S. Navy participated, the economic sanctions reimposed by the United Nations on oil and other trade with Haiti were porous and failed to bring the military authorities to the negotiating table, though they did inflict hardships on the majority of the Haitian people. Subsequent efforts were made to target the sanctions even more effectively on wealthy Haitian elites. The regime was virtually isolated from the rest of the world in diplomatic terms. Although some observers believed these sanctions and diplomatic pressure would eventually succeed in their aims, stiffer measures, including invasion, soon came under consideration. After recurrent problems with refugees flowing out of Haiti's collapsing economy, and a succession of failed efforts from late 1993 through mid-1994 to reach a diplomatic resolution of the crisis, the United States decided to launch a major initiative to bring about a transition to democracy. Aristide's government was ultimately restored to office in October 1994 as a result of the threat of a massive U.S. invasion, accompanied by efforts by a delegation led by former President Jimmy Carter to arrange a face-saving exit for General Cedras. The general backed down, and a U.S.-led military mission to oversee the restoration of democratic institutions is now being conducted under UN auspices.

Modest Success: Peru

When Peru's president Alberto Fujimori, himself democratically elected, dissolved the Peruvian parliament, abolished the judiciary, and set aside the country's constitution in April 1992, the OAS activated Resolution 1080 and denounced Fujimori's actions. With the United States and Japan threatening economic sanctions and Latin American countries voicing harsh criticism of Fujimori's "auto-coup," OAS ministers visited Peru to pressure the president to restore constitutional rule. Partly in response to these pressures, Fujimori attended the OAS General Assembly meeting later that year and reversed his original plan to rule without the constraint of Congress or the constitution. Instead, he held elections to form a body to draft a new constitution. A subsequent plebiscite approved the new constitution, and Peru has returned to at least a modicum of legal normalcy.

Successful Defense of Democracy: Guatemala

The response of the OAS to the May 1993 attempt by Guatemalan President Jorge Serrano to stage a Fujimori-style auto-coup, and to a subsequent claim to the presidency by the Guatemalan vice president, was a more clear-cut success than that achieved in Peru. Meeting days after Serrano's suspension of the constitution, judiciary, and parliament, the OAS denounced his bid for power and dispatched two fact-finding missions composed of the secretary-general and member-state foreign ministers. Meeting with all major sectors of Guatemalan society and government leaders, the missions emphasized the seriousness of the action and urged prompt return to constitutional government.

This initiative reinforced the domestic pressures that had been mobilized by the government's own human rights ombudsman, who escaped house arrest and appeared on television to condemn the coup and appeal for popular action against it. Various sectors of Guatemalan civil society, calling themselves La Instancia, immediately organized to oppose the coup, stating as their primary goal the nonviolent return to constitutional rule. Composed of representatives of labor unions, business groups, and political parties, La Instancia distributed its declarations and analyses of the situation to the general public, including the military. Meanwhile, the Supreme Electoral Tribunal refused Serrano's call for new elections, and the constitutional court met secretly to issue rulings declaring Serrano's actions unconstitutional. Seeing this popular outcry, the military, which had hitherto been indecisive, withheld their support for the assault on Guatemala's democracy. Within two weeks the president caved in. A new government under President Ramiro de Léon Carpio, the former human rights ombudsman, was subsequently voted in by parliament.

WHO DID WHAT AND WHY?
PREVENTIVE AGENTS, INSTRUMENTS, AND MOTIVATION

Before trying to identify the main factors that explain the successful and unsuccessful outcomes in the above cases, let us first review these cases (and selected other conflicts such as Somalia and Moldova) to address some basic descriptive questions: Who tends to be most involved in preventive diplomacy? What policy instruments do they use? And why do actors undertake preventive action or refrain from doing so? While they do not, of course, constitute a comprehensive sample, the cases are sufficiently numerous and diverse to at least suggest some answers.

Typical Actors
Preventive diplomacy is multilateral.
No one country, international organization, NGO, or person has monopolized the practice of preventive diplomacy, and individual conflict arenas typically see several global, regional, and local third parties involved in preventive efforts. These actors have included major powers (not least the United States), middle-rank powers, neighboring states, regional organizations, NGOs, and eminent individuals. Several of these efforts were initiated by the disputants themselves, as well as by local third parties. In every conflict arena, although one actor may have played the most visible role, various other actors were depended upon to provide a range of services and resources: conduct of mediation and negotiations, threat or application of economic

sanctions and arms embargoes, diplomatic leverage, financial and logistical support, preventive peacekeeping deployments, fact-finding or monitoring, and so forth.

Regional organizations, such as the CSCE, the European Community, the OAU, and the OAS, were clearly the most frequently represented type of actor—in fact, one or another played a part in all the cases described. The United States played a prominent role in about three-fourths of the cases. Indeed, the United States appears to have been active in more disputes than any other state, and in all three regions. Almost always it did this not as an independent player, however, but through leadership of or participation in regional and UN initiatives. Other Security Council members or middle-rank powers such as France, Britain, Germany, and Italy also played important roles in the European and African cases, directly or indirectly through the United Nations and regional organizations.

The UN Security Council was involved in less than half the disputes, playing sometimes a mediating role through special envoys, but more often a peacekeeping role. Heavy reliance on UN peacekeeping to monitor cease-fires accounts for the fact that the United Nations was active in almost all the cases that reached the crisis or violent stage (thus those cases that are here considered failures of preventive diplomacy) but in only two of the successes—Macedonia and Estonia.

The invisibility of NGOs in many of these disputes is more apparent than real, for NGOs typically operate discreetly or without fanfare and information about their activities is hard to find. The only apparent third-party involvement in the Russian-Chechen dispute prior to the outbreak of war in December 1994, for example, was a fact-finding mission to the area in 1992 sponsored by International Alert.

Instruments

The preventive instruments used vary widely and involve rewards, penalties, and services.

No single tool of intervention predominated; rather, third parties employed a wide range of tools in which were embodied a variety of both positive and negative inducements, as well as various services. This range included actual or contingent "carrots," such as explicit or implicit offers of membership in regional economic organizations and trade agreements, economic assistance, and diplomatic recognition of new states; and "sticks," such as moral condemnations of violations of human rights or other international norms, the threat or use of economic sanctions and withdrawal of aid or diplomatic recognition, warnings of military actions, and deterrence through preventive peacekeeping.

Another type of instrument was the offer of "tables"—that is, opportunities to facilitate bargaining and negotiations between the disputants and others, such as bilateral negotiations, fact-finding or monitoring missions, peace conferences, track-two informal dialogues, good offices, joint commissions, and binding arbitration.

Reasons for Action

Third-party actors tend to act to avert potential conflicts not because they receive a warning or learn of the outbreak of violence, but rather when national or international leaders judge that particular disputes hold wider regional significance or pose broader symbolic or actual threats.

The cases show that third parties do, on occasion, seek to preempt crises rather than wait for them to erupt and then seek to manage them. Responses have followed warning signs in the form of initial violent or coercive actions or general apprehension that major violence or other destabilizing events might occur if action is not taken.

It is noteworthy that preventive actions were taken despite the absence of palpable and imminent threats posed directly to "vital" national or organizational interests of the third parties. Specific decisions to act may have required some triggering event, such as the violence in Brazzaville, the army riots in Zaire, and the independence declarations of the Yugoslav republics. But in themselves these were relatively minor episodes. Even if they were to erupt in widespread violence, none of these anticipated conflicts would devastate a third party: no third party faced, for example, an attack on its national territory, the cutting off of essential oil supplies, or the complete destruction of an organization or regime. Third parties deemed preventive action advisable because of the possible local and regional or secondary effects of conflict escalation.

Decisions to act to prevent violence were taken by the leaders of third parties without apparent pressure from their domestic constituents or the media to do so. Indeed, most citizens of the member countries of the United Nations, European Community, OAU, and OAS were unlikely to have known of the existence of the disputes that received early third-party attention. More often, domestic constituencies such as Croatians in Germany or African Americans in the United States mobilized only at later stages of major crises, and then in support of one or another party. Leaders acted in response to what, by their lights, were long-term considerations of national interests.

This does not mean that responses were made automatically to every episode of turmoil or sign of impending conflict. Early warnings occurred in several instances but did not precipitate any action. Strong expectations of potential conflict or even the outbreak of violence were not in themselves sufficient to generate preventive action. For example: fighting and grievous human rights violations in northern Somalia were widely reported by human rights organizations as early as 1988 yet provoked no response; International Alert disseminated a fact-finding report and recommendations regarding the Russia-Chechen dispute to the United Nations and other bodies in 1992, but no action followed; in the Danube River dispute between Hungary and Slovakia, the disputants issued several requests for mediation assistance long before any third party stepped forward. Involvement may be spurred by requests for action from the disputants, such as when Macedonia President Gligorov asked for a peacekeeping force in 1992. But not all such requests are honored. Alija Izetbegovic had made a similar request for protective peacekeeping for Bosnia in late 1991 but was turned down.

What, then, does prompt third-party involvement? Often, leading third parties decided if and when to act not because of signs of possible violence, but because the third parties came to conclusions on a case-by-case basis that were particular conflicts to grow they would have wider geopolitical or symbolic impact. The tension between Estonia and Russia over the rights of Russian speakers was deemed of potential geopolitical significance, because Russia was using the issue as a bargaining chip to delay the withdrawal of its troops from the

Baltic states. Ethnic turmoil within the Baltic region might also interfere with U.S.–Russian relations with respect to issues deemed to be of wider significance. The EC and UN action toward Yugoslavia was prompted by the spreading perception that Yugoslavia was especially vulnerable to a violent breakup if the republics continued to show signs of seceding unilaterally, and that this might trigger secessionist moves in many other parts of the region. In Macedonia, the United Nations and Western governments feared a wider Balkans conflict that might not only draw in neighboring countries but also—because Greece and Turkey were among these neighbors—weaken the cohesion of NATO. The West was also moved to take action by the symbolic importance of ensuring the survival of a newly independent state struggling to make multiethnic democracy work. The OAU Secretariat saw the Congo dispute as an opportunity to activate its newly established conflict prevention mechanism, which had just been created in part to improve that organization's declining reputation in conflict management. The members of the OAS responded to attacks on democracy because of concern that events in Haiti, Peru, and Guatemala might invite similar moves elsewhere in Latin America.

Yet, not all third-party decisions to act preventively were based on ad hoc judgments about what was at stake in individual situations. Some responses, such as the work of the OCSE HCNM and the OAS 1080 procedure, followed from a more automatic process, because in those cases a prior mandate was understood to require prevention efforts.

WHAT EXPLAINS SUCCESS OR FAILURE?

Perhaps the most important question to which policymakers and practitioners need answers has to do with effectiveness: Do preventive efforts actually make a difference, or does the nonescalation of disputes have little to do with deliberate preventive action? And if preventive diplomacy does have an impact, why does it? What are the most promising strategies to which policymakers can wisely devote their limited resources? This section sheds light on these issues by presenting initial conclusions from the cases outlined above. This is work in progress, and these generalizations are hardly definitive. But being based on a variety of recent cases examined in light of several plausible hypotheses, the findings are more than merely speculative.

Many factors, of course, explain why emerging political disputes do not always lead to the use of armed force. Some factors are subject to human manipulation and thus are realistic targets for preventive diplomacy. Among these manipulable factors are, for example, the aims, attitudes, and behavior of the leaders of the disputants; the agreements they try to reach; the weapons and resources they have at their disposal; the channels available for resolving the dispute; and the skill of mediators.

But other factors that account for the course of a conflict are less susceptible to deliberate human manipulation (at least in the short run). The presence or absence of these so-called structural or systemic factors may be sufficient to determine whether conflicts erupt or are mitigated. Social scientists list many such more or less nonmanipulable sources of conflicts, and some show up in early warning models. An example would be the general deterrent effect on the origination of hostilities that is exercised by the balance of military power between two countries. Scholars in the "realist" tradition of inquiry regard such effects as very important causal factors in determining the course of international relations and thus the incidence of conflicts. Another factor assumed to be relatively nonmanipulable is the "primordial" attachments or bonds that some analysts of ethnic conflicts in particular regard as powerful underlying emotional and historical forces that tie the members of ethnic groups together and drive such conflicts. In recent literature seeking to explain violent ethnonational conflicts, for example, key nonmanipulable variables include "ethnic affinity," or the bond between members of the same ethnic groups who live in different places; gross inequalities of power and wealth between the parties to a dispute; the extent to which groups have dominated or fought each other in the past; the constraints placed on leaders by outside patrons on which the disputants depend; and limits on war making imposed by geography.

In sum, whether or not a dispute becomes violent or is prevented may be determined as much by the weight of certain basic "givens" as by whether or not anyone has done anything to prevent it. The stronger such systemic causal factors are, the more likely it is that a conflict will escalate and the less likely that intervention can prevent it. The weaker these factors are, the less likely conflict will erupt. A flaw of many firsthand accounts by those directly involved in preventing or resolving a dispute is that they may tend to exaggerate the impact of human action and thus claim credit for results actually brought about by causal factors that are more or less beyond a third party's control. This issue is not academic, because overestimation of human agency can lead to unrealistic policy recommendations.

There is an equal danger, however, of underrating human efforts. Just as historians who focus on warfare may conclude that conflict is an ingrained human trait, conflict analysts may fail to notice the human interventions made to avoid the eruption of violence and may thus be skeptical of the notion of preventability. Contributing to this lack of attention to preventive efforts is the dearth of accounts of preventive diplomacy—a dearth attributable in part to preventive diplomacy's secret process, but largely a result of the fact that those directly involved have not written up their experience. The resulting perspective ignores the possibility that significant variations in conflict outcomes can depend on whether actions are taken to prevent or exacerbate them. This too has policy implications, because ignoring cases of successful prevention can discourage efforts to attempt other preventive efforts.[7]

Even some systemic factors may be more malleable than is often assumed. For example, the legacy of historical enmity between ethnic groups can be downplayed as well as whipped up by the present-day leaders of those groups. Proceeding from the assumption that some conflicts are not inevitable and that some can be prevented, the present study seeks to determine which of those factors that are relatively manipulable make the difference between a violent or a peaceful outcome. How, though, can we tell which manipulable factors might have had an effect? One method is to pick, as we have done, conflicts for examination that share systemic features often deemed of paramount causal importance (such as ethnic content and historical and regional context), but that differ in terms of whether they escalated into violence or did not. In social science jargon, one can control for the causal weight of the systemic independent variables by comparing the cases that share these conditions but that varied in their outcomes. Examples of such constants in this study are the structural changes that after 1989, we have suggested, laid the groundwork for ethnonationalism and the possible disenfranchisement of ethnic minorities in the new states of Central Europe and the former Soviet Union.

All the cases selected were targets of some kind of preventive diplomacy. One then looks to see if hypothesized manipulable factors characterize the cases that were prevented but not the ones that were not. If differences in these factors were in fact significant determinants of the diverging outcomes, one would expect to see fairly consistent differences in these features between the relatively successful cases of preventive diplomacy, on the one hand, and the relatively unsuccessful ones, on the other hand. This "similar systems" logic does not eliminate all possible basic or manipulable factors that may explain the differing outcomes, but it gives one more confidence that manipulable factors that appear in some cases but not others have had some independent influence on the result.[8]

Discerning causal relationships within conflicts is inherently difficult. Even so, preliminary examination of a range of cases suggests that five more or less manipulable factors were often present in the situations in which emerging political disputes were handled through peaceful means and were largely absent in those disputes that resulted in the use of armed force. Three of these factors operated outside the immediate arena of the dispute and pertained to third parties; two were indigenous in nature but are nonetheless instructive for would-be preventers insofar as they reveal points where third parties might usefully apply leverage. The five factors are:

- **Third-party timing:** The extent to which third parties support strong, unequivocal pressures in the form of positive and negative inducements directed at the disputants to advance a peace process before one or the other disputant uses armed force or another type of coercion to attempt to resolve a dispute.

- **Multifaceted action:** The extent to which third parties, acting in coordination, employ not one but several diverse instruments—

including, for example, contingent offers of recognition, consultations, and advice, and provisions for security—so as to address the various aspects of a dispute.

- *Support from major players:* The extent to which major global and regional powers and neighboring states support or tolerate active preventive efforts and refrain from subverting a peaceful process through backing one or the other disputant. In the cases surveyed, this ingredient was often reinforced by the degree to which the United States took an active interest in resolving the dispute and by the high-profile involvement of a regional organization perceived to be acting not as the agent of one or another major power but in the best interests of the region as a whole.

- *Moderate leadership:* The extent to which the leaders of disputing groups display moderation in their expressed views, actions, and policies.

- *State autonomy:* The extent to which recognized states are involved in a dispute and are autonomous from any of the disputants. A sufficiently autonomous state possesses procedures and institutions through which disputes can be impartially negotiated and agreements enforced; the military and security forces of such a state serve the constitutional order and are independent of the partisan aims of political factions vying for control of the state. Established states can also provide the channels through which political elites seeking to achieve or maintain political power can secure support for their positions of power from the international community.

Third-Party Timing

Peaceful outcomes are more likely to the extent that third parties apply unequivocal pressures on the parties to engage in mutual processes and institutions aimed at peaceful settlement of differences—before one or the other party mobilizes its political constituency or deploys armed force or coercion to achieve concrete gains.

As reflected in table 3.1, the widely accepted belief that the earlier that third parties take preventive action the more effective it is finds overall support in general theories of conflict escalation and certain quantitative studies into the correlates of effective mediation. This research is inconclusive, however, as to whether inducements to resolve disputes peacefully can be effective before the parties have actually engaged in some degree of intense conflict. Some analysts suggest that third-party intervention must "wait" until the disputants have already reached some sort of stalemate following an initial engagement or have attempted themselves to come to terms.[9]

The cases reviewed here confirm the generally accepted view that early third-party involvement is vital, and do not support the argument that effective intervention must wait for a stalemate to develop. According to the evidence examined here, political, economic, or military pressures to work toward a mutual solution must be applied before either party has begun to garner political support or use coercive measures or force to achieve substantial gains. Third parties apparently have to be willing not only to encourage and facilitate negotiation but also to engage in what has been termed "muscular mediation"—that is, to provide rewards sufficient to gain the disputants' compliance and/or impose penalties adequate to deter their noncompliance with processes of peaceful negotiation. Because these inducements have to be seen by the parties as outweighing the partisan gains that might be secured through force or other unilateral coercive actions, the impact of such inducements is likely to be considerably dulled if they come into play after one or the other party has already made gains.

In the Hungarian-Slovakian dispute, third-party involvement was not especially prompt. The parties themselves had several times requested and been denied outside assistance before the European Community finally offered mediation; and that mediation did not immediately secure an agreement. Nevertheless, an initial settlement was achieved and later a broader treaty encouraged as well, once it was made clear to Hungary and Slovakia that their membership in the European Community would be hindered if they continued to balk at resolving their dispute. Similar economic rewards were offered to Estonia as an inducement to modify its minority legislation, and Russia was provided an incentive to keep to schedule with its troop withdrawals by the threat that U.S. and other Western economic aid otherwise would be withdrawn.

The several preventive measures in Macedonia were taken to guard against Serbian efforts to destabilize Macedonia either directly or through intensifying the suppression of the Kosovar Albanians, as well as to monitor and to signal international support for the maintenance of internal political cooperation among Macedonia's ethnic groups and their parties. The effectiveness of these essentially deterrent measures may owe much to the fact that they were undertaken largely *before* any party to the disputes within and outside Macedonia had the opportunity to impose its will through force or agitation.

These deterrents included the periodic warnings from Presidents Bush and Clinton to Serbian President Slobodan Milosevic that any Serbian armed movement in Kosovo or against Macedonia would be met by firm U.S. retaliatory measures, which have been understood to mean military intervention; and the UN peacekeeping force deployed to patrol the Serbian-Macedonian border, which was created in 1993 after the Yugoslav army had withdrawn from the area, and serves as a tripwire to deter its return. The fact that Macedonia is recognized in international law as a state by 110 other countries and is a member of the United Nations may also be a significant deterrent of a normative kind. These actions seem to have been more effective than international recognition of Croatia, because Macedonia not only was endowed with the status of a sovereign state prior to any takeover by hostile elements but also was afforded some military protection to guarantee that status (or at least to guarantee vigorous countermeasures should the Serbian army move against Macedonia).

Prompt international involvement also characterized the relatively successful cases of international involvement in the Guatemalan and Congo/Brazzaville democratization disputes. Most OAS members have preferred to rely on a Latin American style of consensus building and facilitation rather than intrusive mediation or intervention for the resolution of domestic problems. Because the OAS has been wary of sanctioning the use of military force as a tool of enforcement and has been unwilling to make economic sanctions mandatory, Resolution 1080 relies on voluntary collective action in the form of moral condemnation, diplomatic persuasion, the glare of publicity, and economic sanctions, not the presence or threat of military force. Nevertheless, the resolution's requirement of prompt investigation of threats to legitimately established democratic institutions and its unambiguous prohibition of coercive actions have been effective because they have created a collective expectation from which it may be hard for governments to deviate. Resolution 1080 not only sets out a clear standard for judging governments' actions and requires OAS inquiry of apparent violations of that standard, but also may have a multiplier effect in mobilizing economic and diplomatic pressures from other states and catalyzing domestic opposition. This combination of international and domestic pressure was sufficient in the case of Guatemala to deter the Guatemalan military from supporting President Serrano.

With regard to OAU and other international involvement in the electoral dispute in Congo/Brazzaville in mid-1993, it is more difficult to determine how critical was the mediator's timing in averting further violence and reaching a peaceful outcome. He seems not to have had much in the way of carrots and sticks. Although no rewards or threats were explicitly made by the mediator, however, the president and opposition realized that outside powers were watching and were supportive of the talks. The electoral agreement agreed to would be monitored and implemented under joint OAU-EC supervision, and the mediator had solicited support for his negotiations from the U.S. ambassador—thus, the parties to the dispute may have entertained the possibility of U.S. and/or EC sanctions should the negotiations have failed or the agreement fallen apart. The mediator also resolved a financial dispute between the government and a French multinational oil company suspected of supporting the opposition parties.

Nevertheless, such factors as the mediator's own skills and the disposition of the disputants themselves to reach an agreement may have shaped the outcome as much as inducements offered and the timing of intervention. After all, the OAU emissary arrived in Brazzaville only after extensive rioting and violence from street demonstrations had left many dead. Although sporadic skirmishes were occurring and the atmosphere was tense, the army's imposition of order had brought about a halt in the fighting. Even so, given the fact that a mediator had been requested by the government and was agreed to by all the parties, the OAU's relatively quick response and the mediator's success over the next several days may well have been essential in avoiding further deterioration in the relationship of the parties and renewed instability and violence. In that sense, timing probably was crucial.

That early forceful international support for peaceful politics may be a requisite for effective preventive diplomacy finds further support from cases of failure. In none of the cases that resulted in violence or deadlock were muscular third-party efforts made before significant intercommunal violence or the preemptive use of armed force occurred.

In the growing conflict between the Yugoslav federal republics after the breakdown of the Communist Party, several outside efforts were made beginning in early 1991 to pressure the republics to stay together or negotiate their differences. In this case, the problem was not that no mediation efforts were made or that the notion of peaceful resolution of differences was left unspoken. In fact, the European Community and the U.S. government made it clear, initially at least, that whether Yugoslavia stayed together or divided was not so much the issue as that some mutual agreement on governing structures, including provisions for minorities, be arrived at without the use of force.

Rather, one problem, at least before late 1992, was that by the time the European Community and the United States acted, the political divisions among and within the republics had already grown very wide and military preparations and actions were already under way. To dissuade the nationalist leaders in the republics from pursuing independence unilaterally, the European Community could urge restraint, withhold or offer recognition and economic assistance, threaten economic sanctions, and proffer negotiations. But these inducements to pursue a peaceful solution seem to have been weak in comparison to the substantial territorial and domestic political gains the republics believed they could continue to achieve on the ground through unilateral faites accompli.

In addition, the initial evenhanded approach adopted by the European Community was itself soon undercut by Germany's recognition of Slovenia and Croatia as sovereign states. Not only did Germany's strategy of "preventive recognition" produce a rift in the community's ranks and a shift in EC policy, but it also backfired, for instead of deterring further hostilities between Serbia and Croatia, it hastened their breakup. No effort was made to insist on or enforce protection of the minority Serbs in Croatia or to protect the Croatians should the ongoing local skirmishes continue to grow, thus increasing the insecurities on both sides.

Even after the short war between the federal authorities and Slovenia had been resolved by Slovenian victory in July 1991, and the longer conflict between Croatia and Serbia had been waging for some months, the international community still had time and opportunity to prevent a similar resort to military action in Bosnia. A legal commission to the European Community recommended in January 1992 that republics wishing to be recognized as independent states hold referenda to determine their citizens' views. By this time Bosnian leader Izetbegovic saw that with Croatia now independent and recognized as such by EC members, Bosnia would be exposed to untempered Serbian domination were it to be part of the tripartite confederation Izetbegovic had earlier proposed. Izetbegovic thus announced a referendum to confirm Bosnia's independence, despite the tensions this would unleash in Bosnia among Muslims, Serbs, and Croats. Predictably, the Bosnian Serbs rejected the referendum and fighting began in April. Here again, the international community was not willing to provide the newly declared and vulnerable republic with any protection. A request from Izetbegovic in late 1991 for the kind of UN preventive peacekeeping force that was to be sent later that year to Macedonia was denied.

The same delay between use of force by a disputant and forceful international efforts at peaceful resolution of a dispute is seen in the Haiti case. When the Haitian military authorities abrogated the democratic presidential election of Jean-Bertrand Aristide in September 1991, the OAS set in train the procedure contained in its Resolution 1080, condemned the action by the Haitian military, and asked the United Nations to impose a trade embargo. But General Cedras's action revealed two shortcomings of the mechanism when applied to military, as against executive, coups—one, that military coups tend to be completed extremely swiftly, leaving little or no time for the OAS mechanism to come into play; and two, that OAS diplomatic and economic actions are no match for military regimes once in power. Argentina, Venezuela, and Ecuador did advocate an immediate

military invasion of Haiti, but the idea was opposed by the United
States and Mexico and failed to win OAS approval.

International pressures eventually led to the negotiation of the
Governor's Island agreement, by which Aristide was to assume his
elected office. However, with sanctions suspended, Haiti's military
rulers saw to it that the UN training force on board the USS *Harlan
County* did not disembark on the island, and in October 1993 the
Haitian junta refused to fulfill its part of the Governor's Island agreement. Despite the relative weakness of Cedras's seven-thousand-man
force, the United Nations was unwilling to consider authorizing an invasion of Haiti. Sanctions were reimposed but had little apparent impact on a regime by now deeply entrenched in its opposition to a
return to democratic rule. Not until faced with a full-fledged invasion
and offered a face-saving deal did the regime give up power peacefully and allow Aristide to return and assume office. By then, sanctions had left Haiti even more economically distressed than usual
and, together with political repression, had prompted the exodus of
thousands of refugees.

Rwanda from 1993 to 1994 presents another instance of international preventive action failing because of insufficient resources early
on. The deficiency in this case was again not the utter lack of timely
third-party action, but the relative weakness of the carrots offered and
sticks brandished when compared to the mounting strength of the
forces driving the use of violence. A civil war had waged between the
predominantly Hutu government and the predominantly Tsutsi
Rwandan Patriotic Front (RPF) since an RPF invasion from Uganda
in 1992. The OAU and United Nations were able to arrange a cease-
fire and inaugurate a plan for achieving power sharing through the
Arusha Accords of August 1993. To monitor observance of the accords
and watch for signs of instability, the OAU and subsequently the
United Nations dispatched a military observation force in the fall. This
force was made up of only five hundred troops, however, and thus
was insufficient to be able to detect the efforts being taken by the
Hutu authorities not only to avoid implementation of the accords but
also to recruit and arm militias ready to retake the country at the first
opportunity.

That opportunity came when the plane carrying the presidents of
Rwanda and Burundi was approaching Kigali airport on April 6, 1994.

The most common criticism leveled against the international role in Rwanda is that the response to the mass killings was too slow and too limited. And it is true that repeated efforts by OAS Secretary-General Salim Ahmed Salim and President Yoweri Museveni of Uganda to mediate the conflict and to raise African troops for a peacekeeping force failed to attract support, not least because other countries were wary of intervening in so violent a situation. But the chief fault of third-party involvement occurred before genocide began. That fault was providing too few resources to monitor the implementation of the Arusha Accords and to discern the strengthening of ethnic militias. In short, in Rwanda as in other cases of failed prevention, the pressure being applied by the international community to pursue a peaceful resolution of a political question was weaker than the forces fueling a slide toward violence.

Similarly, in Moldova, for example, no international body took an interest in the deepening antagonism between the Moldovan government and the Dniestr separatist movement until the CSCE mediated a cease-fire in 1994 and sent an observer mission to monitor it. By that time, the local forces had captured all the territory they wanted. A similar pattern is apparent in the events preceding the war that broke out in Chechnya in December 1994. Although several bilateral negotiations between the authorities in Moscow and the Chechen political leadership had taken place in the preceding years, requests for international mediation had elicited no response. As we have noted, the only third-party effort seems to have been the fact-finding mission sent by International Alert in 1992.

In sum, the cases here reviewed suggest that the level of inducement that third parties must bring to bear in terms of carrots and/or sticks is relative to the scale and stage of development of the violence or coercive power being addressed. Measures applied early in a conflict before these factors grow require less pressure and cost less than do measures applied later. Once the use of force or coercion is imminent or under way, it can only be deterred or reversed by a great deal of counterforce (whether in the form of material rewards or threats of economic sanctions or military action).

Multifaceted Action

Effective preventive diplomacy requires not just a strong enough combination of carrots and/or sticks but also the use of a variety of actions and instruments to address the various facets of a dispute. These actions must be closely coordinated among the third parties participating in the preventive effort.

Parties to a conflict generally need more than rewards for good behavior and penalties for bad conduct if they are to see their way to a peaceful resolution of their dispute. Depending on the resources already available to the disputants, third parties may have to provide not only a combination of carrots and sticks but also a variety of other services, which might include hands-on assistance in building institutions, alleviating distrust, promoting reconciliation, establishing channels through which to pursue negotiations, and formulating settlements. In other words, one of the measures of the adequacy of preventive interventions is their richness or breadth.

Arguably, for example, the effectiveness of preventive effort in Macedonia depends on the *aggregate* impact of U.S. threats of military action and the presence of the UN peacekeeping force, the CSCE observation mission, several NGO dialogue and reconciliation projects, and the widespread diplomatic recognition accorded the new Macedonian government. Together, these official and nonofficial actions have turned the international spotlight on Macedonia and signaled to its various factions and neighbors a significant international presence and interest in Macedonia. In Estonia the great variety of governmental and nongovernmental, bilateral and multilateral third-party entities that became engaged had the same effect. By contrast, in the failed cases of preventive diplomacy in Croatia, Rwanda, and Haiti, only one or two instruments were employed, and these were targeted on only one aspect of the local dispute.

In particularly complex situations with a variety of problems, such as Macedonia, Zaire, Rwanda, and Burundi, a premium is thus placed on cooperation and coordination among third-party actors. Where cooperation and unity of purpose among third parties are weak or absent, preventive effectiveness is compromised. The EC decision to recognize Slovenia and Croatia, for example, was taken against the wishes of the UN negotiator Cyrus Vance, who felt recognition placed further strains on the relationships among the republican leaders and increased the difficulties of reaching a political settlement. The mutual wariness and varying attitudes among the United States, France, and Belgium regarding Zaire has probably contributed to the absence of an assertive effort to resolve that crisis. The head of the UN observer mission in Rwanda in 1993–94 regretted the apparent disparity among the agendas of the third parties there.[10] By contrast, the unified approach displayed in the Congo and the degree of UN-CSCE consultation achieved in Macedonia may help to explain the effectiveness of these efforts.

Concerted third-party action may be greatly facilitated by the presence of an individual diplomat, other single player, or small, united group that, backed by a major power or organization, takes charge and orchestrates a unified preventive strategy. Among examples of the individual diplomatic entrepreneurs who infused preventive efforts with a notable degree of synergy are U.S. diplomat Robert Frowick, the first CSCE head of mission in Macedonia; the OAU's envoy to the Congo, Mohamed Sahnoun; the UN special representative to Burundi, Ould Abdullah; the CSCE HCNM, Max van der Stoel; and the OAS secretary-general, Joao Clemente Baena Soares. By using their personal prestige, diplomatic skills, and authority as de jure representatives of multilateral organizations (and in some instances as de facto representatives of powers), such individuals established local contacts, found the best political leverage points, handled the media adroitly, and employed other tactics to help create a package of inducements, penalties, and services tailored to a given situation.

Support from Major Players

Preventive diplomatic efforts are more effective when major powers, regional powers, and neighboring states agree to support or tolerate those efforts and do not undermine them by overt or covert support for one or another party to a dispute. The participation of the United States and of regional organizations further enhances the possibilities for preventive success.

Although localized and regional conflicts are now much less likely to involve confrontations between major powers than was the case during the Cold War, the outcome of third-party conflict initiatives in regions where dominant powers are present or where they have significant interests is still greatly determined by the attitudes of those powers. Russia, for example, has a proprietary interest in the treatment of Russian minorities in many states of the former Soviet Union, and any preventive efforts in the so-called Near Abroad must depend on Russian goodwill or tolerance if they are to proceed. Even states that are minor players on the world stage may be major players in a local context if their geographical propinquity to, or partisan stake in, a particular conflict endows them with the ability to facilitate or frustrate third-party preventive efforts.

The influence, for good or ill, of major players can be exercised in a variety of ways. One is through approving or vetoing the involvement of the United Nations or a regional organization of which they are members. Serbian objections to CSCE involvement in the former Yugoslavia, for instance, help explain why that organization quickly became less effective than the United Nations and European Community in 1990–91 in trying to negotiate an end to the fighting. As a member of the CSCE at the time, Serbia was able to veto further CSCE involvement.

Another way local actors as well as major powers can impede or assist prevention is through supporting or not supporting one or another disputant, or choosing whether to remain on the sidelines or to themselves become direct parties to the conflict. In Moldova, for example, the support given to Dniestr Russians by Russia's 14th Army was instrumental in their ability to control the left bank of the Dniestr River and in limiting outside efforts to resolve the conflict. Despite repeated appeals for support by Moldovan president Mircea Snegur to the UN Security Council, CSCE, and Commonwealth of Independent States, Russia's influence in the conflict limited the effectiveness of international organizations. An example of this can be seen in the Russian-Moldovan convention on principles for the peaceful settlement of the conflict, signed on July 3, 1992. Without ruling out the use of UN or CSCE observers, the convention mandated Russian Moldovan and Dniestr units to enforce the cease-fire and disengagement of forces and provided for "peacemaking" troops of the Russian Federation to be deployed in Moldova. The CSCE-mediated cease-fire in 1994 took place after the Russian forces left of the Dniestr had consolidated their territorial gains.

A major player can also exert itself through the economic and/or diplomatic influence it enjoys in a given region and that obliges other regional states and outside powers to depend on it or to accommodate its point of view. Russian economic, political, and military dominance in the Near Abroad—particularly the leverage given Russia by its control over the supply of energy to, and the presence of Russian military forces in, many smaller states—allows Russia to play active roles in the conflicts not only in Moldova but also in Estonia, Ukraine, and the Transcaucasus. Even in the former Yugoslavia, an area that is not clearly within Russia's sphere of interest, the West has had to be mindful of Russian sensibilities because of Russia's links to the Serbians. When Russia went to war in Chechnya in December 1994, the United States was initially hesitant to criticize Russia for fear of complicating and compromising U.S.-Russian cooperation on a range of other issues.

Russian dominance in the former Soviet Union is paralleled by U.S. supremacy in the Western hemisphere. The United States has long resisted the introduction of extrahemispheric military forces into conflicts in Latin America, permitting their introduction only recently in Haiti, and then only under the aegis of the United States or United Nations. Significant diplomatic initiatives by outside actors to contain or resolve hemispheric conflicts would almost certainly need U.S. approval. Conversely, U.S. political support of the OAS responses to the executive usurpation of democratic authority in Guatemala and Peru was clearly important to the effectiveness of OAS action. And the threat of economic sanctions from the United States added to the pressure that the OAS exerted and was critical to persuading Guatemala's business community to support the reversal of the coup.

Even major powers lying outside the region of a conflict but having an interest in it will shape the likelihood and success or failure of the prevention efforts made there. In the Middle East, for example, the United States has long been the main peacemaker and a prime actor—although it is not always the only one, as the Norwegian-brokered Israeli-Palestinian talks illustrate.

In some regions, several outside powers may have interests. Although none of these powers will necessarily dominate the handling of a dispute, individually and collectively they may have a profound impact on whether preventive action is taken. Sub-Saharan Africa lies outside the sphere of interest of any single major power, for example, but European powers such as France, Belgium, Italy, and Great Britain have maintained close ties with their former colonies and have been active in many military interventions, mediations, and peacekeeping throughout the continent. The United States has considerable interest and influence in the region, too, particularly in the Horn of Africa, East Africa, and southern Africa. The Baltic states, although formerly part of the Soviet Union, have historically enjoyed close relations with the West and the Nordic countries, a fact that has increased third-party preventive activity and leverage there, as a counterbalance to Russia.

The interest of several major powers in a particular region can enhance the prospects for effective preventive action, but it can also complicate, delay, or even undermine such activity. Differences among the United States, Belgium, and France over how to deal with President Mobutu have not advanced the chances of defusing the crisis in Zaire. More dramatically, France's apparent supply of arms to Hutu groups in Rwanda and Burundi is fueling further violence in those countries.

Whereas competing interests may weaken the efficacy of preventive efforts, the lack of interest among the major powers in a particular region may cause disputes there to be neglected. This direct relation between level of interest and level of activity may partly explain the slow response to developments in Moldova and Somalia, for example, neither of which has high economic or strategic significance for the West.

The Unique Position of the United States. Notwithstanding regional variations in U.S. prestige and influence, the global purview of the United States, its moral standing, and its effective influence as a third party have endowed it with the status of "first among equals" in many preventive efforts. In the cases examined and in others like Somalia, the United States was widely welcomed as a participant, and its role as "prime mover" was often crucial in securing cooperation and resolving conflicts. The positive reception generally accorded to U.S. actors performing the roles of leading energizers, mobilizers, mediators, guarantors, and/or financiers of many efforts stemmed from the widespread perception that the United States is more likely than other states to be nonpartisan and/or that it possesses the political and military power and economic influence to deliver on incentives or threats that might be part of a settlement package.

In Latin America, uncomfortable memories of past U.S. military interventions do not detract from acceptance of the idea that the United States has been critical to several dispute settlements there—and privately, Latin American leaders often indicate as much. The prospect of U.S. sanctions or assistance in the Haitian, Peruvian, and Guatemalan cases surely figured prominently in the calculations of the parties involved. In the Macedonian case, the U.S. government was often regarded as the most important of the third parties involved. The fact that the three heads of the CSCE mission have been American diplomats reflects the desire among local actors for U.S. involvement and has undoubtedly enhanced the local respect accorded the CSCE. Many European nations are encumbered by historical baggage from their colonial experiences or other episodes that discredits them in the eyes of some local groups from serving as impartial mediators. They also may have more nationalist foreign policies and less global reach. The generally good reputation enjoyed by the United States extends also to the work of U.S. NGOs. In Croatia and Macedonia, for example, the initiatives taken by American NGOs often seem to fare better than those conducted by European NGOs. Of course, the United States would bring its own historical baggage to some regions, and thus its direct involvement—in the form of U.S. peacekeeping troops, for example—would not be politically feasible.

But even where, as in many instances, U.S. involvement in preventive activities has been indirect in nature, it has still proven invaluable. Indeed, direct U.S. involvement is by no means always necessary or desirable. In the international involvement in Yugoslavia, the U.S. government often exerted considerable leverage through multilateral channels, such as through the CSCE and the UN mission in Macedonia, rather than through direct, unilateral U.S. action. In the case of Congo, the U.S. government occupied a secondary but nonetheless important role, indicating its desire for a peaceful settlement while leaving center stage to the OAU mediator. In South Africa, too, low-key, uninstructed mediation by the U.S. ambassador played a significant role in averting widespread conflict.

Regional Organizations as Middle Ground. At the forefront of preventive activity in many of the cases reviewed, regional organizations not only helped to advance ideas, marshall regional sentiment and resources, and provide various inducements and facilities for negotiation, but also served to allay suspicions that one or another major power or regional actor was seeking to impose a settlement for its own selfish reasons. By thus legitimizing preventive activity and acting as a buffer between major players, regional organizations create a middle ground for cooperation among third parties and between third parties and disputants. In Eurasia, for example, the OSCE has acted as a useful meeting ground and focal point for both Western and Russian involvement in Estonia, Moldova, and other states of the former Soviet Union. In the Americas, the OAS has helped to legitimize U.S. participation in and support for hemispheric initiatives.

One factor motivating the OAS to adopt and apply the Santiago mechanism was the Latin American members' desire to overcome a pattern whereby their inability to agree to address common threats and conflicts had increased the rationale for unilateral U.S. intervention. The U.S. invasion of Panama to remove President Manuel Noriega from power, for instance, was seen by some Latin American leaders as a failure in Latin American political self-reliance. The OAS's aversion to the use of force thus stems in part from Latin American resentment of past U.S. military interventionism and a desire to substitute other, homegrown methods. As Luigi Einaudi, U.S. representative to the OAS, noted, the adoption of Resolution 1080 was in part a preemptive effort "by the Lilliputians to tie down the American giant."[11]

Moderate Leadership

Peaceful outcomes are more likely when the leaders of the parties to the dispute are moderate in their words, actions, and policies, make conciliatory gestures, and seek bilateral or multilateral negotiations and bargaining to resolve the issues in dispute.

The level of tension and disposition to use violence can be greatly increased if political controversies are intensified by a public "war of words" waged with ultimatums, threats, and divisive rhetoric. Such intemperate and incendiary public debate is especially likely to occur in those areas (such as the former Soviet bloc) where established political norms have broken down and new ones have yet to take their place. The potential for violence is further exacerbated when partisan rhetoric is translated into legislation or policy action that clearly favors one faction or group at the expense of another. The use of force by the police and/or military against political opponents adds yet greater momentum to the slide toward widespread violence.

Conversely, the chances of reaching a peaceful outcome are significantly enhanced in cases where leaders display greater restraint and show themselves willing to accommodate the interests of other parties through negotiation and consultation before enacting potentially divisive or discriminatory legislation. In the Gabcikovo-Nagymaros hydroelectric project dispute and other ethnically charged controversies between Hungary and Slovakia, for example, harsh words and unilateral actions by the parties were nevertheless mixed with efforts to initiate bilateral negotiations and to involve third parties, efforts that eventually resulted in mediated agreements. Moderate leaders from both Slovakia and Hungary have made a number of bilateral efforts over the last two years to maintain an open dialogue on ethnic issues and to keep major crises from developing.

The same tendency to refer issues to negotiation and international bodies was displayed by the leaders of other countries that successfully managed potentially explosive crises over the interests of ethnic minorities whose kin are majorities in neighboring states. Despite Estonia's restrictive legislation and its unilateral seizure of a naval base, for example, its actions were increasingly tempered by a willingness to accept monitoring and policy suggestions by international bodies such as the Council of Europe, the CSCE, and a UN human rights delegation. For its part, although Russia used its control of energy supplies and the presence of its troops as bargaining chips, it also appealed to the international community for support on the basis that Estonia was flouting accepted human rights standards.

In other cases of relative success in dealing with ethnic national-ist movements, moderation too played an important, albeit sec-ondary, role. The breakup of Czechoslovakia on January 1, 1993, into two new independent states, for example, was managed without vio-lence in part because the Czech and Slovak peoples were largely separated in the two parts of Czechoslovakia, but also in part because the Czech and Slovak leaderships tried hard not to inflame the eth-nic passions on either side. With the sobering example of Yugoslavia before them, both Vaclav Havel and Meciar made special pleas dur-ing 1992 to their respective constituencies to avoid raising tensions. Avoiding the Yugoslavian practice of whipping up support for poli-cies with nationalist rhetoric, Czech and Slovak elites took pains to keep popular sentiments out of their debate. Popular referenda were not even held on the breakup.[12]

The peacefully resolved dispute between Russia and Ukraine over Crimea has ingredients similar to both the Estonian case of relative success and the Moldovan case of relative failure: the presence of a Russian-speaking majority in the Crimea and in other eastern parts of Ukraine, who favor retaining links with Russia; Crimean leaders who have risen to power in part because they champion local aspi-rations for independence or autonomy; and a major Russian military presence left over from the Soviet period in the form of the Black Sea Fleet. The abatement of tensions over the possibility of Crimean sep-aratism is explicable chiefly in terms of the larger stakes involved in the Ukrainian-Russian relationship, especially the negotiations over the dismantlement of Ukraine's nuclear weapons and Ukraine's con-siderable economic dependency on Russia. Even so, it is not without significance that Ukrainian policies toward minority rights and in-terests, which are among the most liberal in the region, did not con-tribute to tensions between the two countries. Unlike many other former Soviet republics, Ukraine defines itself as a territorial and le-gal entity, not as an ethnic nation; its people are defined in terms of their place of residence, not in ethnic or linguistic terms; and its leg-islation regarding employment, education, and culture protects every citizen regardless of ethnic origin, language, or religion. Ukraine has also turned to the Organization for Economic Cooperation and Development and the United Nations to help it deal with its local mi-nority problems.[13]

State Autonomy

Preventive diplomacy is more effective to the extent that the state directly affected by a dispute is autonomous from one or another of the disputants. A sufficiently autonomous state possesses procedures and institutions through which disputes can be impartially negotiated and agreements enforced; the military and security forces of such a state serve the constitutional order and are independent of the partisan aims of political factions vying for control of the state.

The cases examined suggest that preventive diplomacy, whether conducted by the disputants themselves or by third parties, is more likely to achieve a peaceful outcome when the parties to a dispute deal with one another within some previously established framework of rules and procedures. In cases of disputes *between* states, that framework may be provided by international organizations, institutions, and norms. In cases of disputes *within* states, the framework could be a political process or national government that is accepted as relatively nonpartisan. Prospects of a peaceful outcome in instances of growing civil discord are thus greatly enhanced by the existence of an autonomous state in which state organs and functions—lawmaking, administration, judicial decision making, international relations, and so forth—operate more or less independently of any one party to the dispute and in which the security and military forces refrain from direct involvement in political contests. In such instances, disputes are about the policies of states rather than the basic character and control of states.

The successful cases of preventive diplomacy occurring within states (among them, Macedonia, Guatemala, Congo, and Czech and Slovak republics) had the benefit of more or less effective governing institutions that had control of their security and armed forces. Guatemala and Peru, for example, possessed strong state institutions that had recently come under democratic control. The military and police forces had lately been constrained from playing a political role and did not automatically support the executive coups but rather paused to consider their effects on the country's economic position and international standing. Congo/Brazzaville had also developed a strong civil service and its military (although divided ethnically) had come to accept in recent years that it should play a neutral role in politics. Thus when the OAU mediator arrived, although the army was not ethnically diverse, it had restored order in the center of Brazzaville and was remaining neutral in the dispute for fear of fragmenting.

In the successful preventive actions undertaken in cases of disputes between states, the disputing governments were constrained in their actions by other states and by international norms. In Estonia, Russia, Hungary, and Slovakia preventive diplomacy was facilitated by the fact that the disputants, as leaders of established and internationally recognized states, stood to lose more in terms of foreign aid, membership in multilateral organizations, and various other benefits in the gift of the international community than they would gain politically from promoting ethnic nationalist causes.

Preventive diplomacy was less effective where there was no tradition of strong independent central governmental institutions (for instance, Moldova), where central state institutions were being torn down (as in the case of the Belgrade government in the former Yugoslavia between 1990 and 1992), or where leaders ran state institutions as patrimonial fiefdoms (for example, Somalia and Zaire). In all these settings, the rules and procedures of political-administrative entities were manipulated for political ends by the disputants themselves; unable to seek redress for their grievances through effective, nonpartisan channels, political opponents sought instead to pursue their aims through rebellion or secession. With each side already mobilizing and arming its support, preventive diplomacy became much more difficult to conduct and further violence more likely.

A major factor impeding the efforts of mediators to keep the dissolution of Yugoslavia from erupting into violence, for example, was the ongoing disintegration of organs of the state (such as the system of economic self-management, the collective presidency, and the Yugoslav army)—a process of fragmentation that had begun as early as 1974 with Marshall Tito's devolution reforms and had been accelerating since the late 1980s. Before and during the debate between the republics over Yugoslavia's constitution, a high degree of control was held by the presidents of the republics over political, administrative, economic, and—increasingly—military resources. A common tactic of aspiring nationalists was first to capture control of their parties, thus pushing moderates out, and then to use well-timed referendums to validate their parties' control of the republic. As early as

1990, republics were not sending conscripts to the Yugoslav army and instead were creating their own armed republican units within the police.

Similarly, the leaders of Moldova and the "Dniestr Republic" shared no common political institutions, and as violence erupted on the left bank, interior ministry forces lined up against a local militia increasingly supported by the Russian 14th Army. In Rwanda and Burundi, civilian institutions of government such as the civil service and legislature are weak, the militaries are dominated by Tutsis, and ethnic group leaders have had relatively free rein to arm their followers.

The Impact of Civil Societies. An autonomous state need not be a fully democratic state. State autonomy requires only that state institutions be effectively governed by a set of rules. Enforcement of those rules can be achieved equally well through compacts, coalitions, and other agreements among competing political elites who effectively control their own constituencies as it can through a process of immediate accountability to broad-based electorates.

Strong civil societies are, to be sure, desirable. But of the successful cases reviewed here, only two witnessed strong civil societies exerting pressure to prevent a political dispute from becoming violent. In Guatemala, a wide network of business, labor, and other groups mounted an impressive campaign to persuade President Serrano to back down; in Congo, leaders from the private sector contributed to pressure on the two factions to reach an agreement. In Zambia, too, trade unions and other social and economic institutions were apparently critical to the management of a peaceful transition from autocracy to pluralist politics.

4

POLICYMAKING AND IMPLEMENTATION

As we saw in chapter 3, preventive diplomacy has been tried and is sometimes effective. But to reap its full potential, it has to be undertaken more deliberately and consistently. It is one thing to apply preventive actions on an ad hoc and occasional basis when one or another organization, government, or person takes a special interest in a particular case. It is quite another to be prepared on an ongoing basis to anticipate and, where warranted, respond to a range of situations that could become deadly conflicts and costly international quagmires.

Fortunately, in developing a preventive diplomacy capacity we do not have to start from scratch. A variety of governments, intergovernmental organizations, private organizations, and individuals are already doing parts of the job. To get the maximum benefit from the scarce resources of these groups, however, their activities have to be better focused, enhanced, and coordinated, with the lessons of past experience incorporated into present and future policy. Preventive diplomacy at the margins must give way to more systematic and regularized strategies, and the institutional resources for carrying them out have to be strengthened.

To implement a more deliberate, informed, and coherent approach, five generic issues and related tasks regarding policy and operations have to be addressed, whatever the particular circumstances facing specific preventive interventions. These issues arise in one way or another for each participant in such actions and for all participants collectively. The five key issues are:

1. Where and when are tensions and disputes likely to escalate into violent conflicts? *(early warning)*
2. Which of these potential conflicts warrant responses? *(deciding priorities)*
3. What preventive responses are the most timely and cost-effective for given conflict situations? *(devising effective interventions)*
4. How can political, bureaucratic, and material support be obtained? *(mobilizing will and resources)*
5. What is needed to organize an ongoing, coordinated system for preventive diplomacy? *(linking international actors in a coherent system)*

In practical decision making, these issues become intertwined, but for purposes of strategic planning it is useful to separate them and examine them individually. This chapter examines issues 1 through 4. Each of the following sections outlines one of the issues, describes current efforts to address it, and offers guidelines for further action. The aim here is to inform and stimulate debate, not to present definitive conclusions. In the same manner, chapter 5 takes up the last issue.

EARLY WARNING

A policy of preventive diplomacy that acts on any and all signs of trouble would quickly exhaust its resources and credibility—and, like the boy who cried "Wolf!" too often, would ultimately leave real dangers unchecked. Thus, a critical task in prevention is ascertaining where and when the most harmful conflicts and crises are most likely to occur, so that appropriate levels of preventive response might be activated and appropriate resources committed to averting these dangers. Such analysis neither requires nor ensures that a response be made. (Whether or not to take action is a subject dealt with later in this chapter.) But the capacity to anticipate and analyze the nature and scale of possible conflicts is a prerequisite for any prudent decision to act and for effective action itself.

Anticipating conflicts is not a matter of forecasting the precise timing and direction of future events—what the intelligence community calls "single-point" prediction. Claims of such precision are, indeed, best left to fortune-tellers. Recent criticism of U.S. intelligence for failing to predict the complete dissolution of the Soviet Union, for example, is hardly fair; the weakening of the Soviet economy was accurately foreseen, though not the rapidity of the decline.[1] Rather, post–Cold War early warning regarding violent conflicts is a matter of gauging whether the relative probability of a course of events leading within a certain period to significant violence or other crises is sufficient to justify early attention.

Challenges

"We don't need more early warnings," runs a common complaint. "Our problem is responding to the warnings we have." This is, however, simplistic. Gaps do exist in the early warning coverage, and interpretation of the information that is available is far from easy, especially given the widespread lack of analytical capacities and skills.

One problem is obtaining complete, regular, and reliable analyses of information pertaining to the range of possible conflicts and man-made crises (both interstate and intrastate) that may be characteristic of the post–Cold War period (such as border disputes, disintegrating regimes, civil wars, human rights abuses, massive refugee flows), especially about those regions and localities where they are most likely to emerge. The total volume of data pertinent to such contingencies worldwide—in print and electronic news coverage, books and articles, government statistics, aggregate data-sets, socioeconomic and security research, and computer mail—has proliferated rapidly in recent years and is plentiful on many problems and areas. What is needed, however, is not simply more of the right kinds of information, but also the reliable interpretation of its meaning in terms of the likelihood of certain feared outcomes. Indeed, although in the post–Cold War period useful information for anticipating conflicts is increasing and largely unclassified, the difficulties of early detection of potential conflicts and crises may be greater than they were during the Cold War.

One reason is the more diffuse nature of both the pertinent information and the criteria for interpreting it. During the Cold War, elaborate, highly centralized, government-funded intelligence-gathering apparatuses routinely collected data about a relatively discrete set of phenomena in relatively discrete places. The places where such data were collected were more or less clear, even if the information was tightly held by defense and security bureaucracies. Predicting a specific event such as a third-world military coup was inherently difficult, and certain mistakes were made. But through spy satellites, clandestine operations, and a variety of other means, these well-equipped organizations could track developments such as the size of military forces, troop maneuvers, and weapons development, at least where they were likely to pose a significant threat to perceived national interests at the time.

In the post–Cold War era, however, the sources and loci of emerging "threats"—if that is still the right word—are more numerous and widely dispersed, and the processes of gathering and interpreting information about them are likewise widely scattered, as well as uneven in their coverage and varied in quality. Rather than being confined largely to potential adversaries of the United States and its allies, potential problems for regional and global security now emerge out of an array of social, political, economic, and cultural conditions and actions as diverse as price fluctuations, popular demonstrations, governments' policies, religious trends, political infighting within regimes, leaders' attitudes, and the flow of small arms. Also, the task of anticipating future developments, which is always based on the interpretation of inevitably equivocal information and is known as "estimative intelligence," is made even more difficult by the "messy" character of emerging post–Cold War conflicts. During the Cold War, the potential impact of, say, border skirmishes and local insurgencies on national and global interests was less ambiguous. Threats to the interests of the United States and its allies, for example, often came from self-declared enemies; interpreting their actions as posing clear and present dangers was relatively straightforward.

Now, however, the more or less predictable nature of the contest between the superpowers and their proxies has given way to much greater uncertainty and ambiguity regarding the direction and significance of observed events. Distinguishing between more and less serious emerging risks and threats (separating "signals" from "noise," or "migraines" from "headaches") has become more difficult. Ominous signs for a given country or region may be detected, but it is hard to estimate what kinds and levels of violence or other problems may actually erupt, as well as when, where, and how. Even if many channels of information or analysis are available, they may provide contradictory and politicized predictions, thus suggesting widely varying degrees of concern and types of response. All information, including early warnings of future conflicts, is subject to the self-interested biases of its producers, and it can be politically manipulated for partisan gains. In short, the post–Cold War era, in Joseph Nye's words, holds fewer "secrets" but more "mysteries."[2]

In a world full of national transitions from one kind of economic and political system to another, for example, change, tension, and political turmoil can have positive as well as negative results. As we saw in chapter 3, increased politicization of ethnic differences can erupt in some settings in violent ethnonationalism, while in other locales it is accommodated through peaceful political processes that may sustain pluralistic communities. A recent quandary for policymakers regarding Central Europe and the newly independent states of the former Soviet Union, in particular, has been to ascertain whether certain successful new nationalist leaders are entrepreneurial democrats or ethnic demagogues. What factors explain which kind of nationalism prevails is only beginning to be grasped. From 1990 into 1992, it may be remembered, a major obstacle to European and U.S. involvement in the Yugoslavian imbroglio was considerable uncertainty as to the wider ramifications of the gathering storm. In sum, the potential import for national, regional, and international security of signs of instability and discontent are harder to decipher, especially when the signs are low level and dispersed.

A linked problem to which post–Cold War policymakers are susceptible is the lack of a set of interpretive categories in relation to which news of emerging troubles can be assessed and its significance judged. Even if one has adequate early warning information, the psychological tendency exists either to interpret it along familiar lines or to filter out its unfamiliar or inconvenient aspects, and thus fit the data into preconceived notions. The effects of this tendency will be increased where few alternative frameworks are available into which to fit new information—as is the case with relatively new post–Cold War phenomena such as ethnic cleansing, grass-roots militias, and warlordism. When the saliency of these problems is low, moreover, they must compete for the limited attention and analytical resources of bureaucracies with larger problems that have more familiar rubrics—such as arms buildups. For example, information received by the U.S. government in late 1993 and early 1994 regarding Rwandan ethnic militias arming and training for attacks on other Rwandan groups had little impact on U.S. policy because, as one policymaker put it, it did not "fit in the box" and competed with incoming information about other, higher-priority regions.

But this heightened uncertainty increases rather than diminishes the value of whatever authoritative analysis is possible. Decisions have to and will be made on some basis or other, whether shaped by informed and cogent analysis or governed by the vicissitudes of public sentiment, the media, bureaucratic politics, and particular events. As events in the former Yugoslavia, Chechnya, and Chiapas have shown, both action and inaction can harm the interests of outside powers. Indeed, in recent years, the absence of authoritative interpretations as the basis for policy has created an intellectual vacuum in the policy marketplace, a vacuum that has sucked in a bewildering variety of radically divergent scenarios regarding the future prospects for and causes of international conflict.[3]

Access to reliable early warnings by no means turns policymaking into an automatized, technocratic process that disregards intuitive, political, and qualitative considerations. No conflict model can ever completely close the gap between data and the judgments that must inform decision making. Nevertheless, compared to occasional media reports, fragmentary information, or the biases of influential individuals, regular weighing of systematic and well-informed assessments of the chances of escalation of situations provides the soundest overall basis for policy decisions regarding possible preventive action, and it has to be done by designated people held accountable for their conclusions.

Another challenge of early warning is establishing tighter conceptual and communication linkages between early warning analysts, on the one hand, and busy decision makers and practitioners, on the other hand, so that the latter receive analyses in concrete forms that are relevant and usable. The common separation between responsibility for intelligence gathering and decision making leads to a tendency to cry wolf for fear of being otherwise caught by surprise and also to an inclination to hedge predictions lest they prove inaccurate. Confronted by intelligence reports that are at once both alarmist and vague, policymakers are left confused and suspicious that they are being "set up."[4] In addition, some early warning databases employ complex formats, terminologies, and methodologies that are unfamiliar to policymakers, and ways to encourage use of such systems in the policy and implementation process are needed.

Recent Developments

Attempts to develop reliable and useful early warning procedures have increased considerably in the last few years. In various universities and policy research organizations, a growing number of highly sophisticated systematic data-sets with quantitative and qualitative indicators of international events, socioeconomic and political phenomena, the sources of wars, and the dynamics of conflict scenarios are being developed and put in computerized form. Efforts are under way to connect these data-sets into research and information-sharing networks so that the various topics and unique strengths of each can be linked and utilized. Based on systematic analysis and modeling of the emergence of past conflicts and crises, this activity is generating a number of empirically grounded indicators that policymakers and political officers in governments and multilateral organizations can use as checklists in watching for possible trouble in their respective geographic and functional areas.

To illustrate this work, the list below indicates some of the generic factors that analysts have identified as local antecedents of possible genocide:[5]

- Governing elites express exclusionary ideologies (beliefs that elevate some ethnic group or class to a position of superiority over other such groups) and use rhetoric that dehumanizes the "out" group.
- A charismatic leadership emerges that attracts a mass following through abstract appeals to a certain people's or group's destiny.

- Severe economic hardship or differential treatment occurs for certain ethnic or other groups, so scapegoats are sought.
- Competition for power occurs among governing elites in a context in which the state security apparatus or paramilitary activities have few constraints.
- New discriminatory or restrictive policies, such as abuses of human rights and restrictions on free speech and the media, are enacted by a regime.
- Capital flight and disinvestment occur.
- Violent episodes, such as clashes between regime supporters and targeted groups, assassinations of group leaders, and attacks on scapegoat groups, occur.
- External rhetorical and material support is provided for politically active groups.
- Terrorist, vigilante, and paramilitary groups come into being.

Efforts are being made to bring analyses of this kind about particular countries directly to the attention of decision makers. The CASCON conflict assessment system developed by Lincoln Bloomfield at the Massachusetts Institute of Technology, for example, is being put in a highly user-friendly computer format to allow policymakers and professional staff at many levels to access it through their desk computers. Similarly, a process for exchanging information about developments and needs in troubled areas that would operate through the Internet, known as Reliefweb, is currently being developed by the UN Department of Humanitarian Affairs for use by governments and humanitarian organizations.

A number of efforts also have been made in recent years to set up within governments and multilateral organizations regular mechanisms not only to collect information but also to analyze its meaning for policy decisions. One long-standing method for gathering information has been to send special envoys or ad hoc factfinding and/or observer missions into volatile areas (traditionally, after considerable violence has already occurred). The United Nations and organizations such as the OSCE are creating such missions more frequently than before and dispatching them for longer periods. As illustrated by the work of the UN secretary-general's special representative to Burundi, who was sent there in 1993 before significant violence had arisen, these information-gathering tools are also being used more frequently for preventive purposes, rather than only for crisis management or conflict management. These ad hoc, hands-on approaches will always be needed to confirm and enrich the more general information provided by early warning indicators. But ways to institutionalize information gathering and analysis on an ongoing basis are also coming into being.

Encouragingly, in a few instances a particular official or governmental unit has been assigned explicit responsibility for monitoring and analyzing such data for specified geographic and problem areas and given a mandate to launch efforts in preventive diplomacy. In the office of the OSCE High Commissioner for National Minorities, for example, regular procedures have been institutionalized to look for and interpret the meaning of such signs in terms of certain kinds of conflicts that are to be avoided in that region. The commissioner and his staff are accountable for anticipating possible minority crises and initiating efforts or recommending other action. In doing so, they can also incorporate the lessons they learn from each effort into their subsequent strategy. Unfortunately, such a process of continuous collection and rigorous analysis of data pertinent to the evolution of crises is absent in many locales and agencies.

Like the OSCE, the United Nations has begun to institute early warning initiatives. After the outbreak of the Falklands War had taken the UN Secretariat by surprise, Secretary-General Perez de Cuellar set up within the Secretariat the Organization for Research and Collection of Information (ORCI). Its purpose was to allow Secretariat staff to monitor developments around the world and report them to the secretary-general for possible preventive action. Although ORCI was disbanded for lack of strong bureaucratic and political support, a similar effort was started in 1993 in the UN Secretariat to create a Humanitarian Early Warning System (HEWS). Established as part of a wider restructuring that had created the Department of Political Affairs in 1992, HEWS aims to track indicators of possible famines, refugee flows, and other calamities that might cause massive human suffering and thus require international relief or intervention.

Until recently, U.S. State Department officials were reluctant to support efforts at early warning except through occasional exercises in political gaming. Beginning in late 1994, however, the State Department conducted a path-breaking, six-month experiment whereby each month a potential crisis area was identified from early warning data, and interagency consultations were held to consider what preventive actions might be taken. Since 1992, warning staffs, training in warning, and weekly warning reports appropriate to the more complicated post–Cold War milieu have been initiated by the CIA, the National Security Agency, and State Department intelligence units.[6]

Other proposals to remedy gaps in coverage involve introducing new technologies (such as worldwide communications technology) and new actors (such as NGOs) into the early warning process. One such proposal envisions electronic mass media playing a bigger role in early warning of impending calamities. This suggestion, however, is not without its drawbacks. Although worldwide television coverage of the kind provided by CNN allows quicker and broader coverage of far-flung hot spots, such news reports may do little to enhance understanding of the complex dynamics of conflicts, especially at their early stages. TV coverage also tends to be uneven and episodic, focusing mainly on crises that have already erupted. This tendency will be hard to reverse as long as this medium is dependent on audience ratings. Furthermore, greater media coverage at the early stages of disputes may actually increase the chances of violence, for local parties may deliberately escalate a conflict in order to win wider exposure for their cause.

The idea that NGOs should play a more extensive role in gathering and disseminating information on conflicts, and in early warning in particular, is currently enjoying significant support. But this expectation has to be tempered by certain constraints. For many years, government abuses of human rights—which can be precursors of bigger crises—have been monitored by watchdog organizations such as Amnesty International and Human Rights Watch through their regional branches and country informants. These groups perform invaluable services in highlighting situations that local governments would prefer went unnoticed and governments far away are reluctant to deal with, but which could grow into major international crises. The human rights records of all nations are now tracked and publicized in an annual U.S. State Department report. These efforts, though, leave many other signs of impending conflict unmonitored and do little to enhance understanding of the broader context and wider set of value tradeoffs that effective preventive action has to address. Encouragingly, more multifaceted monitoring of localized conflicts is being undertaken through on-line computer and fax networks stimulated by NGOs such as the Carter Center and multilateral agencies such as the OSCE and the Department of Political Affairs in the UN Secretariat.

Furthermore, NGOs are remarkably varied in their aims and activities, and by no means all would be able or willing to assume early warning roles. Humanitarian NGOs, for example, are primarily in the business of alleviating human suffering, and that mission could be compromised were a host government to learn that an NGO was supplying foreign audiences with information critical of government policies. Those NGOs that undertake dispute management or preconflict peace building need to retain some independence from the governments of the countries where they are headquartered if they are to be accepted by the parties to a conflict. Even if an NGO faced no such constraints, there is no guarantee that its early warnings of impending crises would be listened to. Conversely, the danger exists that successful efforts by an NGO to draw attention to an area of potential conflict could (like the effect of sudden media coverage of a previously ignored trouble spot) lead to an escalation of violence.

In sum, while NGOs are often the only source of local information about troubled areas and can make valuable contributions to an ongoing, analytical, and rigorous early warning process within official governmental and intergovernmental channels, they cannot be a substitute for such a process. Ultimately, official mechanisms have to be developed that are responsible for regularly gathering and interpreting information for use by accountable officials.

Guidelines

1. Effective tracking of the range of contingencies that may produce international crises requires the creation of comprehensive systems of early warning geared to characteristic post–Cold War conflicts. Such systems must be user-friendly and make explicit analytical links between their problem indicators and the range of options available to particular policymakers and implementers of preventive diplomacy at specific levels. Such analysis must focus on long-term and medium-term, as well as short-term, phenomena and responses.

2. Long-term, structural factors that should be monitored are the characteristic economic, political, cultural, and technological forces at work in the post–Cold War international system and their impacts, especially in vulnerable developing regions, on the social and institutional fabrics of societies, the strength of states, and the stability of international relations among countries in particular regions.[7]

Each region should be analyzed in terms of the problems likely to be encountered there over the long term. In the case of sub-Saharan Africa, for example, analysis might focus on the combined effects of population growth, environmental degradation, associated food and resource scarcity, and economic reform and democratization pressures on the ability of existing states to achieve ethnic harmony, maintain order, and provide basic human needs such as food security. In the case of Asia, an assessment might be made of whether the growth of its middle classes and demands for greater democracy and respect for human rights will encourage one-party, authoritarian, or highly statist regimes to broaden political participation rather than resist more pluralism. In the Middle East, the effects of cultural modernization, economic decline, Islamism, and the ending of the Arab-Israeli conflict on the stability and behavior of long-established one-party and autocratic regimes might all be assessed in terms of their long-term impact. In Latin America, the effects of economic change and international competition on the durability of the region's new democratic institutions might be studied. And in the former Soviet republics and Central Europe, analysis might focus on whether the interplay of economic opening and the resurgence of ethnic and nationalist sentiments will undermine the viability of new states and lead to the return of authoritarian regimes or the birth of new autocracies.

3. Medium-term analyses are needed that model the interaction of the underlying sources of conflict with more immediate political dynamics and events in particularly vulnerable places that could trigger civil wars, ethnic violence, and so forth. Development of empirically based theories of the origination of crises would illuminate the stages and sequences through which political disputes pass on their way to escalation or resolution. This work can help refine existing indicators of incipient conflicts and identify moments of "ripeness for prevention"—points at which preventive leverage is most likely to be effective.

4. Both long-term and medium-term analyses need to factor in the impacts on these countries and societies of existing international policies—such as the structural adjustment and economic aid requirements of international financial institutions, military assistance, and the arms trade—to discern the roles they play in worsening or ameliorating social conflict and political turmoil. A system of "conflict impact statements," for example, might be introduced to determine the likely impact of economic reform and democratization programs on vulnerable areas.

5. Vis-à-vis post–Cold War conflicts and humanitarian crises, regularized early warning procedures need to be further institutionalized in the U.S. government and the United Nations, and newly established in regional organizations such as the OAU and OAS that lack them but seek them. At the same time, these various processes need to be more closely coordinated, thereby allowing the development of an efficient division of labor among them.

The threat agendas of the Cold War–born information-gathering and analytical mechanisms of the U.S. government— the several intelligence agencies, the State Department, the Defense Department, and the National Security Council—should be reoriented to the collection and interpretation of data on the wider range of likely post–Cold War phenomena and threats. Budgetary pressures on the CIA and other parts of the U.S. intelligence community are leading to reductions in staffing levels; meanwhile, the community is being given additional responsibilities in the fight against commercial sabotage, criminal syndicates, terrorism, regional nuclear threats, biological and chemical weapons, and drug trafficking. The net effect may well be that high-profile issues will receive the lion's share of attention, leaving few or no resources for the monitoring of low-level but potentially tragic and consuming conflicts and humanitarian crises.

Within the State Department, several forms of de facto and more explicit early warning and information gathering already operate (through the geographic and functional bureaus, the overseas posts, Intelligence and Research, Policy Planning, and the Executive Secretariat and its Operations Center). These need to be looked at as a whole in terms of the respective targets of their coverage and their comparative efficiency in gathering and assessing information pertinent to a range of characteristic post–Cold War threats and the particular linkages they each have to specific policy response procedures. Although access by top-level policymakers to multiple sources of information, analysis, and advocacy helps to avoid the adoption of blinkered policy strategies, the plethora of other U.S. intelligence-gathering units outside the State Department point up the need for some consolidation and harmonization. A first step might be to inventory what kind of information is presently collected, who collects it (and what indicators they use to interpret it), who receives it (which agencies and which levels within those agencies), and what diplomatic, military, economic or other policy tools are at their command. Wherever concerns to protect information vital to national security do not preclude the possibility, the United States should pool or otherwise coordinate its early warning capabilities with those of its allies, the United Nations, regional organizations, and NGOs.

6. More explicit and accountable intraagency and interagency mechanisms for aggregating early warning information and linking it to contingency planning and the implementation of preventive responses need to be created. The divorce of intelligence gathering and analysis from policymaking—a separation intended to avoid compromising the former or preempting the latter—has sometimes led to failures to follow up on warnings of impending crises that did in fact erupt. There is, analytically, no sharp line between threat assessment and policy response; the two occupy an area of several gradations of gray in which neutral analysis of potential conflict situations shades into advocacy that presses for specific actions. Thus, more iterative procedures are needed that link the functions of early warning and decision making, so that the former remains independent of political influence yet can be acted upon promptly and effectively.

7. U.S. and multilateral official information-gathering and interpretive capabilities can be enhanced by drawing more heavily on the expertise and resources of NGOs and the academic community, as well as other documentary and human sources of information. More collaborative networks, procedures, and relationships for the regular collection, coding, sharing, and assessment of early warning information need to be created (perhaps on a region-specific basis) among governmental agencies, multilateral organizations, NGOs, and research centers and universities.

Universities and nongovernmental think tanks might be most fruitfully employed in tackling more generic and long-term but nonetheless policy-relevant problems, leaving government analysts and decision makers to keep tabs on more medium- and short-term, tactical, time-sensitive, and situation-specific information. Such interaction between official and nonofficial circles, though it would require instituting procedures to protect sensitive information and to guard against politically inspired manipulation, would enhance analytical reliability and ultimately generate broader support for final policies.

8. Databases and conflict scenarios, though valuable, are no substitute for the judgments of well-informed individual practitioners on the ground and policymakers at headquarters. Indeed, because of the time lag between events and their interpretation at various bureaucratic levels, these two sets of actors may become aware of a troubled area even before the analysts have made policy sense out of it. To enhance their understanding of the nature of post–Cold War threats, the value of long-term thinking, and the usefulness as well as limitations of early warning information sources and procedures, U.S. diplomats, policymakers, and NGO professionals should be encouraged to participate in simulations, gaming exercises, and other forms of education and training in analysis of complex conflicts. Such training might be especially useful for mid-careerists such as ambassadors, deputy chiefs of missions, and junior officers about to assume their posts abroad, as well as for staffs of multilateral organizations.

DECIDING PRIORITIES

Early detection and warning of a potential conflict do not themselves require that action be taken to prevent that conflict. It falls to policymakers to decide whether action is called for. In doing so, policymakers are faced not merely with the problem of distinguishing "real" from "false" warnings, but with a much more difficult task: making informed policy choices from among a range of "real" warnings—all potentially serious but none absolutely imperative—as to which warrant attention and which should be ignored or minimized. Because policymakers rarely if ever enjoy the luxury of facing only one place where preventive efforts might be made, priorities have to be set. Thus, the challenge is deciding which, if any, among several potential trouble spots identified by early warning mechanisms demand or deserve attention, and if so, how much attention is warranted.

The Problem of Overload

This challenge arises whatever the identity of the would-be preventer and the resources at its disposal. The United Nations, the United States, and most other bureaucratic governmental or nongovernmental entities active abroad have multiple competing demands on their time, staff, and resources, and therefore cannot devote unlimited energies to every problem within their domain. When an array of apparently reliable sources generate credible warnings of potentially serious conflicts, choices among policy priorities have to be made. Too often, however, those choices are made by accident or as a result of political pressures, rather than through deliberate decision making. In the absence of explicit procedures for deciding where and how to marshall their resources, organizations may be pushed to take on too much and spread their resources too thinly across problems both large and small, thus squandering them, or respond chiefly to highly visible problems and leave other problems to ferment and grow.

The problem of prioritizing is exacerbated in large, complex bureaucracies such as the U.S. government and the United Nations that tend to centralize decision making, in the process overloading the capacity of their top decision makers to deal with the vast number of issues brought to their attention. Indeed, the failure to respond promptly to recent crises has resulted in part because of the huge organizational gulf between, on the one hand, information gathering and analysis at the lower and middle levels of the bureaucracy and, on the other hand, decision making by overloaded officials at the higher levels, who are either oriented to current crises or to the management of the ongoing programs of peacetime diplomacy. Thus, even high-quality early warning information has been condemned to irrelevance by bureaucratic overload. Supplying early warnings without sufficient recognition of the issue-processing limitations of government bureaucracies, for example, contributed to the ineffectiveness of an expensive program of national intelligence estimates (NIE). This program involved U.S. agencies and embassies around the world in collecting a variety of country-by-country information. However, when officials in Washington were presented not with a carefully selected list of the more ominous developments but with a flood of reports, the officials simply stopped reading them.

The UN Secretariat offers another example of overload. With sixteen UN peacekeeping operations now deployed around the world, the secretary-general himself considers the UN Secretariat to be stretched beyond its capability to manage them effectively—and yet more peacekeeping forces will be required in the near future. The secretary-general's recent efforts to provide good offices and deploy special mediators to conflicts around the world has also been strained in recent years. The obvious dangers of such overextension include not only reduced ability to handle particular problems, but also loss of credibility, as has befallen the United Nations since the early 1990s.

In trying to ration their attention and energies, bureaucracies concentrate on problems that have already reached the stage of crisis, that have attracted significant public attention (the so-called CNN factor), or that are advanced by the most persuasive policy entrepreneurs and most forceful interest groups. The tendency to focus only on immediate crises is especially problematic for preventive diplomacy, however, because its long-term and medium-term concerns tend to be pushed off the agenda by short-term pursuits. Even government policy-planning units that were specifically set up to take the longer view seem inevitably to get swallowed up in current operations.[8] Understandable though this tendency is, it not only runs the risk of ignoring important, albeit less visible, threats that may impose high costs in the future. It also invites other states or organizations to interpret inattention as indifference and to act accordingly, perhaps thereby worsening the future problem and raising future costs even higher.

Like the task of early warning, the task of deciding prevention priorities is more complicated today than it was during the Cold War. During the Cold War, foreign policy priorities from the point of view of the United States and other major Western powers tended to be defined clearly by the imminence and scale of self-declaring threats that were posed to basic interests, such as national survival, containing the spread of communism, or maintaining the stability of key strategic regions such as the Middle East. Threats usually took the form of a major war, crisis, or hot spot (Berlin, Korea, Cuba, and Vietnam, for instance) or less demanding regional conflicts in which U.S. interests were believed to be indirectly affected (for example, the 1956 Suez Crisis, the Ogaden war between Ethiopia and Somalia in 1977 and 1978, and the Nicaraguan civil war in the 1980s). The point is not that preventive policies were absent. Preventive actions were taken, under rubrics such as containment, deterrence, security alliances, and military assistance, but their targets presented themselves more urgently and conveniently for policymakers.

The pervasive security ambiguity of the post–Cold War era, however, makes prioritizing where to launch proactive preventive efforts a less straightforward matter. True, fewer imminent threats exist, leaving more time, in principle, for the analysis and avoidance of future ones. But that same dearth of pressing concerns makes it harder to decide which among the broad range of potential problems merit focused energies. A few clear and dangerous threats still exist, of course, such as North Korean development of nuclear weapons, terrorism, and continued turmoil in the oil-rich and heavily armed Middle East. These tend to compel close attention more or less automatically. But a larger proportion of the international agenda is made up of less imminent, smaller-scale, and more localized problems, such as ethnic tensions, human rights abuses, and national power struggles. These have little or no immediate strategic importance in themselves, but they have the potential to escalate into crises that would seriously affect the interests of the United States and other nations.

Adopting a stance of indifference toward any but the most conspicuous and apparently threatening of these problems is an attractive option, especially to many now in the U.S. Congress. But expectations of U.S. involvement in a variety of international problems have also risen in recent years among both domestic constituencies and the international community. Thus, demands for action may increasingly outstrip resources, both material and political, accentuating rather diminishing the need to prioritize.

Recent Developments

Some analysts have tried to fill the vacuum of clear and present threats by redefining and broadening the concept of "international security" and thus the threats to it. Under the rubric of "common security," this approach would expand the list of threats to international security beyond traditionally accepted ones like nuclear war, cross-border aggression, and arms proliferation to encompass a host of current and future international and "transnational" problems, including ethnic strife, degradation of the environment, population growth, famine, refugee flows, poverty, organized crime, and drug trafficking. Usefully, this approach seeks to break out of the Cold War mindset, the main focus of which is on large-scale confrontations and inter-state wars, and identify a wider range of sources of international instability. At the same time, however, it produces a long wish list of problems to be tackled but fails to prioritize among them. If adopted as some sort of official world or U.S. agenda, it would place a huge burden of responsibility on the international community, especially on its leading underwriters such as the United States, for tackling a multitude of regional and national problems. In short, adopting such expansive, undifferentiated notions of "security" would exhaust resources and exacerbate the problem of prioritizing.

For the United States, the president's annual National Security Review does try to define foreign policy priorities as each administration sees them. But it covers all U.S. foreign policy goals, not just future conflicts; is closely identified with particular administrations (and thus changes significantly from one administration to another); is not widely read; and may not be an influential guide to policy even for the executive branch that produces it. Nor, of course, can one automatically equate U.S. foreign policy goals with those of the international community—as seen in U.S. decisions to depart from the decisions of the United Nations, to act outside of the World Trade Organization, and so on.

Clearly, policymakers have to perform triage if their scarce conflict prevention resources are to be used most effectively—no matter whether the would-be preventer is the international community as a whole, a regional community of nations, or an individual nation. But how can such priorities be set? What criteria should guide these choices? What potential threats should be addressed through early action?

Guidelines

1. Prevention priorities must be established through an analytically comprehensive and deliberative process that addresses four fundamental questions:

- What goals and interests does the would-be preventer wish to preserve, defend, or expand? In the ambiguous post–Cold War world, before one can decide the question "What areas and conflicts should be priorities for preventive diplomacy?" one must first be clear about the more fundamental question "What are the preventer's most important goals and interests?"
- What trends and forces in the regions of the world are likely to threaten the attainment of those goals in the coming years? Answering this question requires assessing data from long-, medium-, and short-term trends analysis and early warning indicators against the specified goals and interests.
- Which of these risks and threats are most important vis-à-vis one's specified goals? The identified threats have to be ranked in terms of their comparative impacts, as measured by their probability, likely magnitude or scale, temporal and geographical proximity, and potential for contagion.[9]

These three questions arise at the *strategic* level, that is, where the task is to develop guidelines that delineate which generic sets or classes of threatening situations around the globe should be addressed through preventive action as a matter of general policy. A fourth question must be addressed at the *tactical* level as well, where the task is deciding which among the various cases that fall into the generic classes will receive priority attention at a particular time:

- Must this or that particular threat be addressed? The preventer must judge whether the short-term costs of trying to prevent a situation's worsening are worth the likely long-term costs of ignoring it. Thus, a decision not to act in some instances does not mean that a general threat is being ignored. These tactical judgments are subject to idiosyncratic and circumstantial considerations of efficacy, political support, and technical feasibility.

This four-step analytical process is not precise or omniscient. Its conclusions need not be regarded as rigid and fixed and can be modified as changes occur. But some such deliberative process is the only way to protect preventive diplomacy decision making from the inevitably more short-term and parochial pressures of the media, public opinion, bureaucratic agendas, and partisan politics and the related danger of taking on too many priorities.[10]

2. As stated in the first of the four questions outlined above, the targets of preventive diplomacy must be determined by the goals of the would-be preventer. Unfortunately, however, those interests are in some cases unclear. To be sure, as discussed in chapter 1, the post–Cold War era shows an unusual degree of international consensus around certain overall principles and norms. This growing awareness of common ideals does not, however, mean that nations no longer have differing views of the relative importance of these values and differing perceptions of the particular threats to the values that require a preventive response. Nor does it mean that nations necessarily always subscribe with equal enthusiasm to collective initiatives to protect international security that are activated by the multilateral organizations to which the nations belong. Multilateral preventive diplomacy will always have to contend with the problem of reconciling, accommodating, or at least respecting these inevitable differences.

Differences among the interests of nations are one problem. Uncertainty within nations about what their own interests might be is another. To the extent that a nation is unclear about the character and hierarchy of its basic interests, it will be unable to develop a coherent preventive policy. And if that nation is, or is expected to be, a key player in many multilateral preventive efforts, then the effects of its incoherence will be very widely felt. Sadly, the United States is today prey to a high degree of uncertainty and disagreement regarding its national interests. Indeed, the confusion at present over what foreign policy goals, values, and interests the United States wishes to promote in the post–Cold War world has not only impeded the development of a coherent U.S. preventive diplomacy strategy, but also contributed to recent U.S. foreign policy indecisiveness and failures.

How would the development of a U.S. strategic foreign policy compass that so many observers have urged, proceed? This is not the place for a lengthy discussion of "the U.S. national interest" and U.S. international priorities. But we can sketch the steps entailed and offer some provisional directions for consideration. The United States's foreign policy goals abroad are always subject to debate, and it is unwise to try to pin them down in an overly precise and rigid formula. Nonetheless, the current amount of intellectual agnosticism and promiscuity is excessive. If U.S. preventive diplomacy is to realize its potential, this clearer sense of U.S. interests is essential.

Fortunately, a number of scholars have already embarked on such a process. Drawing on their work, the illustrative lists below define four basic U.S. national interests and then indicate more locale-specific threats to one or more of these interests that could arise in the coming decade.[11]

U.S. Post–Cold War Basic National Interests
- Protection of the territorial integrity of the United States against attack or intimidation.
- Preservation of U.S. economic well-being and creation of opportunities for increasing prosperity, including the maintenance of an open system of international trade.
- Preservation of U.S. political freedom, individual rights, and democratic institutions.
- Basic assurance of international security through maintenance of a relatively stable global and regional order in which states generally resolve their differences without the use of force, most nations enjoy political stability, and an increasing number of nations either have adopted stable democratic institutions or are engaged in meaningful movement in that direction.

A more explicit list of interests such as this then compels inquiry into the particular location and sources of potential international threats that may thwart the pursuit and protection of those interests. Such a schedule is given below. These emerging manifestations of the threats can then be prioritized as a guide to allocating the limited resources of the United States and international community according to the relative importance of the threats and their magnitudes in different regions. This review should seek to identify which threats are going to be of primarily local or regional significance and which of global importance, and which will have short-term and which long-term impacts.

Possible Threats to U.S. National Interests
(in descending order of importance)

- Confrontation or conflicts between the major market democracies and other major powers (the United States, Western Europe, and Japan versus Russia and/or China), including direct attacks on the United States or its allies or the emergence of tensions and conflicts over regional issues (e.g., the Balkans, Taiwan).

- Nuclear or conventional regional wars fought to gain regional dominance (e.g., Iraqi invasion of Kuwait) or settle long-standing rivalries (e.g., India versus Pakistan, Israel versus Syria) or because new instabilities within established regimes tempt aggression (e.g., between unstable Arab regimes such as Libya versus Egypt).

- Transnational threats to the economies and democratic institutions of the Western market democracies, such as those posed by criminal syndicates, drug trafficking, terrorism, political extremism, and massive migrations.

- Irregular interruptions of democratic governance through threat or use of force (e.g., Guatemala) or reversal of democratization and economic reforms in major states such as Poland, Hungary, India, Brazil, Argentina, and South Africa.

- National political breakdowns and conflicts in large (e.g., Ukraine, India, Nigeria, Zaire, Pakistan, Turkey, Algeria) or small states (e.g., Liberia, Rwanda, Burundi, Georgia, Bosnia) brought about by secessionist wars, revolutions, civil wars, ethnic conflicts, repression of minorities, and so forth.

Whether or not the specific interests and threats listed above are widely accepted, it is clear that the U.S. policy community needs to engage in a more vigorous and explicit debate about the main interests that should drive U.S. foreign policy in the post–Cold War era. With a clearer sense at the highest levels of the U.S. government of the relative importance of primary goals, those goals can be articulated vocally and forcefully to audiences at home and abroad. Where U.S. goals and limits overlap or fall short of those of the wider international community will also be brought into sharper focus. They can also be operationalized by the creation of benchmarks by which to judge the behavior, policies, and actions of other nations in promoting or obstructing U.S. interests. Time lines can be established that lay out acceptable rates of progress toward each goal or interest. These criteria can help determine current U.S. policies on matters such as aid, trade, and commerce with particular nations. If such benchmarks and time lines are not established, the defined goals and interests will remain vague rhetorical aspirations, the realization of which will continue to be shaped entirely by ad hoc responses to short-term crises and the vagaries of domestic politics.

3. Procedures must be put in place that link this continuous gathering of early warning information to specific decision makers at specified levels within relevant bureaucracies. These decision makers must be given explicit responsibility for judging which warnings would significantly harm the national interest if ignored and thus merit a response, and they must be authorized to initiate procedures to formulate an appropriate preventive policy.

4. Although goals and threats need to be more explicitly prioritized at the highest levels, to avoid overload at the top, the routine business of actually monitoring and assessing early warning signs and devising possible preventive responses might be delegated to lower bureaucratic levels and to other organizations with smaller bureaucracies, depending on the nature and scale of the threat. Indeed, once priorities are set and program synergy improved, the implementation of threat management and crisis prevention must be decentralized to avoid overload at the top. A more decentralized and multilateral system for conflict prevention would push down to lower levels, as well as local and regional actors, under appropriate international rules, explicit responsibility for issue processing, prioritizing, and responding to potential areas of difficulty. The way in which the explicitly preventive OSCE high commissioner for national minorities (HCNM) functions provides a suggestive operational model. On the one hand, the HCNM depends on high-level backing: he is ultimately accountable to the members of the OSCE as a whole, must operate within its agreed-upon rules and norms, and reports periodically to the OSCE's political executive body, the Committee of Senior Officials. On the other hand, the HCNM is given a relatively open mandate and considerable discretion with regard to which situations he addresses and how he handles each one.

A clearer vertical division of labor could be established over time in which smaller-scale problems such as national ethnic conflicts and human rights disputes would tend to be engaged early by lower levels of foreign affairs bureaucracies and multilateral organizations (at least those of the larger governments and organizations, which have the greater capacity), in conjunction with their counterparts among other local and regional actors. Larger-scale issues, such as possible major interstate wars, potential nuclear crises, and the unprevented local crises, can then be reserved for the attention of ministerial and chief executive levels. The eventual effect might be to reduce the number of such major crises rising to the central levels (see chapter 5).

DEVISING EFFECTIVE INTERVENTIONS

Even when interests and possible threats to them have been prioritized and a mechanism exists to determine whether responses are warranted, the particular actions to be taken must be determined on a case-by-case basis. Effective prevention depends on finding ways of engagement that are appropriate to specific circumstances. No one formula will fit all circumstances, and to pretend otherwise is both presumptuous and risky. Because every emerging conflict situation differs, a great deal of latitude and flexibility must be given to those who devise and implement preventive strategies both on the ground and at headquarters. Fortunately, unlike the severe time constraints characteristic of crisis management, the process of formulating preventive diplomacy strategies benefits from the fact that conflicts emerge more gradually than crises develop, thereby allowing poli-cymakers more time to consider and evaluate a range of options; some opportunity even exists for learning through trial and error which options work best.

Recent Developments

Some efforts to assess the effectiveness of U.S. government programs devoted to such interrelated but potentially conflicting goals as re-gional security, conflict resolution, democracy building, human rights, civil society building, and economic development have already begun to occur, through steps to tally the programs and existing bud-get allocations devoted to programs with these ostensible purposes.[12] Facing a confusing array of potential risks and threats and under pres-sure to conserve the declining resources for U.S. international in-volvement, the U.S. government in recent years has also inaugurated policy reviews in foreign policy functional areas. The purpose of these reviews is to ascertain how specified agencies' policy tools and personnel can be used more cost-effectively in meeting post–Cold War challenges. One example is a commission that has been created to examine the appropriate targets and roles of the U.S. government's several intelligence units. Another is the review begun in mid-1995 of U.S. humanitarian response policy, undertaken to determine how well prepared foreign assistance programs are to prevent and remedy potential humanitarian crises caused by natural disasters, famine, col-lapsing economies, civil strife, and the like. A third example is the searching analysis of U.S. defense posture to determine military read-iness for a range of regional conflicts. The issuing of PDD-25 regard-ing peace operations is yet another example.

Guidelines

Whatever the circumstances of a particular case, effective preventive diplomacy depends on making wise tactical decisions with respect to four generic issues:

- *Timing:* What is the most propitious time in the emergence of a conflict to conduct a preventive effort?
- *Tasks and methods:* What tasks must prevention action undertake, and how can those tasks best be accomplished?

- *Sequencing interventions:* What short-term, medium-term, and long-term objectives should be pursued? How should methods or tools of intervention be modified in relation to the different stages of a conflict over time?

- *Disengagement:* When should the effort be terminated?

Each of these issues is discussed below, with some guidelines for reaching sound decisions offered in each case.

Timing of Intervention

As mentioned above, one of the most influential ideas in the field of conflict management is that conflicts cannot be resolved at just any point in their development but must be "ripe for resolution." According to this approach, an essential condition making for ripeness is a "mutual hurting stalemate" between the parties to a conflict—that is, a point in a conflict where neither party can prevail over the other. Once they recognize that they have reached such a stalemate and cannot achieve their objectives by armed struggle, the parties become more willing to enter into negotiations.[13]

Although this theory clearly deals with the advanced stages of conflicts in which armed struggle has been waged for some time, some analysts have suggested that its logic makes preventive diplomacy inherently futile. If disputants refuse to negotiate until they have engaged in significant, albeit fruitless, violence, then attempts to engage them in a peaceful process of settlement before violence has occurred are doomed to failure. The interveners will have to wait at least until war has begun.[14]

The concept of ripeness for resolution is at least helpful, for it raises the key question of what conditions may be needed in the relationship of the parties and their circumstances before preventive diplomacy can make headway. Nevertheless, the application of the theory of the mutual hurting stalemate to previolent stages of conflicts is suspect. It does not seem to match those situations (such as the case of Congo, as sketched out in chapter 3) where low-level violent conflicts have gone no further than early skirmishes. The existing theoretical literature does not seem to suggest that parties have an ineluctable desire or tendency when a dispute arises to prosecute it to the bitter end through armed force. This literature suggests instead that, *once some level of significant violence has begun*, it is prone to escalate because an interactive process of attack and retaliation leads to a self-perpetuating cycle.[15] To end such a cycle, a mutual hurting stalemate may indeed be necessary, but the cycle itself is not inevitable.

Still, an analogous notion of "ripeness for prevention" may apply to early stages of conflicts, even to their previolent stages—though mutual and prolonged bloodletting is not its necessary content. That is, a party may be open to preventive efforts only after it has both asserted its interests and encountered some level of resistance to its pursuit of its cause. Thus, those who would head off potential conflicts may need to choose their moments as carefully as those who seek to mediate and terminate them. Preventive diplomacy must avoid the twin horns of a dilemma: action that is either too little, too late or too much, too soon.

The problems of action too little, too late were illustrated in the cases of Croatia, Haiti, Moldova, Somalia, and Rwanda. These problems boil down to a mismatch between the (limited) influence would-be preventers can bring to bear on the parties to a conflict and the (large) gains those parties have made through exercising coercion or taking up arms—a mismatch that can be corrected only if the preventers are willing to employ a proportional, and thus possibly extremely costly, amount of counteractive pressure, whether in the form of a negative or positive inducement.

But what would it mean for preventive diplomacy to be too much, too soon? Can preventive action be taken too early? Conflicts at their early stages must contain certain ingredients before violence becomes possible. At a minimum, they require 1) discrete parties who are conscious of possessing common interests, which they perceive at risk because of the actions of other parties; 2) particular disputes over issues that reflect this clash of interests; and 3) assertive statements or activity by the parties to realize their interests.

If preventive diplomacy efforts are made before these conditions exist, they may fail. Not only is there, in effect, no "audience" for the preventive action, but also the intervention may itself fuel tensions and discord by creating an awareness of a dispute, stimulating demands and expectations, and provoking countermeasures from one or another party. Marxist revolutionaries have tried to achieve a similar result by removing the veil of "false consciousness" from their working-class constituents. And community organizers have learned to "rub raw the sores of discontent" to rouse supporters who are habitually apathetic after years of discouragement. But preventive diplomats are not in the business of revolution. Even once a dispute has surfaced in some form, there is a danger that by calling attention to it too early, the third party can contribute to its escalation. The parties might use the heightened attention being given to an issue—by the media as well as the would-be preventers—as a platform from which to inflame emotions within their constituencies and to appeal to outside audiences for support.

Guidelines for Timing of Intervention

1. Early warning procedures need to be able to follow emerging developments in specific locales with a great deal of sensitivity so that the most opportune moments for preventive action can be determined. Achieving a highly nuanced understanding of the situation requires supplementing quantitative and qualitative data compiled by officials distant from the site of a dispute with news reports and detailed consultations with knowledgeable observers on the ground. Before undertaking a local mission, for example, the OSCE HCNM not only takes great pains to digest all the reports his office receives but also reads the local press, talks personally with experts, and consults with local diplomats.

2. Preventive action is best launched at points when there already exists sufficient interest and motivation on the part of the disputants to seek a peaceful resolution, yet not so early that the disputants are incited to intensify their confrontation. Early action is vital if violence is to be preempted and the disputants are not to entrench themselves in rigid positions from which it is difficult to withdraw. But preventive diplomats must be wary of acting solely on the basis of hypothetical presumptions and speculative fears of conflict escalation.[16] When early action is taken, ordinarily it must adopt a low-key and low-profile approach that does not invite the attention of the media or otherwise provoke widespread comment.

Such timing was suggested to the HCNM when he sought advice from the Conflict Management Group in October 1992 about how best to help resolve the dispute between the Estonian government and the

Russian-speaking community in Estonia over proposed language laws. The commissioner was advised to intervene once the Estonian parliament had begun debating the language laws but before any law had been passed and policies perceived to be discriminatory were implemented. He was also cautioned to choose only disputes that were "real," in the sense that more than mere fears of possible discrimination were evident.[17] In short, the commissioner was advised to give priority to such crises at their incipience but to act at those points when he can preempt moves by one or the other party to establish a decisive gain that is hard to reverse.

Tasks and Methods of Intervention

What kind of actions, methods, and tools of intervention will effectively prevent escalation of a dispute into unmanageable violence? Although obviously central to the conduct of preventive diplomacy, this question often seems to be paid only lip service and is dealt with implicitly rather than explicitly. One reason for this is that each would-be preventive actor tends to answer the question according to that actor's perspective, resources, and favored modus operandi. A good deal of governmental decision making and policy analysis dealing with conflicts is done reflexively rather than reflectively, because it occurs within bureau-level agencies whose jurisdiction and job are defined largely functionally in terms of the implementation of one or two particular tools—arms control, peacekeeping, diplomacy, track-two problem solving, economic assistance, election monitoring, and so on. Expected or eager to do something, a government agency may not stop to consider whether its particular intervention technology is in fact even appropriate to a specific context and may fail to assess first what a given situation actually requires.

Furthermore, some of the most familiar state-sponsored and multilateral policy tools that are almost automatically considered and employed have had disappointing results. The record of economic sanctions imposed by the Security Council against recalcitrant parties, for example, is decidedly mixed. Sanctions are difficult to enforce. The economic and arms embargoes imposed against Serbia and Haiti were hampered by those countries' relatively porous borders. Whether or not sanctions succeed in putting pressure on a targeted regime or group, moreover, they often have adverse side effects on other groups within the targeted state or on neighboring countries. In Haiti the poorer sections of the population suffered far more than the military regime from the sanctions intended to secure the return of democratic rule. The economies of Hungary, Romania, and Macedonia have been severely affected by the embargoes against Serbia. Sanctions were considered as an option after Peru's anti-democratic coup but rejected because Peru trades with five bordering countries, thus making sanctions unenforceable and undesirable.

NGOs too can err in their use of favored tools. For instance, human rights advocacy groups approach a potential conflict from one angle: how local behavior measures up in terms of certain international human rights standards. Thus, the "intervention" envisioned almost exclusively involves international pressures—and chiefly negative pressures—on an offender to refrain from violations of human rights norms. But if such pressures increase the insecurity of entrenched regimes sufficiently to provoke a backlash and violence ensues, the cause of human rights may be further set back.

Similarly, because those NGOs that focus on conflict prevention, management, and resolution depend heavily on the receipt of grants or contracts, they may seek funds for whatever conflicts are "popular" with foundations or relatively conspicuous in the media, even though the particular tools they have at their disposal (track-two diplomacy and the like) may have relatively little efficacy in highly militarized situations. Indeed, it is often doubtful that track-two diplomacy is very cost-effective with regard to highly advanced violent conflicts; concrete results are more likely in tense situations that are potentially violent but have not erupted. Nevertheless, scarce funds continue to go to such projects in places such as Tajikistan. Although some argue (not without some justification) that even in the midst of war-torn situations track-two efforts can have an impact on the future elites who will emerge after the cessation of current hostilities, it seems wiser to concentrate those efforts where disputes exist but hostilities have not begun, for there the NGOs can have an impact on current leaders.

This tendency to look at an incipient conflict from the perspective of one type of intervention not only wastes resources on areas that may not need or benefit from such an intervention but also leads to serious policy errors. For one thing, policies that have been successful in one locale or conflict at one time are by no means guaranteed to work in another. From late 1993 to early 1994, for example, the UN/OAU observation force placed in Rwanda to watch for further bloodshed was touted as a success story of preventive diplomacy (perhaps because a similar preventive peacekeeping force had been put in Macedonia a year earlier and appeared to be effective). But in April 1994 one of Africa's most savage interethnic massacres occurred. A question worthy of further inquiry is whether the mere fact that *someone* is doing *something* in a given locale dissuades others in the international community from undertaking efforts that may in fact be better suited to local circumstances.

Locating intervention decisions in particular functional bureaus can also lead to shortsighted decisions *not* to act in a prudently preventive way. If the question of whether to intervene is posed in the context of one particular method of intervention, the answer is subject to the particular outlook and bureaucratic culture of the organization that deploys that method and its operational limitations. For example, the possibility of the United States intervening in Somalia was raised in 1991, after the civil war had begun but before there was massive famine, and thus before the decision was taken to launch Operation Restore Hope. Because the issue was brought up within the Defense Department, the assumption was that involvement meant the deployment of a U.S. peacekeeping force. Because peacekeeping at the time was seen as a particularly dangerous endeavor, a task better suited to the United Nations and warranted only in strategically vital areas, the idea was rejected. Nevertheless, when the situation worsened within a year, a U.S. peacekeeping force was in fact sent into Somalia, but at perhaps much greater cost than an earlier deployment would have incurred.

Guidelines for Tasks and Methods of Intervention

1. A more synoptic and interorganizational approach to developing preventive interventions is clearly required, one that is based on an assessment of the preconflict situation. Responses should not be deduced automatically from past experience or an organization's preferences; what has worked in one place may not work again in another, and a third party's preference for one or another policy instrument should not itself dictate the type of preventive action undertaken.

Accordingly, some analysts have tried to be more systematic about the ways a possible violent conflict might be averted.[18] The options or choices one faces can be classified in a number of ways. One emerging approach is to list the various policy tools or instruments one might use. Analysts have begun to catalogue and classify the array of instruments in terms of functional categories such as military, economic, judicial, official diplomacy, and so on, and/or in terms of whether they are coercive or noncoercive—carrots or sticks—along the lines of the "Preventive Diplomacy Toolbox" described in appendix A. Such tool typologies are definitely useful in enlarging the options normally entertained, but for the purpose of considering possible options for action, they skip an important step.

After being alerted to such a situation by early warning, the would-be preventer's first question should not be "What tool should I use?" but rather "What is the problem on the ground?" Rather than invoke familiar remedies simply because they are convenient or available, policymakers and practitioners should proceed inductively, working from the ground up to tailor a response that meets the particular circumstances of each conflict situation. Only after the needs of the local situation have been diagnosed and corresponding tasks identified can a suitable choice be made of the tools that best fit the tasks. Early warnings undoubtedly will have provided some of this information, but they cannot provide enough detail to fine-tune a response. As we have seen, managing or preventing conflict is likely to take a variety of efforts and resources, contributed by a range of actors. Multi-pronged comprehensive strategies that draw on several sources and use both positive and negative pressures are usually necessary.

2. The first step then in tactical preventive diplomacy is *needs assessment*—close scrutiny of the preconflict situation itself to see what is required to keep it from becoming a violent conflict. Chapter 2 argued that the purpose of preventive diplomacy is to keep political disputes from becoming violent, or to manage incipient conflicts peacefully, and that it comes into play when regular peacetime diplomacy (in both its international and national incarnations) is increasingly unable to handle the strains caused by major change. Each situation where a potentially violent conflict exists has its own configuration of diplomatic, strategic, security, political, economic, and cultural-psychological elements, which may be moving a situation in the direction of violence or away from it. Thus, the relevant question is "What is absent in the situation that otherwise might keep it from escalating?" Or, turning the question around, "What factors are present that might bring this unstable situation to crisis or violence?" Posing this central question at the outset focuses the preventer first on the needs of the situation and then on the tasks, functions, or services required, rather than the other way around.[19]

When one asks why violence could erupt in a particular setting, the list of generic factors knowledgeable analysts would identify is unlikely to be long. As intimated in the definition of preventive diplomacy presented in chapter 2 and suggested by the case studies in chapter 3, disputes become violent or peaceful depending on one or more of the following six deficiency or need factors:

1. *Lack of restraints on violence*: Few limitations restrict the ability of the parties to resort to armed force to achieve their demands.
2. *Lack of a process:* No procedures or institutions exist through which the dispute can be discussed and solutions sought.
3. *Lack of resources:* The parties may have neither an immediate desire to use violence nor the means to do so, but they lack the material wherewithal to engage in any effort to keep the dispute from worsening.
4. *Lack of solutions:* The parties are at the table and seem willing to negotiate but lack proposals for settling the issues that divide them.
5. *Lack of incentives:* Solutions abound, but the parties lack sufficient motivation to accept any of them.
6. *Lack of trust*: The perceptions and attitudes of the parties toward each other are so negative that they are unable to contemplate particular solutions or to comply with them.

Specific dispute arenas will likely vary a great deal in how many of these factors are present. Comparing the case studies in chapter 3, for instance, the Hungary-Slovakia dispute was typified mainly by factors 4, 5, and 6, but not 1, 2, or 3. In Macedonia, 2, 3, 5, and 6 were evident. In Rwanda in 1993–94 and in Burundi in 1994–95, all six factors were present.

This inductive needs assessment can be particularly helpful in alerting those who would seek to prevent escalation of a specific dispute to the particular configuration of problems where preventive action is required. Unfortunately, many previous preventive efforts have neglected to match actions to all the needs of a situation. For example, Yugoslavia in 1991 showed evidence of need factors 1, 2, 5, and 6, but the international community addressed mainly 2, 4, and 5. That is, although the most obvious manifestations of the conflict were the verbal debates among the leaders of the republics over the future of the federation, arming of militias was imminent or actually under way within the republics, and state institutions were being actively sabotaged. The main "service" provided by the international community, however, was a peace conference in which various specific constitutional outcomes were presented as options. While this offered a process and some solutions, it did not provide negative or positive inducements to the parties that would enforce, through sufficient punishments or rewards, the peaceful pursuit of their differences. Apparently, the main ingredient assumed by the European Community and the United Nations to be lacking was substantive solutions, rather than restraints on the use of force and sufficient economic inducements to negotiate peacefully through existing governmental channels.

The needs question also calls for explicit examination of what indigenous (whether local, national, or regional) capacities, resources, and "will" exist in the preconflict situation that may already be helping to keep the dispute from intensifying. One should not presume that everything that needs to be done or can be done must be done by newly alerted third parties. Where indigenous institutions and processes for the peaceful settlement of disputes already exist, for example, they should be buttressed and built upon rather than replicated. By performing a needs assessment before action is taken, the preventer can discover not only what it needs to do but also what it can leave the disputants to do, and thus what amount of pressure and influence is required from third parties.

3. Once the needs of a given situation have been pinpointed, the *required tasks and appropriate tools* of preventive diplomacy become more readily apparent. How tools might be matched to tasks is illustrated as follows.[20]

- Lack of restraints on violence.

  Tasks: Suppress or contain violence or threats of violence; deprive parties of arms; provide protection against the use of arms.

  Tools: Preventive peacekeeping force, targeted deterrence, enforceable demilitarized zones, safe havens, emergency measures, protectorates, war crimes tribunals, military assistance, and so forth.

- Lack of a process.

  Tasks: Engage the parties in communication and dialogue; create channels and processes for discussion or negotiation; set up or strengthen permanent political institutions (such as legislatures and executive bodies) through which such negotiations can be regularized.

  Tools: Good offices, mediation, peace conferences, arbitration, adjudication, institution building, problem-solving workshops, democracy building, trusteeship.

- Lack of resources.

  Tasks: Provide elemental needs; alleviate extreme social and economic conditions that provide the occasion for incitements to armed force.

  Tools: Humanitarian relief, technical assistance, economic assistance.

- Lack of solutions.

  Tasks: Address particular disputes; generate a range of possible settlements.

  Tools: Brainstorming, menus of alternative options for governance from similar places.

- Lack of incentives.

  Task: Induce parties to adopt solutions.

  Tools: Positive inducements, such as security guarantees, provision of foreign aid, offers of membership in international entities;

negative inducements, such as coercive diplomacy (sanctions, threats of force), threats of exclusion from international organizations, elimination of foreign aid, and so forth.

- Lack of trust.

  Tasks: Provide mutual assurance; change attitudes and perceptions; reduce tensions when they arise.

  Tools: Nonofficial dialogues, educational and informational efforts, media programs.

In sum, such a needs assessment helps to set the particular priorities for a preconflict arena among different tasks and corresponding methods of intervention. Although in most instances, *all* the above tasks will have to be performed to *some* degree, ordinarily, a given situation will call for greater emphasis on some tasks than on others. The extent and nature of local capacities and resources will determine in part where third parties should focus their efforts. Success depends on finding the right combination of tools that address the deficiencies of a particular situation.

4. A needs assessment reveals the tasks that a specific preventive effort must undertake, and this list of tasks in turn suggests the types of tools required. Thus, once a needs assessment has been performed, a *tools inventory* must be undertaken. (See appendix A for an inventory of preventive policies and instruments.) This involves surveying institutions, organizations, and individuals at local, national, and regional levels to see which of them might be able to contribute to the preventive effort. Such a wide-ranging inventory is likely to uncover resources that otherwise would be overlooked in the formulation of strategies. And it may avoid automatic adoption of methods that are inadequate or counterproductive.

Many tools may not, of course, be available; the range of feasible options available to a would-be preventer may be limited. The means the U.S. government has to influence North Korea, Zaire, and militant Islamic movements in the Middle East, for example, are relatively few. In the case of North Korea, U.S. economic sanctions would not be effective and military options or positive inducements are limited because of the isolation of the North Korean regime. But given the growing interconnectedness of societies, economies, and cultures, society-to-society channels of influence as well as state-to-state diplomacy should be explored wherever possible. The repertoire, or "toolbox," of policy instruments is enlarging to include a wider range of direct and indirect policies and programs, and the work of nongovernmental as well as governmental bodies. Even private for-profit corporations and businesspeople may have roles to play.

In sum, rather than assuming that one organization necessarily should undertake all the preventive diplomacy or conflict management activities within a particular nation or region, the international community needs to think in terms of appropriate divisions of labor and complementarities. The experience in Yugoslavia clearly shows that no single multilateral organization possesses the full range of tools and resources that an effective preventive effort is likely to require. NATO is still mainly a defense alliance reliant on military force; the CSCE has until recently served chiefly as a forum for arms control and human rights promulgation, and operates by consensus; and the European Union remains primarily a common economic market. If several intervention tools—financial, logistical, negotiating, military, technological, administrative, and leadership skills and resources—are required, and yet it is assumed that a single organization should have a virtual monopoly over the conduct of a preventive effort, that effort is almost inevitably doomed at best to partial success, at worst to utter failure.

5. An especially powerful factor in preconflict situations that helps decide which positive or negative inducements suit which circumstances is how remote or close at hand a threat of violence is—or, put another way, the degree of cooperation or hostility that exists between the parties to a conflict. The greater the use of, or inclination to use, armed force by the parties to the dispute, the more preventive force that needs to be applied. This fundamental insight has long been recognized in dealing with conflicts, as early as the just war doctrine's notion of proportionality in the use of force and the UN Charter's provision of a sequence of increasingly coercive actions in Chapters VI and VII. Yet its application has been largely ignored in current policy discussions regarding recent regional conflicts.

Where violence is imminent, for example, preventive diplomats, if they are to succeed, have no choice but to take whatever steps are necessary to block or deter the threatened hostility. The kinds of preventive actions required might include specific deterrence provided by a powerful state, economic sanctions against a state, preventive peacekeeping, or even the creation of a judicial system, including a war crimes tribunal, to deter violations of human rights.

Where violence is possible but not imminent, preventive diplomacy has more time to address other needs of the situation. For example, it can reduce, restrain, or regulate the weapons that might be used in the future through some form of disarmament, arms control, and/or nonproliferation enforced by international agreements. In an interstate context, security guarantees provided by a defense alliance may be required. Sufficient breathing space may also permit preventive diplomacy to set about strengthening existing local, national, or international political institutions and procedures such as power-sharing arrangements, special commissions, legislatures, and multilateral forums.

Where existing institutions that are normally used for resolving political disputes exist but are weak, preventive interventions should concentrate on strengthening these institutions and should avoid policies that may destroy them. At the same time, opportunities for dialogue should be sought through track-two diplomacy. Where these institutions do not exist, preventive diplomacy should concentrate on creating them, thereby allowing future disputes to be channeled into peaceful mechanisms of resolution.

Specific substantive grievances at issue among established and politically secure governments may be resolved through the formal arbitration and other judicial or quasi-judicial procedures of multilateral commissions or the International Court of Justice or through the less formal good offices, mediation, and negotiations offered by a third-party government, the United Nations, a regional organization, or a prominent individual. Where egregious inequities and resource shortages tempt violence, preventive diplomacy should act rapidly to provide economic assistance targeted to especially vulnerable countries or regions within them.

6. This matching of tools to the needs and scale of particular conflicts seems commonsensical, but many conflict management and international policy analysts seem to recommend the deployment of certain tools of intervention with little or no prior consideration of the impact those tools might actually have on a dispute or of indigenous factors that affect whether a dispute can be handled peacefully. A more elaborate effort to match appropriate tools to the stages of conflict is provided in table 4.1.

The destructive consequences of inattention to local vulnerabilities and capacities is illustrated by the current enthusiasm for exporting policies from the post–Cold War liberal agenda such as human rights, economic reform, and democratization as if they were cure-alls for the ills of all nations. In countries and regions where liberal institutions, policies, and values are already present to a significant extent, further economic reform and democratization are likely to prove mutually reinforcing and to come into tension only at the margins. Governmental respect for human rights helps to guarantee against civil violence, for instance; the rule of law is needed to sustain markets; stable democracies are required for economic growth; and so on.

But in areas where few of these institutions and policies are evident, promotion of political and economic liberalization may either fail for the lack of fertile soil or, if reforms are promoted too vigorously, may have the unintended consequence of eroding the social fabric necessary to maintain minimum social order and material well-being. The promotion of a single goal—democratization, say—without regard to the possible consequences for, say, minority rights, domestic social and political stability, or economic well-being, may produce more harm than good. Sudden advancement of democratization in the form of self-determination within a given area can (as the case of Yugoslavia showed) destabilize its established patterns of authority and encourage groups to seek further political power through violence. Without appropriate constitutional guarantees, populist democracy can often become "a tyranny of the majority" in which the rights of minorities are neglected, thus causing only strife and oppression. The reform of centralized economies along market principles can cause severe unemployment and other social instabilities, which increase the chances of civil violence, crime, political upheaval, war, and the return of authoritarianism.

The point is not that preventive diplomacy should tolerate oppressive policies and gross economic and political inequalities for the sake of preserving order and the status quo. It is rather that those who seek to prevent violent conflicts have as their first obligation to keep potentially explosive disputes from breaking out of manageable processes for *eventual* resolution. Stimulating and maintaining a peaceful *process* of managing political disputes should take precedence over the immediate attainment of discrete substantive goals as ends in themselves. Achieving this requires pursuing both the "negative" goal of keeping the lid on imminent violence in the short run, and the "positive" goal of promoting economic and political transformation that will help avoid violent conflicts in the future.

This raises the question of what should be done in situations of what is called "asymmetrical conflict," such as in present-day Kosovo, Myanmar (Burma), and Nigeria, where "negative peace" prevails largely because governments hold predominant coercive power and maintain a kind of stability by controlling the political activity and other behavior of their populations. In these situations it is not enough to counsel pacifism in order to avoid bloodshed. Unless these authorities are pressured to change, their oppression is likely to continue, thus continuing a state of injustice and possibly only postponing the day of eventual violent confrontation. But the answer still includes preventing violent conflicts. Rather than encourage or support revolt, third parties and supporters of oppressed groups must put other forms of pressure on the regime. For governments outside the area, this may mean applying various forms of sanctions, as well as making efforts to mediate. For the oppressed groups themselves, it may mean adopting a strategy of nonviolent protest, boycotts, or resistance; assertive participation in whatever political channels remain open; and pleas for international condemnation of, and measures to reverse, a regime's policies. This strategy may include destruction of property, but it does not include armed revolt and terrorism.

Deciding on grounds of prudence and feasibility not to act equally vigorously in every situation on behalf of certain cherished general principles is not a denial of the validity of these general principles, nor does it constitute blind acceptance of a stable but politically

Table 4.1. Stages of Conflict and Corresponding Intervention Methods or "Tools"*

Stage of Conflict	Priority Tasks	Tools
War		
Sustained fighting between organized armed forces. Characterized by breakdown of civil society and disintegration of central government. Rule of law abolished or threatened by military or emergency rule. Deteriorating health situation with decreasing life expectancy. Displacement of populations and growing dependence on imports of food and other humanitarian supplies. (E.g., World War II, Vietnam, Sudan, Somalia, Algeria, Bosnia War.)	End war and stop violence. Enact and enforce cease-fires. Disarm. Create sense of accountability and security to inhibit cycles of revenge killing. Provide humanitarian relief to meet basic needs. Provide shelter and resources for displaced persons and begin process of repatriation.	Military force (or threat). Arms embargoes. War crimes tribunals. Demilitarized zones. Diplomatic and economic sanctions. Third-party mediation (e.g., UN and EU mediators in Bosnian conflict). Delivery of humanitarian relief, possibly with military protection. Refugee assistance.
Crisis		
Tense confrontation between armed forces. Existence of threats and low-level fights. High probability of the outbreak of war. Often characterized by regime repression, insurgency, and systematic violation of human rights. Marginalization of communities. Communication almost nonexistent. (E.g., Columbia, Cuban missile crisis of 1962, Burundi, the U.S.-Soviet relationship in the late 1950s.)	Contain crises. Prevent (re)escalation to all-out war. Stop violent or coercive behavior. Limit arms. Reduce tension. Open communication, transparency. Create atmosphere of basic security. Provide consultation to analyze conflict. Change expectations of victory/defeat. Provide humanitarian resources to minimize additional stress and tension.	Title VII peace operations. Coercive diplomacy or "mediation with muscle." Crisis management procedures (e.g., U.S.-Soviet hot-lines). Confidence-building measures. Bilateral negotiations. Peaceful settlement of disputes mechanisms (e.g., OSCE's procedure). Track-two diplomacy (e.g., nonofficial dialogues and shuttle diplomacy). Military-to-military consultations. Institution building (e.g., interim power-sharing arrangements and national debates). Reconciliation projects.

Unstable Peace (the main realm of preventive diplomacy)

1) Near Crisis Major violence probable. Sporadic low-level violent acts. Increasing use of inflammatory rhetoric. Taking up of arms and threats. Decreasing communication. (E.g., North Korea.)	Block violent acts. "Freeze" hostilities. Reduce tensions. Improve relationships. Foster positive communications. Enhance cross-cutting ties. Maintain basic security. Create nonviolent means for addressing issues in conflict. Limit arms.	Diplomatic and economic sanctions. Preemptive peacekeeping forces. Multilateral peace conferences. Economic assistance. Track-two diplomacy (e.g., Transnational Foundation Project in Kosovo). Arms control regimes and their monitoring.
2) Low-Level Conflict Conflict over particular issues with increasing tensions. Polarization of communities and "enemies" defined. Violence mainly structural but overt violence possible. Often erosion of political legitimacy of national government and rising acceptance of sectarian politics. (E.g., Estonia, Burma.)	Address disputes. Channel specific grievances into negotiations. Engage parties in dialogue. Discourage extreme actions that can precipitate violence. Create processes to improve relationships and reduce tension.	Arbitration by International Court of Justice. Track-two problem-solving processes. Conciliation. Elections monitoring. Special envoys and good offices. Third-party mediation. Conciliatory gestures (e.g., GRIT, Tit-for-Tat).
3) Unstable Peace General level of tension and suspicion among parties. Diffuse political instability, uncertainty, distrust, and anomie, Growing levels of systematic frustration and increasing social and political cleavages along sectarian lines. (E.g., Macedonia, Ukraine.)	Create channels for dispute resolution. Build or strengthen political and civic institutions. Alleviate worst conditions breeding conflict.	Conflict resolution training. Human rights standard setting and monitoring. Peace committee structures (e.g., South Africa, Nicaragua). Fact-finding missions. Commissions of inquiry. Economic reform, standards, and integration. Collective security regimes. Rule of law programs.

continued on next page

Table 4.1. *continued*

Stage of Conflict	Priority Tasks	Tools
Stable, "Cold" Peace Relationship of wary communication and limited cooperation (e.g., trade) within overall context of order. Value or goal differences exist, but mainly addressed through established, non-violent channels. Political protests and violence against property and national symbols may occur. Communication basically open and prospect of confrontation or war is low (E.g., U.S.-Soviet détente of late 1960s, U.S.-China 1995, South Africa 1994–95, Israel-PLO accommodation, Nicaragua 1993–95.)	Promote cooperative relationships and peaceful integration of identity groups. Build or strengthen institutions capable of resolving conflicts that arise and maintaining dialogue. Promote methods of participatory decision making. Sustainable development of economy and environment.	Confidence-building measures (e.g., joint development of resources and development projects). Early warning systems. Preventive economic development aid and private investment in conflict-prone areas. Democracy building. International human rights standard setting. Creation of power-sharing arrangements.

Durable, "Warm" Peace

High level of cooperation. "Positive" peace prevails based on shared values, goals, institutions, economic interdependence, and sense of community. Peaceful, institutionalized settlement of disputes alleviates need to maintain ready arms to safeguard security. Basic needs met for majority of population. High degree of regime legitimacy with regular peaceful transfers of power between government and opposition. (E.g., U.S.-Canada, EU's Maastricht goal of common economic institutions and foreign policies, unified Germany.)	Maintain cooperative, nonadversarial relationships. Promote, environmentally sustainable economic growth. reduce inequality. Promote peaceful integration through a level of shared identity.	Regular dialogues and consultations (e.g., G-7 summits). Cooperative security pacts (e.g., NATO Partnership for Peace, European Union Stability Pact). Disarmament and arms control arrangements (e.g., NPT). Regional economic arrangements that allow for equitable distribution of resources. Establishment and strengthening of international principles and laws regulating use of the environment.

* This chart illustrates various "tools" or intervention methods that may be used to address conflicts at varying levels or stages of escalation. The strategy advocated is to match a particular intervention strategy to a specific stage of conflict and implement it at the appropriate time in order to preempt the conflict from escalating through the stages identified above. Thus, the stages represent a continuum of fluid states of conflict/peace. It should be noted that the list of tools given above is illustrative and not exclusive. Although certain tools are particularly appropriate for a given stage, they may not be limited only to that stage.

unjust status quo. Preventive diplomacy must be informed by intensive assessment of local conditions and recognition of what can and cannot be achieved without destructive upheaval. Its objectives should be set with reference to the specific power and capacity of the governments and social forces that preventive policies are seeking to influence. Case-by-case, country-specific estimates of material needs and institutional capacities, of the stage of socioeconomic and political development reached, and of the possibilities of further development: all should inform analytical judgments as to the primary and secondary benchmarks to be achieved. For example, the abundant research available on the dynamics of political change during transitions from authoritarian to more liberal political and systems could be applied more directly in developing appropriate preventive interventions and benchmarks.

In short, preventive diplomacy is not simply a moral campaign but a pragmatic enterprise. The international community should not leap from a Cold War era in which opposed blocs sought to force their ideologies on one another to a post–Cold War era in which the singular promotion or enforcement of democracy and human rights becomes itself a cause of increasing violence and destruction, which then requires costly international remedial efforts.

Even so, certain generic situations are likely to call for broadly similar mixes of positive and negative preventive methods. For example, various differentiated options can be suggested, depending on the extent to which countries carry out their foreign and domestic policies through authoritarian institutions backed by coercive armed force, at the one extreme, or are legitimate democracies at the other.

• Where a "rogue state" such as Iraq, North Korea, or Sudan threatens use of force or employs subversion outside its borders and tightly controls the political life of its own people, the best form of short-term prevention may be effective deterrence and containment of potentially dangerous aggression or subversion of other countries, meeting force with force wherever necessary. To the extent a state grossly represses its own people, economic sanctions and diplomatic isolation may be used. But if "authoritarianism" means the lack of democracy rather than the active oppression of a population, "carrots" such as the contingent benefits of economic assistance and membership in trading blocs, rather than "sticks" that distract from the source of the oppression, should be used. Thus, it may be advisable in some situations to maintain contact with the offending regime through educational and cultural exchanges with an eye to the regime's eventual political transformation.

Support for opposition groups to overturn an offending regime through violence risks not only tremendous human suffering but also costly involvement in the difficult job of national reconstruction after a civil war has ended. Opposition groups should instead be encouraged to use nonviolent means to keep pressure on the regime, thereby allowing their cause to retain the moral high ground and thus international support.

• In the case of relatively benign socialist or other politically centralized regimes that are not belligerent but stubbornly maintain control of large portions of their citizens' lives, such as Cuba, active engagement to promote democracy, human rights, and economic integration may help to head off future conflicts by gradually eroding state power and creating channels for evolutionary internal change. Imposing economically oppressive sanctions on such regimes, however, might entrench them in their nondemocratic positions or even destroy their economies and lead to more "failed states," the humanitarian consequences of which would have to be remedied by the international community. Indeed, in regard to regimes of this kind that are resistant to political change but possibly very vulnerable to violent overthrow or sudden collapse, the best preventive strategy may actually be to help stabilize the existing regime but simultaneously attach conditions to the foreign aid and economic benefits it receives, thereby permitting the preservation of some degree of order and human welfare and avoiding the outbreak of violence or total societal breakdown. Longer-term goals of promoting democracy and respect for human rights thus need not be abandoned but can be pursued gradually (through nondestabilizing policies) to transform basic institutions.

• Where predemocratic economies and societies are shifting toward greater economic openness and political pluralism but their economies are weak and their state institutions in danger of collapse, international policies should provide active support for democratization but should not promote such rapid sociopolitical change that it threatens social stability. The international community should avoid undermining existing indigenous institutions that are essential for the provision of basic human needs.

• Where newly democratic countries are threatened by reactionary forces that would subvert fledgling institutions, preventive diplomacy requires firm deterrence against any attempt at coercive takeovers, such as military or executive coups.

In sum, the consistent principle is that preventive diplomacy strategies should always seek to avoid exacerbating political tensions to the degree that they erupt into violent conflict or bolster oppression. Preventive diplomacy should instead aim to preserve or wherever possible create those conditions and procedures through which regimes can be transformed through peaceful political dialogue.

7. Preventive diplomacy thus also needs to be modulated, not only from place to place but also as a single conflict situation evolves. The sequence over time in which coercive and/or conciliatory or positive inducements are used is therefore important. Elements of both may need to be present at every stage of a conflict but their relative proportions within a particular "preventive package" may well have to be graduated as a dispute intensifies. Just as finely calibrated preventive diplomacy strategies must be tailored to reflect realistic assessments of what is and what is not attainable in a specific country or regime at the moment, so they must also be planned and operated with an eye to realizable future medium- and long-term goals. Thus, early warnings of troubled areas must continue to operate beyond the initial alarm to help set short- and long-term goals, and strategies must remain flexible and responsive to changing tactical and political considerations.

Generally speaking, in a situation where little violence has erupted or little coercion has been exercised, positive, conciliatory, non-threatening, nonintrusive, and noncoercive methods should be emphasized, with the threat of penalties or force made known to the parties but acted on only if violence escalates. Premature use of force or coercion may provoke a conflict rather than avoid it, while the absence of any potential negative sanctions may deprive initial conciliatory diplomatic overtures of sufficient clout. If more violence or coercion is used by the parties and conflict escalates, however, the graduated use of force or threats of force may be increasingly necessary. By the same token, higher levels of coercion have to be ready at hand and their possible use made clear to disputants, so that the disputants are not left free to pursue their aims during the imposition of less stringent measures.

The importance of thinking in terms of achieving specific goals through specific methods at particular times, and thus postponing some in order to achieve others, is especially well illustrated in the tensions that frequently arise between the values of stability and change, or peace and justice. Some tools of intervention are aimed primarily at "peace" (the preservation of order, stability, and physical security against violence) and others at "justice" (the advancement of human rights and/or constitutional democracy through social and political change). In terms of the definition outlined in chapter 2, this difference is seen in the tension between the objectives of "crisis avoidance" and "preemptive initiatives" on the one hand, and "preconflict peace building" on the other hand. In more academic terms, the tension is between achieving "negative peace" (preserving basic security and stability) and promoting "positive peace" (advancing democracy, human rights, and economic growth).

Four examples illustrate the kinds of trade-offs among values that have been made, for good or ill. In Kosovo, the international community has had to accept that Serbian domination makes it currently impossible to achieve full political justice for the Albanian majority, and has urged that only a policy of nonviolence will avoid worse repression by Serbia or possible civil war and thus wider regional instability. Similarly, for many years U.S. policy toward Zaire operated on the basis that the only choice was between "Mobutu or chaos," and thus the U.S. government supported Mobutu SeSe Seko and was very cautious toward the idea of opening up the Zairian political system to wider political participation. This kind of logic guided the initial U.S. reaction to the outbreak of fighting in Chechnya. Preserving smooth relations with Moscow was seen to be more important than peaceful resolution of Chechen grievances. In the case of the Bosnian war, the Vance-Owen peace plan and the U.S.-sponsored peace settlement of late 1995 for partitioning the country along ethnic lines were regarded by their proponents as the quickest ways to minimize further bloodshed and thus end the war. But this approach was even repugnant at one time to the U.S. government itself and other observers because it appeared to give international sanction to Bosnian Serb territorial gains achieved by force and to legalize the cantonization of ethnically based political communities.

In each case, the value of maintaining order or preventing further violence in the short run was regarded as more important by at least some third parties than the immediate achievement of democracy or some other more just solution to a political dispute or conflict. This has not necessarily meant that other values have been ignored or their attainment postponed indefinitely, but preventive strategies must incorporate an awareness that individual objectives must be pursued on individual timetables.

An apparent failure to recognize that different policy goals may require very different timetables is illustrated in the prime foreign policy priorities of the Clinton administration. The administration's early announcement of its "global issues" priorities—population control, "enlargement" of democracy, economic reform, free trade, control of arms proliferation, and protection of the environment—have more recently been described as policies aimed at conflict or crisis prevention. They may indeed play a preventive role over the long term, but save for policies intended to stem arms proliferation, they are of limited value in dealing with conflicts likely to arise in the short and medium term, particularly in countries vulnerable to violent resolution of political disputes. In fact, equal emphasis of these goals everywhere may provoke violent conflict, thereby setting back rather than advancing their achievement. Low-level turmoil and incipient conflicts of the kind we have seen in recent years could go undetected beneath the sweep of a conceptual radar that measures movement only in terms of progress to the more distant goals of population control, democratization, and so on.

In sum, tactical policy strategies must be developed that reconcile future and current objectives by indicating what amount of change is acceptable at a given moment in light of the concomitant need to deter the use of force, preserve political stability, and so forth. Before effective tactical preventive strategies can be launched and carried out effectively, such goal trade-offs must be addressed. Their consequences can be lessened by recognizing candidly that goal conflicts exist and trade-offs have to be made, and by establishing a clearer sense of appropriate or acceptable balances among the competing values.

8. Because of the need to calibrate the application of various preventive methods geographically and, as circumstances change, modify their relative importance over time, a preventive effort normally benefits from the presence of a "prime mover" that orchestrates the design and implementation of a multifaceted preventive strategy. The prime mover can be a single individual (such as an enterprising diplomat), a government, or a multilateral group, team, or task force. When several multilateral organizations operate simultaneously in one area, their separate functional tasks will not necessarily work easily in tandem. The challenge is to cut across the boundaries that divide governments, their agencies, and other organizations with different functional mandates and loyalties in order to focus their respective energies on common goals in local situations.

9. The need to combine and modulate various methods of intervention for specific local preventive strategies also has major implications for how and where policymaking and program planning is done in the bureaucratic hierarchies of governments and international bodies. In essence, the full range of policy tools—economic, diplomatic, military, and so on—should be viewed at certain decision-making levels as the multiple parts of a unified apparatus by which potential conflicts are anticipated and addressed.

The U.S. policy reviews of peace operations, intelligence, and humanitarian response mentioned above represent a useful start. But none seems to have been shaped by thorough analysis of what risks and threats may lie around the corner for the United States, and none proceeds from a single, coherent statement of what are the U.S. interests that therefore compel attention to the various risks and threats. In addition, more thorough cross-budget analysis and evaluation of the impact of these and other programs—not simply in terms of their program objectives, but more broadly in terms of the avoidance or intensification of violent conflicts—are needed to develop effective, coherent preventive diplomacy strategies within the context of overall U.S. planning and budgeting for national security. Among other beneficial results, closer coordination of programs in different functional areas will enhance their cost-effectiveness.

10. Rigorous empirical research using policy-relevant variables is needed to assess the respective costs and benefits of the full range of preventive policies and instruments that might be applied to different types and stages of interstate or internal conflict and different forms of political repression or instability. Such research could examine cases of comparative success and failure in the use of alternative strategies in varying contexts, identifying those factors and conditions that are conducive to avoidance of escalation. The effectiveness of interventions such as sanctions, war crimes tribunals, preventive peacekeeping, or the use of force varies considerably from case to case, particularly in relation to the level of violence. Setting up war crimes tribunals, for example, may intensify rather than deter violence, depending on the stage of conflict and the state of mind of the antagonists. This evaluation of a variety of preventive responses should then be fed back into early warning models.

Some preventive tools, such as deterrence, sanctions, coercive diplomacy, and third-party mediation, have been studied relatively extensively, but usually in relation to advanced stages of conflict and confrontation, not to precrisis stages. Thus, their utility in previolent situations needs further consideration. The performances of other promising preventive techniques have escaped evaluation at any conflict stage.

For example, among the less familiar preventive techniques worthy of much greater study are preventive peacekeeping, elections, freezing of the personal assets of members of offending regimes, civil society–building programs, and military-to-military programs.[21] Increased evaluation of track-two efforts (both those staged by NGOs and those undertaken by multilateral bodies such as the OSCE's HCNM) might reveal whether and under what conditions low-key consultations can tangibly affect a volatile situation. If track-two diplomacy can be shown to be effective, then a strong argument could be made for governments "contracting out" those tasks of an overall preventive strategy best performed by track-two specialists.

Particularly in regard to potential interstate tensions and instability in regions, such as Asia, without strong regional organizations, confidence-building measures (CBMs) and confidence-and-security-building measures (CSBMs) should be further examined and encouraged. CBMs and CSBMs have the advantage of not requiring comprehensive agreements; instead, they can be pursued on a step-by-step basis, as seen in the case of the CSCE with the 1975 Helsinki Final Act, the 1986 Stockholm Accord, the 1990 Vienna Document, and the 1992 Vienna Document. They can be both formal and informal, established through negotiated agreements in some instances and through tacit cooperation and declaratory policies in others. These measures can contribute to regional political-military stability and conflict avoidance through a variety of ways:

- building trust among parties whose relations have been characterized by mistrust;
- reducing fears of surprise attack as well as the likelihood of miscalculation or misrepresentation through greater transparency, communication, and military cooperation;
- establishing agreed-upon procedures and mechanisms for conflict management, which can help to avoid escalation of conflicts that do arise;
- facilitating and complementing arms control agreements as well as political and diplomatic agreements; and
- creating a favorable climate for the forging of other regional linkages, such as in trade and resource management.

CSCE-type consensus-building organizations are also worth considering in areas where they have been proposed but do not yet exist, such as Africa, Asia, and the Middle East. In relation to powerful regimes such as China that resist efforts at unilateral U.S. enforcement of its priorities of democratization and respect for human rights, the U.S. government might try instead multilateral efforts to promote regional consensus around those values through the development of regionally based multilateral, norms-setting processes. Notwithstanding these regions' cultural and political differences with Europe, such a strategy could draw on the successful experience of the CSCE in Eastern Europe in encouraging cross-cultural and scientific exchanges and emergent nongovernmental civic groups and organizations to peacefully promote domestic political change.

Disengagement

Once a third party has chosen to involve itself in a preventive diplomacy effort, how can it limit its commitment so as to ensure that it can withdraw? Any effort to prevent a single local, national, or regional problem comes up against other, perhaps inextricably interlinked problems. Preventive efforts themselves may open the door to new problems or even cause them—especially if, as is increasingly the case, these initiatives involve the internal affairs of societies and nations. Thus, skeptics have asserted that preventive diplomacy may not avert potential quagmires but may mean simply that "one bogs down earlier rather than later."[22]

In Zaire, for example, if a major U.S. diplomatic effort were to be effective in facilitating a democratic transition, where and how would this effort come to an end? Even if Mobutu were removed, there would remain the problems of setting up a new government, monitoring elections, providing economic aid, and so on. The successful negotiations to dismantle Ukraine's nuclear weapons, for example, involved U.S. and British security guarantees for Ukraine's present borders. But it is unclear how these guarantees would be redeemed in the event that pro-Russian secessionist sentiment and ethnic strife rise in the Crimea and eastern Ukraine, precipitating a backlash in the rest of the country and increasing Russian-Ukrainian tensions. Ensuring progress toward dismantling Ukraine's nuclear weapons thus also requires U.S. attention to domestic problems that go to the heart of Ukraine's continued viability as a legitimate state.

Understandably, the experience of past and recent U.S. quagmires from Vietnam to Somalia has engendered a strong aversion to future military involvements. As noted in chapter 1, the results of the eventual intervention in Somalia stimulated the preparation of PDD-25, which spells out the criteria that have to be met before the United States will commit resources to UN peacekeeping forces. U.S.

reluctance to become entangled in further operations is also accentuated by the fact that the United States has funded about 30 percent of the bill for the current sixteen UN peacekeeping missions worldwide.

Guidelines for Disengagement

1. The current concern about becoming trapped in quagmires is to some extent exaggerated because of a confusion between preventive diplomacy undertaken prior to conflicts and the recent peacekeeping missions sent to nations already devastated by violence. The danger of entanglement may be further overstated because attention has been focused on the problematic interventions, not on cases of successful prevention. Thus, one must keep clear the conceptual distinction between the goals of preventive diplomacy and those of crisis management or conflict intervention.

Preventive diplomacy has as its goal the avoidance of such demanding intervention through selective and modest early engagement. Rather than leading to deeper involvement, preventive diplomacy seeks to obviate the need for it by strengthening or creating nonviolent mechanisms for coping with political differences. Where indigenous institutions and processes are in danger of breaking down but still exist, such as in Estonia and Hungary, the risks of becoming inextricably involved are relatively small.

Those risks do increase significantly, however, where third parties are required to restore law and order, create political institutions, foster social reconciliation, and assist in economic reconstruction. The difficulties of disengaging become particularly great in instances where third parties have intervened through military force, such as occurred in Panama and Somalia. Military interventions are perhaps especially likely to create local dependency on the intervening third party, since where considerable disorder already exists, military authorities may find it difficult not to assume almost full responsibility and accountability for running the country. But preventive diplomacy, of course, looks to intervene before violence has destroyed the institutional fabric of a country.

2. To be sure, misconceived preventive diplomacy could lead to open-ended commitments to vulnerable areas even after the most

immediate dangers have passed. Here, the distinction between preventive diplomacy, on the one hand, and peacetime diplomacy and
long-term development, on the other hand, comes into play. Preventive diplomacy, it must be remembered, aims not to achieve good societies in every land but to prevent various destructive forms of
violent and coercive resolution of political differences, which if ignored often require even more extensive international involvements.
Rather than taking on the immense tasks of national development
through increasingly costly and intrusive efforts, it seeks only to restore and build up a society's *self-regulating* processes of dispute management, including not only indigenous social, cultural, judicial, and
democratic institutions but also less-than-perfect governments.
Where such processes already exist, preventive diplomacy needs only
to buttress these mechanisms against strains and threats to their functioning, rather than displace or destroy them. Priority is given to
strengthening and adapting traditional mechanisms for dispute resolution that draw on local history and customs, rather than substitut-
ing new, externally imposed mechanisms.

3. To avoid encouraging even higher levels of conflict as a result
of the third party's preventive effort itself, thought needs to be given
to which levels of government and what kinds of governmental or
nongovernmental actors are most appropriate to the scale and nature
of the conflict. Involvement by high-level officials (such as the U.S.
secretary of state) and bodies (such as the UN Security Council) may
be counterproductive in suppressing low-level conflicts because of its
effect in raising the stakes and increasing incentives to "grandstand"
before an international audience.

4. Limits in the form of "sunset" provisions should be put on the
potential responsibility and financial costs that a third party (whether
the United States, the United Nations, or some other entity) could in-
cur in a preventive effort. In implementing a specific prevention effort, its sponsors should specify in as much detail as possible the
mutual obligations of local, regional, and other parties and arrange
strict, quid pro quo contractual agreements with the parties in a dispute. Awareness of what preventive diplomacy does and does not
seek to accomplish might also be enhanced by developing a set of criteria for direct U.S. involvement in preventive diplomacy initiatives—

as a counterpart to the (quite different) criteria laid out in PDD-25 for peacekeeping.

5. It should be remembered that specific preventive initiatives have, in fact, come to successful conclusions. Further analysis of those cases where third parties have intervened and disengaged without conflict recurring would be extremely instructive both for those people wary of taking preventive action and for those responsible for its planning and conduct.

MOBILIZING WILL AND RESOURCES

Even if a situation is well understood, goals and trade-offs are relatively clear, and a promising course of action is apparent, it may be difficult to generate the necessary domestic, bureaucratic, and international support and resources to act. Preventive diplomacy must come to terms with the lack of national and international political will to act decisively and concertedly in launching and persisting with preventive efforts.

Because of national budget deficits, preoccupation with domestic problems, and the lack of clear enemies abroad, the task of galvanizing and maintaining resolve behind a coherent course of action is perhaps harder today than during the Cold War, especially if the action contemplated is likely to be multilateral. In an era of scattered, local conflicts, major powers appear to see few reasons to intervene in conflicts that do not *yet* greatly affect their national interests. Those same powers most able to intervene effectively and head off escalation tend to be geographically remote from and/or to feel themselves under little direct and immediate threat from the sources of conflict. And today, rather than being direct or indirect objects of possible attack or interested supporters of one side in a regional conflict, the United States, its allies, and other major powers are usually involved in conflicts as third parties.

National leaders in democracies attend to their political fortunes mainly by addressing domestic concerns, and their domestic constituencies rarely evince much interest, or at least much enduring interest, in international initiatives. But it surely falls to the government, not the general public, to generate political support for action to head off remote future conflicts. Thus, the problem of mustering will is rooted mainly within national executives, foreign policy bureaucracies, and legislatures. Bureaucratic inertia and a focus on the conduct of established policies rather than the anticipation of new problems explain much of the resistance to or lack of interest in preventive diplomacy. Another factor contributing to the dearth of preventive enthusiasm is the absence of career incentives for bureaucrats to launch preventive efforts. Merit recognition goes to those bureaucrats who help to arrest visible crises. Agencies are more likely to increase their budgets by demonstrating the continuance of major current problems than by arguing that future problems can be avoided. This problem, it is often claimed, stems from the difficulty of demonstrating that specific prevention efforts actually prevented a conflict. How does one prove that one prevented something that didn't happen?

However it occurs, the disinclination of individual nations to take responsibility for international problems remote in both place and time has a demonstration effect, by dissuading the leaders and citizens of other countries from picking up the slack. The lack of international agreement on the need to act thus reinforces national lack of will. The resultant vacuum may be filled by countries that act toward a dispute in such a way as to promote the interests of one side or another, thus worsening the situation.

Guidelines

1. The problem of generating political will and securing cooperation to undertake preventive initiatives, like that of disengagement, has been overestimated because of a mistaken equation of preventive action with recent UN peacekeeping missions. These missions are often costly and risky forays into advanced conflicts and raise (especially in the United States) highly charged questions of foreign command and control of national forces and the (too narrowly framed) question of "vital" national interests. But cheaper, less dangerous preventive efforts require mobilizing correspondingly less political will and fewer resources—especially if burdens are shared with other governments through multilateral organizations. For example, no controversy attended the sending of three hundred Americans to patrol Macedonia's borders as part of a UN preventive peacekeeping force.

2. To foster necessary political support, proponents of preventive diplomacy need to educate citizens as to the estimated gains and risks in both preventive action and inaction. A particularly persuasive approach might be to quantify and publicize the total costs incurred when conflicts are left to escalate in terms of lost lives, property damage, peacekeeping, humanitarian relief, reconstruction aid, and lost trade and business opportunities, and then to compare these costs with the more modest costs of preventing escalation.[23] Efforts should be made to publicize the recent success stories of preventive diplomacy, which the media tend to neglect in favor of coverage of active conflicts, In view of the recent quagmires in which UN missions have become trapped, the argument that prevention is cheaper than these later interventions could prove very marketable politically among both politicians and voters.

3. General public support may be less important than support from policy elites, however. Indeed, the chief value of broad popular support for preventive diplomacy may be that it helps persuade government leaders to reallocate some budget resources away from existing programs and toward preventive action. Because of their low cost and low saliency, preventive initiatives can be launched if they win the approval of sufficient legislators and officials within national agencies. This does require, however, that policymakers work closely with legislators to explain the need and risks of such initiatives. As seen in arms control negotiations, executive-congressional consultation has been very helpful in developing coherent policy and being able to maintain the determination to enforce it.

4. The difficulty of providing incentives for bureaucrats to undertake preventive efforts may also be overestimated. Although the conventional wisdom holds that because "the dog doesn't bark" there is no way of telling if preventive diplomacy was responsible for the avoidance of a conflict, on closer examination this may not be the case. As we have seen, in Estonia, Congo, and Hungary and Slovakia timely efforts appear to have reversed the escalation of developing disputes. It is in fact possible to argue plausibly that prevention efforts by a diplomat or other actor had an impact, and thus to bestow credit for their success.

During the Cold War, conflicts and crises seemed to arise overnight, and thus simultaneous actions to contain them were visible. If successful, such efforts naturally received the credit for preserving peace. In the post–Cold War era, although most incipient violent conflicts will be less visible, they still have antecedents. Where evident trajectories toward increasing escalation—as measured by increasing violence, demonstrations, and so forth—are halted or reversed after significant prevention efforts have been made, a strong case can be made that the preventive efforts were at least in part responsible. Accordingly, appropriate credit and rewards can be conferred on those third parties involved. Indeed, career promotions might be based on whether growing incipient threats are defused, rather than allowed to become crises. The fact that individuals who have been active in preventing conflicts in recent years, such as the OSCE HCNM, Max van der Stoel, and the U.S. negotiator of the agreement to dismantle Ukraine's nuclear arsenal, Ambassador James Goodby, have received accolades for their work seems to belie the notion that such rewards are infeasible.

Thus, reorienting foreign policy bureaucracies to undertake early preventive actions depends largely on high-level attention to the creation of appropriate career incentives. A step in this direction has been taken in President Clinton's letter of instructions in 1993 to newly assigned chiefs of mission, in which he urges them "to practice preventive diplomacy, to anticipate threats to our interests before they become crises and drain our human and material resources in wasteful ways."[24] Further progress could be achieved by writing preventive diplomacy requirements into the routine guidance and instructions (post reporting requirements, mission priorities planning, and country director evaluations, for example) given to officials in the U.S. State Department and other agencies. Training and orientation programs for new ambassadors, deputy chiefs of missions, and junior officers could include sensitization to early warning concepts and the range of low-level tools that might be employed.

5. Another perceived obstacle to gaining political support for preventive diplomacy is that remote post–Cold War conflicts are perceived by national legislatures and publics to lie outside the interests of most citizens of the major powers. This obstacle might be overcome, at least in part, by assigning to local actors the responsibility for launching an initial preventive response to a threatening situation.

In other words, prevention responsibilities should be "downloaded" by the major powers and, through them, by the UN Security Council to other third parties (such as the states and organizations within a region) that are conscious of the potential harmful effects of a nearby conflict but may need assistance in promoting a peaceful outcome.

The U.S. government is uniquely well placed to press for such decentralizing of responsibility while also taking a leadership role in energizing and supporting local and regional multilateral conflict prevention efforts. As discussed in chapter 5, this latter task can be accomplished by stimulating collaborative local preventive projects and building the capacity of regional organizations and NGOs through funding and logistical support.

5

ORGANIZING A PREVENTIVE REGIME

Of the five generic issues of preventive policy and implementation outlined at the beginning of chapter 4, one remains to be addressed: linking international actors in a coordinated system. As we have seen, post–Cold War preventive diplomacy is best served by tailoring a strategy that meets the needs of a given situation with a combination of well-timed actions implemented with a variety of well-honed tools. Given that no single actor is likely to possess all the tools required for a specific preventive effort, preventive diplomacy is typically and necessarily a multilateral endeavor. As we have also seen, however, the aims and actions of multiple actors have not always coincided, and where disagreements and/or disorganization have been evident, preventive effectiveness has been severely compromised. Thus, a crucial question for the future of preventive diplomacy is *how* that coordination and organization might be achieved, both within particular preventive interventions and on an ongoing basis.

THE EXISTING "SYSTEM"

Although the total number of individual initiatives being undertaken by one or more actors seems to be growing, the overall approach of the international community to preventive diplomacy is still fragmented and patchy. As we have seen, where they occur, preventive diplomacy efforts usually have involved several international actors, including individual states, groups of states, the United Nations,

169

regional organizations, NGOs, and eminent individuals. While the potential exists for burden sharing and some division of labor, current energies still are dispersed. Because the participants each have different jurisdictions, mandates, funders, and constituencies, each proceeds largely independently, often without explicit reference to what the others are doing and where. The several tasks of preventive diplomacy are carried out largely unilaterally by the many actors and dispersed both across many organizations and at many levels within their individual hierarchies. Although exceptions may exist—such as the effort in Macedonia, perhaps—rather than work together to ensure that the characteristic strengths of each actor complement one another and that their limited resources are put to best use, the participants all too frequently adopt divergent approaches, and consequently leave gaps in overall preventive coverage. As a result, particular efforts may fail for lack of coordination, some disputes may receive more attention than is actually warranted, and many disputes may become violent with little effort being made by anyone to stop them.

While no official or organization is barred from monitoring potential conflicts or taking preventive action in any part of the world, neither is anyone required to do so. Overall, international preventive diplomacy is like a social welfare activity, dependent on volunteers and charitable contributions. Whether a given incipient conflict is addressed preventively and to what degree depends almost entirely, therefore, on whether particular third parties or disputants take an interest in doing so. This does not pose a major problem with regard to major threats, such as rogue states threatening to develop or deploy weapons of mass destruction, because their danger to the international community usually compels considerable attention and effort. But it presents a serious problem with regard to the range of potential conflicts that are less widely threatening but that may evolve into tragic and costly international crises, for fewer international bodies or states may step forward to undertake the tasks required.

Efforts have begun in a few regional organizations and within the UN Secretariat to institutionalize early warning and preventive responses to previolent crises through earmarking staff and resources for proactive monitoring and political intervention. Perhaps the closest to a mandatory authority that is expected to provide consistent coverage of certain kinds of conflicts in a specified region is the OSCE's HCNM. The operation of more such units would both facilitate the coordination of the actors in particular places and increase the likelihood that some action is taken wherever necessary within a given geographic jurisdiction. Most of these mechanisms, however, are not fully operational. And even where they are already relatively well developed (as in the case of the OSCE), they are geared for certain potential crises, such as ethnopolitical conflicts, but not others, such as border disputes. Furthermore, they often lack the staff and other resources even to attend to those tasks that they are mandated to accomplish.

The present uncoordinated and patchy nature of preventive diplomacy reflects the absence of any accepted international conflict prevention regime or system of governance—that is, agreed-upon arrangements through which geographic jurisdictions are allocated, functional responsibilities assigned, norms and procedures formulated, and actors held accountable for their responsibilities. Although the existence in some regions of many channels, venues, and actors at several levels available to assist a preventive process can be useful insofar as the range of options is broad, this absence of set preventive procedures invites disputants to maneuver incessantly without committing to any process of engagement, to shop for the most favorable arrangements, and to play different parts of the international community off against one another.

To suggest that preventive diplomacy needs a better "system" is by no means to conclude, however, that a single, highly integrated and formalized worldwide machinery is either feasible or desirable. To a great extent, preventive diplomacy will always require the spontaneous energy and unique ingenuity of many kinds of actors in the different regions who assume responsibility and decide how to take action in their own ways. Nevertheless, if preventive diplomacy is going to achieve better results than the occasional success story, more regularized, widely established arrangements are needed. In view of the post–Cold War era's dual problems of constrained resources and overloaded bureaucratic agendas, letting a "thousand flowers bloom" in preventive diplomacy may foster creativity but it can also squander very scarce resources—hence the need to explore how preventive activities could be better blended, resources pooled, tasks divided up, comparative advantages exploited, and economies of scale realized, thus maximizing the benefits of collaborative action. Account should be taken of the lessons of recent experience and of the strengths and liabilities of likely actors.

To the extent that enlightened national and global leaders are persuaded of the advantages of preventive diplomacy and increasingly practice it, the need for this more structured approach is likely to become more apparent. As ad hoc endeavors grow in number, their sponsors sooner or later will search out ways to enhance their efficiency by adopting more coherent, coordinated strategies. The only question is how soon such a system will be perceived as advantageous. To hasten this process, we present here one approach to a more institutionalized structure and the advantages it might yield.

RECENT PROPOSALS

Before sketching the design of such a preventive system, it seems wise to review the advantages and disadvantages of those few proposals that have already been made for organizing an overall system of preventive diplomacy. Two of these proposals envision most if not all of preventive diplomacy's tasks being placed within one or more multilateral organizations: in one case, the United Nations, and in the other, regional organizations. A third approach envisions early warning and preventive diplomacy being carried out more extensively by a network of NGOs. Although no one has proposed leaving these activities to individual states, their roles in any preventive effort are inevitably crucial, and thus states, too, are examined here as possible loci of preventive activity. The following review allows us to inventory the characteristic strengths and weaknesses of each of these actors for the tasks of preventive diplomacy and to identify which roles each actor plays best.

All proposals to coordinate and rationalize the existing system must grapple with the question: *Where should responsibility for the tasks of preventive action (early warning, the decision to act, the formulation of a response, and the provision of bureaucratic and political support) be located both horizontally (across different organizations or actors) and vertically (up or down their chains of command) in relation to preventing what type and scale of conflicts, and in which geographic regions of the world?*

A UN-Centered System

The Australian foreign minister Gareth Evans has proposed that the recent creation of the Department of Political Affairs in the UN Secretariat be carried further. Evans proposes that more trained staff be added to the unit to monitor the six geographic regions that have been delineated, and that teams of mediators who are well trained in both conflict intervention techniques and specific regions be deployed as needed to UN regional offices. The mediators would be deployed routinely to potential trouble spots to offer their services to head off crises and to urge the parties to engage in peaceful negotiations if they do not themselves request this aid. In addition to collecting and assessing early warning information and providing good offices and mediation services, they would arrange negotiations and monitor progress, assist the parties in drawing on other resources from the UN system, refer the parties to other channels if appropriate, and monitor compliance with any agreements made.

This unit could be supplemented by staff permanently located in the regions themselves at "Peace and Security Resources Centers," which might be situated in the same cities as the headquarters of regional organizations. The officials in the regional centers would report to the UN secretary-general (and periodically to the Security Council), however, rather than to regional organizations. In effect, the Evans plan would make the UN Secretariat the central headquarters of a worldwide early warning and preventive diplomacy capacity.[1]

It certainly makes great sense for a plan for organizing preventive diplomacy more systematically to start with the single organized body that includes virtually all the countries of the world and already carries out a variety of functions in conflict management and peacekeeping. In principle, the United Nations has several other assets too.

- It can take advantage of the resources of its worldwide organizational network, calling upon the services of a wide variety of specialists and ancillary UN programs (humanitarian, human rights, arms control, development, and so forth).

- It can bring the parties together through the good offices and other tools of diplomacy available to the secretary-general.
- It has the option of bringing an issue or conflict to the world stage, if necessary, through the Security Council or the secretary-general (as laid out in Articles 35 and 99 of the UN Charter), thus focusing the pressure, moral and otherwise, from the international community on the parties in dispute.
- It can draw on the many years of diplomatic experience gained by a wide variety of professional diplomats from member countries and on its staff.
- It can gain the attention and rally the political power and resources of major powers behind threats of formidable preventive measures, if necessary, such as economic sanctions or aggregations of national military forces for preventive peacekeeping or peace enforcement actions.

At the same time, however, trying to locate a single, global process for early warning and preventive diplomacy in the New York headquarters of the United Nations has serious drawbacks.

- Both the secretary-general and his staff and the Security Council are already under serious strain because of their overloaded agendas and limited resources. With many issues and actors competing for UN attention, the organization tends to focus chiefly on major world problems that have already reached the stage of crisis and thus have garnered the interest of the members of the Security Council or of large blocs of member states. The earlier practice whereby secretary-generals first used their own good offices to mediate disputes, and later assigned UN special envoys and regional fact-finding missions to this task, became overtaxed because of the great demands placed on the Secretariat. Even though the new Department of Political Affairs is mandated to anticipate conflicts and take preventive actions, it too has become increasingly preoccupied with current crises, and its new area desk officers so far lack needed training in early warning and preventive options.
- Although the UN Charter under Articles 39 through 42 permits the organization to act in regard to any potential "threat" or actual

"breach of the peace," whether intrastate or interstate, the United Nations deals mainly with disputes among states and governments and finds difficulty addressing claims and conflicts involving nonofficial parties, such as grass-roots political movements or opposition groups.

- By giving world visibility to a conflict, UN involvement might sharply raise the stakes of a dispute by internationalizing it, thus creating incentives for the parties to strike more adversarial postures and become more, not less, combative. Thus, the United Nations may inadvertently widen a conflict and encourage other parties to take sides.

- Because major security actions require the approval of the Security Council, the ability of the United Nations to act is constrained by the ever-present possibility of a veto from one or more of the permanent members and by the difficulty of achieving consensus. Although the veto has been used rarely since 1990, signs suggest that it may be wielded with increasing frequency. Actions that require the approval of the General Assembly (such as the dispatching of an observer mission) are similarly constrained by the need to obtain support from a large number of countries.

- Because of their fear of failure, states may be reluctant to bring their disputes to the United Nations in case those disputes ultimately come before the Security Council, which has the authority to exercise highly coercive, adversarial, inflexible, and typically partial policy tools, such as economic sanctions, that favor one side or the other. Although the secretary-general's good offices are more flexible, states may still be apprehensive of the high stakes that accompany the involvement of the office of the secretary-general in dispute resolution. For some developing countries, the Security Council's actions may still have the taint of neocolonialism.

- Although it is in the process of trying to achieve managerial reform, the United Nations still suffers from major organizational inefficiencies and a reputation for wastefulness among many politicians and influential observers in the West. Until its image improves and/or the current political climate in countries such as the United States becomes less intemperate, the United Nations is unlikely to secure the additional resources it would need to expand the Department for Political Affairs.

- The proposed regional centers are likely to duplicate the efforts of regional organizations and create uncertainty over whether those organizations or the United Nations has the main authority over particular disputes. It also seems politically unpalatable for the UN Secretariat to appear to be directly interfering in national and regional affairs.[2]

On balance, it appears that an attempt to aggregate more resources in a highly centralized early warning and preventive system may meet serious political and bureaucratic obstacles, and even if achieved, could delay response to potential crises to the point that it is already too late. The United Nations clearly has certain roles to play in preventive diplomacy, but it may be unwise to promote a UN-centered system as the only option.

Regional Organizations as Hubs

As an alternative or supplement to the creation of new regional centers at decentralized levels of the United Nations, Mohamed Sahnoun and others have suggested that existing regional multilateral organizations (RMOs) be transformed into major centers of early detection and response within their regions. As we have seen, mechanisms for conflict prevention and management have already been created in the OSCE, OAU, and OAS, and are being developed by subregional organizations such as the Economic Community of the Central African States (ECCAS) and the Intergovernmental Authority for Drought and Development (IGADD) in the Horn of Africa. Ad hoc initiatives focusing on particular disputes have been undertaken by ASEAN and other regional organizations. The *Agenda for Peace* clearly envisions a role for such organizations, and the UN secretary-general has met with the heads of several RMOs to encourage UN-RMO cooperation.

RMOs do, indeed, have a number of advantages.

- Their close geographical proximity to developing conflicts makes regional organizations more likely, at least in principle, to learn of threats before they have reached crisis proportions and more likely to respond before they have adversely affected the interests of the organizations' member states.

- With fewer actors around which to form a consensus in favor of action, and with fewer items competing for attention on their agendas, regional organizations may be able to respond to a problem situation more quickly than the United Nations can.

- Regional organizations can bring to bear on the parties to a conflict the peer pressure of neighboring states and can appeal to the regional pride of their membership to handle disputes through indigenous rather than external mechanisms. The preventive methods they use and the norms they espouse—often based on traditional regional customs and practices—are often more acceptable to the parties in dispute than methods and norms imposed by external forces.

- Regional organizations can provide a legitimizing "political cover" under which major outside powers can become effectively involved in settling a conflict.

However, regional organizations have significant shortcomings.

- In regions such as the Middle East and South Asia, regional organizations have historically been weak and ineffective and are thus ill suited to assume major conflict prevention responsibilities.

- Even where regional organizations are relatively strong, they rarely possess the financial, logistical, and human resources necessary for effective preventive action, and they lack sufficient professional experience in conflict resolution. This has been a serious problem for organizations such as the OAU that have at least been very active and aspire to play larger regional roles.

- Because of rules requiring unanimous consent and their lack of coercive measures akin to those available to the Security Council, regional organizations often cannot easily mobilize joint military forces for peace enforcement, sanctions, or other coercive actions.

- Regional organizations often find themselves constrained by their member states' fierce determination to maintain their individual sovereign national prerogatives.

- The need to cater to the preferences of major hegemonic regional powers (for example, India in South Asia, Nigeria in West Africa, and China in North Asia) often makes it difficult for regional organizations to mobilize political support for regional action where such powers have vested interests or resist preventive initiatives.
- Regional organizations may not be impartial in a given conflict, because they often reflect in their own politics the very disputes and clashes of interests that the organizations are supposed to settle.

Thus, although some RMOs (such as the OSCE) are in fact leaders in the field, and while other RMOs might have the potential to legitimize regional preventive efforts and assume more preventive responsibility in the future, at present RMOs generally lack the financial resources and political backing to undertake preventive diplomacy entirely on their own.

An NGO Preventive Network

A third idea—proposed by, among others, International Alert—is to create a network of NGOs that would work with the United Nations and regional organizations to provide early warning and play a more active role in formulating and implementing preventive responses. This proposal aims to exploit the distinct advantages in dispute resolution and conflict prevention that NGOs enjoy over both multilateral entities and individual states. These advantages include:

- extensive grass-roots contacts and intimate knowledge of many countries and areas, which together foster a sensitivity to the possible trajectories of local disputes and the chances of violence erupting;
- the ability to engage the parties to a conflict, including opposition or "rebel" groups, in dialogues that, being informal, low-key, and nonthreatening, neither oblige the disputants to commit themselves to a binding agreement nor compel them to play to their respective constituencies;
- the ability to forge a variety of links directly between professional, commercial, and educational bodies and other NGOs that bypass governments and cut across national boundaries; and

- the services, at relatively low cost, of a wealth of professional, specialized, and typically highly motivated personnel.

At the same time, however, NGOs:

- are usually short of resources and financially dependent on their donors and thus are often unable to persevere for as long as official entities can;
- lack the financial and military clout necessary to provide guarantees or sufficient inducements that might prompt the parties to a dispute to reach a durable agreement;
- cannot build up the high-cost communications and logistical capabilities that states and large multilateral organizations can provide;
- may have purposes and agendas that are incompatible with those of governmental entities and may thus have to act independently of governments; and
- are ultimately not held accountable to given political constituencies, which even multilateral organizations are, however indirectly.

Thus, although NGOs can make unique contributions within an overall process of conflict prevention, they must rely largely on other parties to provide essential political and material support.

Individual States

It is, of course, neither politically nor economically feasible for every state, large and small, to establish its own capacity for early warning and preventive response. And although the major powers must be relied on to provide political leadership and financial, personnel, and other resources (see below), no one has yet proposed that a single nation house the central headquarters and field offices of an ongoing global system of preventive diplomacy. Some observers, however, have pointed out the inherent advantages that individual states, especially major or medium-sized powers, have over multilateral organizations in conflict management, and thus possibly also preventive diplomacy.[3] For example:

- a state may have a more or less direct interest in the stability of another state and thus be strongly motivated to prevent disputes there from escalating beyond control;

- a state can respond more quickly than a multilateral organization to an international problem, because the state does not have to go through the cumbersome process of gaining an international consensus for action; and

- a powerful state is likely to have formidable diplomatic resources, military forces, and technical resources already in place and at its command.

But states, too, have their shortcomings:

- unless a state happens to have a special strategic, economic, or other interest in a particular dispute abroad, it is unlikely to act to prevent that dispute from worsening—thus, no one state can be expected to "cover" more than a few such situations;

- a government may be unable to act until it has secured the support of its public and/or political elite, especially in cases where a nation's military forces will be involved;

- a state will approach a conflict in a way that favors its particular national interests, which are not necessarily in the broader interests of the international community; and

- for historical reasons, particular states may be unwelcome in a particular region and thus lack the moral legitimacy necessary to gain the respect and cooperation of the parties to a conflict or of other third parties.

In sum, as chapter 3 revealed, individual states are often essential supporters of particular preventive actions, and their tolerance, if not active support, for preventive initiatives is crucial. But they are not necessarily the most appropriate or effective direct actors in those initiatives.

A STRATIFIED, MULTILATERAL REGIME

All the above proposals seek to locate most, if not all, preventive tasks in one or another type of entity. But as the case studies and the preceding discussion suggest, each of the principal players—the United Nations, regional organizations, the United States and other major powers, and NGOs—has its weaknesses as well as strengths. None can perform all the tasks of preventive diplomacy adequately by itself or some tasks necessarily as well as some other players. In short, an adequate, cost-effective, and politically feasible global system of prevention cannot look primarily to one type of actor.

But if effective preventive diplomacy cannot be left to the vicissitudes of international politics and the NGO marketplace, then responsibility and the resources necessary for early warning and preventive diplomacy must be pooled and tasks assigned in some more deliberate fashion. The most promising approach to developing a system of preventive diplomacy seems to lie with the development of a preventive regime—or a set of norms and procedures—that is explicitly multilateral and multilevel. Such a regime would make more deliberate and coordinated use of the respective political, moral, and material advantages of the several types of third parties already involved in conflict regions around the world. Unlike a system whose headquarters and hierarchy are housed within a single organization or state, this layered, multiactor regime would capitalize on the comparative strengths of various global and regional actors already active in the field, coordinating their activities as much as possible within an optimal division of labor that takes advantage of economies of scale. Some actors are needed to provide legitimacy, whereas others are needed to provide political power, security, reconciliation opportunities, economic resources, logistical support, and other vital ingredients.

What would such a system look like and how would it be established? A useful way to sketch out its features is first to outline the system as it typically would operate when eventually achieved, thereby indicating its basic organizational dynamics and normative principles. We can then suggest how this ideal setup would have to be approached incrementally in the short run to accommodate present political realities and capabilities of the actors in various regions.

This two-step analytical approach mirrors the kind of strategy that would be necessary to establish such a regime. The required implementation strategy would, that is, be two-pronged, with one prong being directed toward eventually institutionalizing a more formal and regularized structure that assigns particular responsibilities to particular actors and progressively strengthens them to carry out, and to be accountable for, preventive diplomacy on a regular basis. The other prong would be directed toward achieving effective conflict prevention that is practicable in the short term.

As regards the eventual structure, the international community should begin developing a prevention regime, the parts of which are linked loosely within a single system but which function in a highly autonomous way. The basic structure of the system would be organized by dividing up tasks *both vertically and horizontally*.

A *vertical* differentiation of activity is necessary because responsibility for conflict prevention needs to be located as close to an impending conflict as possible, with the level of resources and actors brought into play matched to the severity and scale of the hostilities. For a number of reasons, including those Dag Hammarskjöld understood, at the low-level stages of violent conflicts, the visible involvement of powerful external actors is frequently neither welcome nor useful; local third parties may be much more effective on this first line of prevention.[4] Thus, as the UN Charter itself enshrines in Chapter VI, responsibility for conflict avoidance should be pushed downward as much as possible to local and subregional actors.

This means that policies and procedures should keep the "response time" between early warnings and the implementation of preventive action—and thus the physical and organizational distance between an emerging conflict and the application of decisions to address it— as short as possible. To borrow from the language of cybernetics, the "feedback" loop that sends messages (in this case, information about disputes) through a hierarchy of interpreters to the implementers of preventive responses should be as short as possible. Accordingly, within the United Nations and other global organizations, such as the U.S. government, current operations should be decentralized to country-level and field offices to achieve a vertical division of labor determined by and large by the seriousness and scale of given conflicts.

However, this means a *horizontal* differentiation of labor is also necessary. Because all the authority and resources that are needed to fulfill the tasks of preventive diplomacy will not be obtainable from local actors or the lower levels of one or another organization within the vertical hierarchy, collaboration and coordination among the pertinent and capable international or national entities that operate within a given geographic area must be encouraged. In many cases, local representatives of the most capable actors (such as major regional or extraregional states) might take the lead, acting as "prime movers" to create and energize international lateral teams of third parties to work together and with disputants. Let us elaborate on each of these concepts in turn.

The Vertical Hierarchy: Thresholds for Preventive Diplomacy

The vertically stratified structure follows a principle similar to that employed in the U.S. federal system for allocating responsibilities between the federal government and the states, as well as by the European Union in defining the respective responsibilities of the union and its member states: subsidiarity. That is, those problems that can be handled by a lower level of government or organization should be handled by that level, and only those problems that cannot should be brought up to the next level. The vertical division of labor in preventive diplomacy would be achieved by pushing explicit direct responsibility and accountability downward—wherever possible and not all at once, but increasingly over time, as the capabilities at those levels permit—to the parties to the conflict themselves and to subregional and regional actors. At the same time, extralocal and extraregional states and the United Nations would provide appropriate facilitative, technical, political, and (if necessary) military support.

Thus, actions to prevent conflicts would be undertaken first in terms of direct involvement by local actors such as the disputants themselves, but with the indirect support of other actors outside the arena of conflict, acting through their representatives present at the local level, such as the ambassadors of major or medium-sized states. Only if greater resources and muscle seem necessary to bring the parties to an agreement would higher-level actors become directly involved—in the first instance at the regional level and in the second at the global level. Thus, each of the three levels—local, regional, and global—would come into the foreground as necessary.

The Local Arena: The First Level of Prevention. At present, the dominant image of intervention by the international community in an interstate or intrastate conflict is that of UN peacekeepers arriving on the scene of a raging conflict to ensure the delivery of humanitarian relief and, at best, to stabilize the situation. This omnipresent image has largely obscured recognition of the multiple ways in which less risky, less costly, and lower-profile action at the local level has been and can be taken before major violence erupts. If low-level sources and signs of interstate and intrastate conflicts are included within the purview of the international community and monitored more consistently, and local resource used more deliberately, the chances for focused, effective preventive initiatives increase.

Preventive diplomacy is not needed when the parties to a conflict themselves choose to settle their disputes without violence, as the leaders of the Czech and Slovak peoples did when they peacefully divided their nation. Preventive diplomacy becomes an issue only when the parties are unable or unwilling to negotiate successfully. Indeed, the ideal system of third-party prevention would be one left unemployed because disputes are resolved locally and at low levels of escalation. Accordingly, one normative principle a global preventive system should promulgate and enforce wherever possible is that the first step toward conflict avoidance is local self-help by conflicting parties. This is, in fact, already laid down in Chapter VI, Article 33, of the UN Charter: "The parties to a dispute, the continuance of which is likely to endanger the maintenance of international peace and security, shall, first of all, seek a solution by negotiation, enquiry, mediation, conciliation, arbitration, judicial settlements, resort to regional agencies or arrangements, or other peaceful means of their own choice." Yet, although this seems an obvious first step, it is not always taken and should be more forcibly and consistently advocated by the international community.

Specifically, when early warning signals of a deepening dispute are given, the international and/or regional community should explicitly and vocally reiterate through well-publicized statements and appeals the expectation that the parties to the dispute will seek their own bilateral solutions by engaging each other peacefully as early as possible. The parties should be discouraged from waiting for others to come to their side, although assistance in problem-solving dispute resolution should be offered and local requests for them promptly honored. If no such requests are made, the parties should be urged to accept mediation assistance wherever it appears necessary.

With intercommunal and intergroup disputes within existing states now widely regarded as posing the most common type of threat to international security, the political institutions of existing states should be expected to serve as the first venue for negotiation and mediation. Where these institutions and similar local channels exist but are weak, third-party action should seek to buttress, extend, or otherwise strengthen them; they should not be displaced by preventive efforts unless absolutely necessary. Direct third-party involvement in mediating a dispute should thus be avoided and the focus placed instead on indirect support.

Unfortunately, in many recent civil conflicts, national institutions have failed or have themselves been part of the problem, such as in the case of the suppression of minorities, when parties vie for exclusive control of the state or seek to escape its control entirely. In such situations, responsibility for preventive diplomacy often must shift from the disputants themselves to subregional or regional organizations, where they exist and can handle the task.

The Regional Arena: The Second Level of Prevention. Where disputants within a state are unable to handle their own disputes or national institutions are a source of the problem, responsibility for prevention must shift to the regional arena. Despite the historic limitations of many of them, RMOs can and should play a more active role not only in strengthening regional interstate security but also in the peaceful resolution of ethnic and other internal political conflicts within member states.

Where mature subregional and regional organizations have some capacity to function cooperatively and effectively, the wider international community should seek to enlist and strengthen them as preventive agents. Although the UN Charter encourages that disputes first be dealt with by RMOs (and only thereafter by the United Nations), too often all RMOs have been dismissed as ineffective and/or unmotivated entities, undeserving of support. The United Nations has not been inclined to explicitly "subcontract" diplomacy and security issues to regional organizations, except when the initiative has been assumed by regional entities backed by major powers. Such an approach is based in part on the frequently demonstrated weaknesses of such organizations in attending to especially dangerous and escalated conflicts. But if applied automatically, it ignores the fact that several RMOs are now establishing conflict prevention procedures and realizing, albeit to modest degrees, their intentions to deal more assertively with national and regional conflicts. As we have seen, RMOs such as the OAS and OSCE are taking on the roles of guardians of democracy and leading proponents of the peaceful resolution of conflicts that arise within as well as among member states. Other RMOs are experimenting with procedures to address shared security concerns; ASEAN, for example, is doing so through its Regional Forum. RMOs possess certain advantages over higher-level third parties when it comes to conflict prevention: regional legitimacy; firsthand knowledge of complex problems; the potential to respond speedily and flexibly to emerging disputes; personal ties; the ability to apply peer pressure on disputants; and awareness of distinctive indigenous cultural mores and methods for managing disputes peacefully .

The international community should seek to capitalize on these assets by giving RMOs progressively greater authority to engage in local conflict prevention activities, developing commonly accepted rules for RMO initiatives, and providing more financial and logistical support to equip RMOs to perform their new responsibilities. Material and political support from individual states such as hegemons inside a given region and outside parties with a long-standing interest in the region will be necessary. But such assistance should be provided only under the auspices and in accordance with the norms of RMOs and within the parameters of the UN Charter, not through a tacit understanding that a given region lies within the exclusive sphere of interest of one or another state. The preponderant influence of regional hegemons (for instance, the United States, China, India, Russia, Brazil, South Africa, and Nigeria) could be counterbalanced by the smaller countries in those regions combining their weight by working together within the appropriate regional organization.

In regard to the promotion of democracy, for example, more RMOs should be encouraged to elicit binding and accountable commitments to democracy by states within their regions. Such commitments must be supported on an ongoing basis—and as far as possible at the "low end" of the conflict spectrum—through such means as international monitoring of respect for human rights, the provision of financial assistance and expertise in the building of democratic institutions, and the dispatch of preventive observer missions (such as those of the OSCE) to monitor compliance with agreed-upon procedures.

Certainly obstacles must be overcome if RMOs are to carry out preventive diplomacy effectively. The process of decision making must be streamlined while respecting an organization's preference for consensual rules and practices. Member states should be pressured to provide the necessary financial and human resources. Threats once made must be carried out, thus enhancing the credibility of the RMO involved. In the short term, member states may decide to act chiefly because of the fear that inaction will lead to greater external involvement in regional affairs. In the long term, success in the preventive field may foster the will and the capacity not only to respond to deepening crises but also to oversee—whether by themselves or in partnership with the United Nations or a regional military alliance such as NATO—compliance with agreements negotiated by the parties, and thus prevent relapses into further conflicts.

For the moment, many subregional and regional actors and institutions are incapable of handling localized disputes, thereby obliging higher-level actors to become involved more swiftly. The nations of some regions are relatively well prepared to handle their common conflict and security concerns through institutionalized collective mechanisms. Effective "regional security communities" or de facto "zones of peace" do exist in certain regions, such as Western Europe and Latin America, for example. But other regions do not yet have this capacity. Among the requisites for these regional relationships are reasonably secure established states, the prospects for economic growth, an ideological or value consensus on forms of governance, benign or supportive regional powers, the lack of egregious imbalances of power between states, and the existence of functioning common regional institutions.[5] Thus, developing regional-level agreements and understandings that facilitate effective preventive action will take much time in regions lacking these attributes, such as the Middle East, South Asia, Northeast Asia, Central Asia, the Horn of Africa, and Central Africa.

In these latter regions, the international community has little choice for the time being but to patch together coalitions of whatever state, multilateral, and nongovernmental actors and resources are available for a given arena to address specific, serious threats. Heavy reliance may need to be placed on ad hoc coalitions of major powers with the ability to energize preventive efforts by providing political leadership and logistical, personnel, military, and other resources. In some cases, powerful extraregional states or enlightened regional powers might be "deputized" to carry out such efforts, albeit within a multilateral framework and with respect for the norms of the United Nations and regional organizations. But over time, the aim should be to create a system that will obviate the need for such ad hoc responses.

In short, despite the present shortcomings of RMOs, the only alternatives to empowering such organizations may be reacting with indifference to emerging local conflicts or continuing to look to a wary and busy UN Security Council and reluctant major powers to reestablish peace amid chaos. If RMOs are to fulfill their preventive potential, a dual strategy is called for—one that works over the long term to prepare RMOs to assume greater preventive responsibilities while accepting the short-term need for more direct international involvement in ad hoc regional preventive efforts.

The Global Arena: The Third Level of Prevention. As conflict prevention responsibilities are progressively pushed downward, global-level actors such as the UN Security Council and secretary-general are freed up to concentrate their attention and resources on three types of problems more appropriate to the visibility and power those actors possess: large-scale crises that local and regional efforts are unlikely to be able to handle, such as major wars and nuclear threats; lower-level conflicts that local and regional third parties have tried but failed to prevent; and the creation of backup peace enforcement forces for possible deployment into new local and regional conflicts in those instances when regional military resources are inadequate to the demands of those conflicts. To the extent that the system at lower levels works, these standby forces would not need to be deployed; yet the existence and possible use of such forces is nonetheless necessary to *deter* escalation of low-level disputes into full-blown conflicts. Sometimes, the UN secretary-general and/or Security Council may be the only entities capable of resolving a dispute; they have in the past succeeded where others have failed.

The Horizontal Axis: Graduated Responses and Lateral Collaboration

The division of labor necessary to institute a multilateral system of conflict prevention must operate through a horizontal division of tasks, as well as vertically. This means that at each of the vertical levels—local, regional, and global—third parties involved must engage in greater lateral cooperation, coordinating their actions, pooling their resources, and assigning responsibilities as required by the circumstances of a given conflict. Thus, a number of actors would be working at each level to keep the dispute within the bounds of that level. The outlines of this laterally collaborative approach are sketched below.

Decentralized Multilateralism. Inevitably, governments, multilateral organizations, and NGOs have different agendas that reflect their differing interests, aims, and priorities. With each of these entities tending to function in a highly centralized fashion—making policy at headquarters and implementing it through regional- and country-level offices—coordination between two or more entities is comparatively rare; far more common is the simultaneous but uncoordinated pursuit by several governments and organizations of differing policies in a particular area. When it comes to conflict prevention, this fragmentation of local effort denies to third parties opportunities to keep local disputes from escalating to the point that they eventually demand the higher-level attention of those same third parties. More damagingly, it may exacerbate local problems (either by sending conflicting signals to the disputants that encourage them to pursue partisan causes through force, or by the pursuit of discordant or uncoordinated preventive strategies), raising the level of conflict and the level of resources needed to prevent its escalation. Although divergent agendas are not completely unavoidable, the growing interest in conflict avoidance among a large number of like-minded powers and multilateral organizations at their top levels suggests they may be receptive to considering the mutual benefits of much greater coordination of activities and policies at regional and country levels.

A more economical approach to preventive diplomacy would have several entities look for opportunities to pool resources and pursue joint local strategies directed toward early action against incipient conflicts. When faced with a potential conflict at, say, the local level, the relevant local-level personnel and agencies of the United Nations, United States, other major states, RMOs, and NGOs should—in conjunction with cooperative local actors and with the encouragement of a prime mover equipped with the necessary resources and stature—create informal multilateral task forces or contact groups. Prominent, widely respected local or regional figures—retired diplomats or heads of state, for instance—might be recruited to head such efforts. These bodies should inventory available local resources; determine how best to fashion a comprehensive, coherent local preventive strategy; and allocate tasks and responsibilities according to the strengths of the participants.

Of course, not all states and organizations represented in the vicinity will be willing to participate; indeed, the participation of some may not be desirable. But the opportunities for attracting seemingly indifferent entities or even coopting seemingly hostile ones should not be dismissed out of hand. Because much less military and political clout is needed for interventions at low than at high levels of conflict, conflict prevention offers one of the easiest ways to initiate multilateral burden sharing and international cooperation

An essential corollary to the idea of local collaboration is the principle of *benign intervention*, whereby third parties, even if not actively involved in preventive efforts, at least refrain from political, diplomatic, or military actions that encourage one or both combatants to intensify their hostilities or that support one side militarily against the other. The aim of third-party intervention (save for collective peace enforcement actions) should be to present a united front of nonviolent engagement aimed both at isolating and de-escalating the conflict.

As the example of Macedonia suggests, agreement among neighboring countries and major powers to refrain from partisan intervention may help to delegitimize outside partisan involvement. And even in the former Yugoslavia as a whole, the fact that no major power or neighboring country has intervened, at least militarily, on the side of one or another local party has served to prevent the bloody dispute spilling over into neighboring countries. Of course, some countries, including long-established democracies, will persist in pursuing foreign policies in vulnerable regions that contribute to the sources of violent conflicts, thus making those countries part of the problem rather than part of the solution. Looking for ways to collaborate in prevention, however, may help to isolate the effects of such troublemaking.

Once a multilateral task force has been established, it should design a "preventive package" of negative, positive, and facilitative techniques tailored to the various facets and peculiar conditions of the conflict situation. Proceeding from the ground up (rather than from the top down, as unfortunately is typically the case with interventions in the prevailing bureaucratic culture), the designers of a preventive strategy should begin by assessing the prevention requirements of the local arena, and then, on the basis of that assessment, consult on the role each third party is best suited to play. Action should no longer be based exclusively on the existing decision-making processes of the third parties' respective central headquarters and their particular policy tools.

As discussed in chapter 4, these strategies should then be applied in measured ways appropriate for the intensity of a conflict and/or capacity of local institutions and societal capacities for change and transition toward the norms and standards of the international community. Rather than pressing for specific substantive outcomes or solutions for disputes, third parties should focus on furthering specific informal or formal political processes and procedures for resolving disputes peacefully among the parties.

Graduated Response. As chapter 4 suggested and table 4.1 elaborated, the most effective preventive strategies would involve a *sequence of preventive responses and tools*, ready at hand and in place, but introduced on a contingent basis, depending on the level of intensity of a conflict. Such strategies might ordinarily start at each level with informal, noncoercive, conciliatory, and discretionary tools and move to more overt, coercive, legalistic, and inflexible approaches only if necessary. For example, at the local level, informal, nonthreatening,

quiet diplomacy conducted by NGOs (albeit backed by interested outside parties) might be most effective initially and should be used
before official bodies or states seek to exert direct and visible influence on the disputants. Similarly, low-key involvement by representatives of RMOs should precede action by the political councils of
those bodies. By the same token, at the global level, the quiet efforts
of eminent world statesmen should ordinarily precede the efforts of
the United Nations. But if the United Nations were to become involved, quiet diplomacy by the secretary-general should ordinarily
precede Security Council action.

But to exert the strongest conflict-suppressive and deterrent effects,
all the pertinent actors should be in place at the outset and able to be
deployed if and when needed in this graduated response system. This
is not to say, then, that the level of involvement of different actors
would necessarily be high throughout the prevention initiative; as has
been noted, each actor would be more or less involved depending on
the appropriateness of its tools and capabilities to the various stages
through which a dispute becomes a conflict. Even so, the load borne
by each level and actor would be lightened by the existence of other
levels and actors. Furthermore, potential participants would be more
likely to commit themselves if they could be convinced that their involvement would be required only if other parts of the preventive
system fail.

Public-Private Partnership. At each level of response, the cast of preventive actors should include not just official entities but also NGOs
active in the fields of track-two diplomacy, conflict resolution training, and democracy building. As noted above, by virtue of their private auspices, nonthreatening presence, transnational contacts, and
peace-serving rationale, NGOs enjoy a legitimacy and a degree of access to the disputants in a low-level conflict that is often denied to
powerful states with coercive military power and their own security
agendas. These advantages are especially apparent in the field of
track-two diplomacy. As suggested by a term sometimes used in place
of track-two diplomacy—*prenegotiations*—the kind of informal, unofficial dialogue that NGOs typically arrange is, or should be, often the
first form of engaged consultations among the parties to a dispute.

The behind-the-scenes, nonbinding environment of track-two diplomacy discourages public posturing and encourages flexibility, thereby opening the way for subsequent official negotiations. Track-two diplomacy, it should be noted, is not the exclusive preserve of NGOs; a version of it is also undertaken by diplomats from states and multilateral organizations who provide "good offices." Thus, as Giandomenico Pico has argued, the secretary-general might play an effective role as an independent mediator, if he is not directly in charge of, and thus associated with, peace enforcement actions of the Security Council.[6]

Just as official diplomacy can vary in terms of its visibility and the amount of leverage applied, so too can nongovernmental diplomacy. Whereas some efforts involve the grass-roots projects of particular organizations, such as Search for Common Ground or the Carter Center, other attempts at nongovernmental track-two diplomacy can involve the offering of good offices by eminent individuals, such as former president Jimmy Carter himself. In the cases of North Korea and Haiti, Carter was able to present himself to stubborn disputants as a "good cop" who could offer a better alternative than the "bad cop" represented by the U.S. government or other heavyweights in the international community and the coercive forces they might apply.

NGOs can be used more extensively (and cost-effectively) not only for track-two diplomacy but also for a wide range of other valuable tasks, ranging from provision of early warning information and interpretation through preconflict peace building (for example, assisting in the writing of constitutions and the development of civil institutions) to the implementation of agreements (for instance, election monitoring).

Incorporating NGOs into the overall preventive system thus requires greater lateral coordination and closer, albeit informal, ties at each level between governments and multilateral organizations, on the one hand, and NGOs, on the other. Although NGOs are already becoming more important agents in preventive diplomacy, both independently and in cooperation with governments and multilateral organizations, so far they are typically involved only on an occasional basis. NGO participation must become a matter of deliberate multilateral policy—and thus, perhaps, a reason for greater government funding of NGOs.

The barriers to such public-private collaboration that existed during the Cold War, when governments and NGOs were frequently at odds over one another's policies and activities, have largely been removed by the end of the Cold War—although differences in their respective mandates still exist. By significantly increasing the present, limited degree of consultation and dialogue between governmental agencies (such as the U.S. State Department) and NGOs at both central and local levels, broad and coherent strategies could be developed to address incipient local and regional disputes. The creation of a more deliberate partnership between, say, U.S. NGOs and the U.S. State and Defense Departments in the field of preventive diplomacy might allow those NGOs to draw on the stature of the United States while also maintaining their independence. The extensive experience in the United States with public-private partnerships and the use of the nonprofit sector in economic development and the provision of social services suggests that issues of control of funds, recipient autonomy, and avoidance of undue governmental or political influence are not insurmountable. If the government-run U.S. Peace Corps was generally seen as maintaining this independence at the height of the Cold War, it certainly seems possible for NGOs to do so after the Cold War.

TOWARD A PREVENTIVE "CONCERT" OF POWERS

Incentives for Action

The remaining essential issue to consider is how the various pieces of such a regime would be put in place. It is hard to envisage the multiple participation of different actors and the fine-tuned application of different tools being operationalized rapidly. One key to its initiation would be the promotion and support of such a regime by the United States and other major powers using the forum of the UN Security Council and other multilateral institutions. But many commentators, especially from within the realist school of thought, question whether a preventive regime has much to offer to the major powers in return for their support of it. In fact, such a regime has several advantages for the leading states of the international community.

First, major states have more at stake, politically and economically, in global and regime stability than do smaller powers. Second, major states have no desire to be constantly plagued with decisions as to whether to make costly interventions to salvage humanitarian disasters or thwart regional threats to security. Although no one state will be motivated to deal with each and every crisis and conflict, all major states share an interest in responding collectively to *several* such situations. This common interest can best be served by turning the job of preventive action over to others through agreed-upon procedures carried out by the United Nations and other multilateral organizations. In other words, by paying a relatively small premium to a preventive regime, major states can insure themselves against the risks of localized conflicts escalating out of control. Third, a major state is unlikely to watch with equanimity when other major powers (including allies) take leading roles in the handling of particular localized disputes while it remains on the sidelines. For example, if Great Britain, France, and Germany, acting through the European Union, are moving toward a policy of conflict prevention in the developing world, this increases the stakes for the United States to follow suit, so that its influence and status are not largely downgraded. A preventive regime allows all major states to conduct themselves according to agreed-upon a priori rules.

The U.S. Role: Support and Leadership

Given that effective preventive diplomacy depends on support from major or medium-sized states and that interest within the U.S. government in preventive action is rising, it is somewhat surprising that the question of what role the United States might play in any preventive regime has so far escaped serious consideration.

If the idea of a multilateral, stratified regime of preventive diplomacy is to become a reality, it must be championed by an actor or actors of global stature, able both to advocate the adoption of such a plan and to actively support it at the local, regional, and global levels. For several reasons, the United States is not necessarily the only, but clearly one of the best candidates to undertake this role. In the first place, the United States has the world's most extensive foreign policy bureaucracy and information-gathering apparatus, thus affording it unparalleled opportunities to become involved in or supportive of preventive diplomacy at each of the vertical levels described above.

Second, the United States is the only country that is effectively a "member" of all regions—in some cases by virtue of formal membership (in NATO, OSCE, OAS, APEC, NAFTA, and so forth), in others by dint of joint interests (OAU, ASEAN, the Middle East multilateral peace process). Third, while it is true that few international issues can be resolved by the United States alone, it also is true that many international issues cannot be resolved without U.S. leadership. Thus, while the United States should welcome, encourage, and seek to enhance the international roles of other states and entities, both bilaterally and through the United Nations and other multilateral bodies, it remains the one actor on the world stage that can marshal the political will to provide leadership and resources on the widest range of issues.

When it chooses to play this role, it is the hub around which many key international institutions and relationships revolve at each level in the prevention hierarchy. Although U.S. leadership regarding the Bosnian conflict was not forceful until military conditions on the ground changed in August 1995, at that point the United States did help to galvanize international action and sponsored the best hope so far of ending the conflict. Other recent events indicate yet more clearly what the United States can accomplish when it chooses to take a lead. Whether it has been spearheading the West's support for Russian reform, charting the course for the transformation of NATO, launching the vision of an Asian Pacific Economic Community, seeking peace in the Middle East, responding to the North Korean nuclear threat, or breaking deadlock in the GATT Uruguay Round—the United States in each case has provided leadership to galvanize the international community.

Following up on its earlier support for the reassessment of options for international cooperation represented by *Agenda for Peace*, the United States thus could take the initiative by proposing the creation of a conflict preventive regime along the lines spelled out here. The United Nations would clearly be an appropriate place to launch such an effort, for the world body would play a prominent role in that regime. Before taking such a step, the United States should first seek to gain support for the initiative from the other major powers—Great Britain, France, Germany, Japan, and Russia, if not China—all of which have expressed through their presidents, foreign ministers, or UN representatives support for preventive diplomacy. U.S. leadership could be exercised not only by legitimizing the concept of early intervention as a sound strategic idea, but also by furnishing resources to multilateral organizations and NGOs on the front lines of prevention; supplying diplomatic muscle, sponsorship, and energy behind particular preventive diplomacy efforts; and providing experienced individual diplomats to mediate incipient disputes under multilateral auspices.

The attention and resources of the United States are not unlimited, of course; but rather than dampening enthusiasm for a broad multilateral regime, that fact should serve only to underscore the need and the opportunity for the United States to download current and future responsibilities onto other capable actors.

If the United States is to energize activity at local and regional levels, however, its traditional style of foreign policy decision making has to change. Whether literally true or not, the statement that the U.S. State Department's eighth floor (where the top officials have their offices) is unable to handle more than three world problems at a time illustrates a feature of U.S. foreign policymaking that emerged out of the need to deal with Cold War global confrontation and regional military crises: highly centralized bureaucracies in which security policy decisions are made and priorities established mainly at the top. This feature is perhaps most evident in the case of the Defense Department and its separate branches, but it also characterizes the "high politics" of international diplomacy in which the State Department engages, and the intelligence-gathering and decision-making processes conducted by the intelligence community and the National Security Council (NSC).

Many of the challenges confronting preventive diplomacy—linking early warnings to levels of response, reducing bureaucratic overload, prioritizing values, and generating political will—could be diminished or circumvented if the U.S. government were to reorient its thinking and operations and fully accept that high-level decision makers need not be directly involved in most preventive initiatives. Although top-level personnel would need to encourage such initiatives, the responsibility for their conduct could be decentralized, with lower bureaucratic levels both undertaking early warning tasks and overseeing preventive responses in local and regional arenas and enlisting the cooperation of NGOs to do so, as described above. Thus, within its own hierarchy, the U.S. State Department needs to move to a new type of diplomacy that would train and empower local and middle-level officials (such as ambassadors, country directors, desk officers, and deputy and assistant secretaries) to undertake preventive diplomacy tasks. The role of ambassadors should be reshaped so that they are seen as serving on the front lines of U.S. foreign policy, tackling problems as they emerge rather than waiting for them to escalate and then asking for direction from Washington as to how to respond. The increased availability of instant communications brings with it the opportunity for drawing on worldwide technical and political expertise, but need not bring in its train more centralized control.

As we saw in the case of Congo, for example, American emissaries have already used the latitude currently allowed them to engage incipient problems with considerable success. This latitude could be further widened by changing bureaucratic procedures, offering merit awards, unburdening embassy staff of the reporting and administration that no longer is essential, and altering the existing high-level crisis orientation to allow the most creative and enterprising ambassadors and country directors to pursue preventive solutions to local problems. At the same time, local field offices of U.S. aid and information agencies could be encouraged to work with one another more closely and with NGOs and other states, as well as regional organizations, pooling their resources and coordinating programs as they engage host governments and indigenous civic organizations in the prevention of local conflicts. Indeed, at each of the levels—from the country and regional level up to the headquarters and NSC level— procedures are needed that can coordinate the application of the various diplomatic, economic, military, and financial instruments required to stem an escalating conflict.

The highest levels of the U.S. State and Defense Departments and the White House could then concentrate their limited time and attention on major potential conflicts and crises that pose direct threats to international security at the global level and those escalating disputes that local and regional organizations and the United Nations have been unable to handle, working wherever possible with and through the United Nations and coalitions of states. Direct attacks on the United States, interstate aggression, regional nuclear threats and arms buildups, and other dangers to the credibility of U.S. alliances and international arms control and security regimes: these would be the areas for top-level concern.

The design sketched here for a multilateral preventive regime that seeks to link the respective virtues of various international actors in more formal and deliberate preventive strategies is not a detailed blueprint, but it does highlight what the basic elements of the operating strategy of such a regime might be:

- proactive monitoring of and early response to previolent or low levels of conflict;
- preventive action to ensure interstate and internal political disputes are settled without the use of force;
- a ground-up policy perspective that focuses resources and attention on the needs of especially troubled areas;
- assertion of the normative primacy of the peaceful transformation of societies and governments undergoing destabilizing change;
- local and subregional actors authorized and enabled to act as the first line of prevention;
- coherent local conflict strategies;
- a graduated sequence of contingent responses based on the intensity level of conflicts and the power of the antagonists;
- when necessary, higher-level, more coercive responses by major powers and other global actors;
- multilateral cooperation and coordination at all levels led by prime movers such as major powers;
- public-private partnership between official bodies and NGOs; and
- U.S. leadership in promoting a coordinated system within the fora of the United Nations and regional bodies.

Woven together, these features would form the fabric of a regime able to respond proactively to post–Cold War threats and to make the most cost-effective use of the limited resources available to governments, multilateral organizations, and NGOs.

A WINDOW OF OPPORTUNITY

Other designs, more detailed than the one sketched above, might ultimately prove more feasible and effective; the chief purpose of setting out here one possible architecture for a multilateral preventive regime is to stimulate further debate on how best to proceed. It is interesting to note, however, that events and constraints are already driving current programs and projects of the U.S. government and the other entities toward an approach that is consistent with the ideas outlined above. The financial aid the U.S. government has given to the OAU to strengthen its conflict prevention and management mechanisms; the several local tools used by the OSCE in conflict prevention; the role played by the U.S. ambassador in Estonia in helping to reduce Russian-Estonian tensions; and the Burundi Open Forum, whereby several agencies of the U.S. government consult regularly with one another, with a range of multilateral and nongovernmental organizations, and with the UN secretary-general's special representative in Burundi: these are but four examples of recent initiatives that reflect parts and principles of the ground-up, decentralized, multilateral regime proposed here.

In any case, in view of both the threats and constraints confronting the global system of nations today, an intensified, systematic, and relatively low-cost effort to create a collective, strategic approach to multilateral prevention seems more sensible than the alternatives. The current occasional ad hoc preventive initiatives invite duplication of effort, turf battles, value confusion, and exhaustion. A laissez-faire approach to emerging problems—refusing to act until those problems reach crisis proportions—may seem attractive in the short term but is sure to prove extremely costly, and not only to the parties engaged in escalating disputes but also to all states with an interest in a more stable, peaceful, and democratic world. Ironically, perhaps, a workable preventive regime would achieve the same goal—the avoidance of costly interventions—pursued by many U.S. politicians who support the reduction of funding for U.S. international programs.

Despite the growing tendency within the United States to embrace isolationism or unilateralism, the decline in international cooperation as Russia and even U.S. allies begin to reassert themselves, and the deepening skepticism about the viability of multilateral action that is being fueled by growing frustration at the past results of peacekeeping in Bosnia, there still exists a window of opportunity for the United States and other governments and organizations to create collaborative, low-cost, low-risk procedures and mechanisms with the real potential to reduce the number of major regional and global crises that will emerge in the next five to ten years. Instructed by the lessons of past preventive efforts and inspired by hopes of a future more consistent with the norms of peaceful and democratic societies, perhaps far-sighted leaders of the post–Cold War era will see that their nations' interests would be well served by a multilateral regime that makes the best use of today's limited resources.

APPENDIX A

●

A PREVENTIVE DIPLOMACY TOOLBOX

POLICIES AND INSTRUMENTS FOR PREVENTING VIOLENT CONFLICTS

I. MILITARY APPROACHES

A. Restraints on the Use of Armed Force

Arms control regimes (including their monitoring)
Confidence-building measures
Nonaggression agreements
Preemptive peacekeeping forces (for deterrence and containment)
Demilitarized zones, "safe havens," peace zones
Arms embargoes, blockades
Nonoffensive defense force postures
Military-to-military programs

B. Threat or Use of Armed Force

Deterrence policies
Security guarantees
Maintaining or restoring local or regional "balances of power"
Use or threat of limited shows of force

This taxonomy draws in part on ideas from the following sources: George Kennan, "Measures Short of War," in Giles D. Harlow and George C. Maerz, eds., *Measures Short of War* (Washington, D.C.: National Defense University Press, 1991); Boutros Boutros-Ghali, *Agenda for Peace* (New York: United Nations, 1992); Ruth Lapidoth, "Diplomatic versus Adjudicatory Means for Settling Disputes" (paper presented to National War College delegation, United States Institute of Peace, Washington, D.C., spring 1991); Harold H. Saunders, "International Relationships: It's Time to Go Beyond 'We' and 'They,'" *Negotiation Journal* 3, no. 3 (July 1987): 245–277; William Dixon, "Democracy and the Management of International Conflict," *Journal of Conflict Resolution* 37, no. 1 (March 1993): 47–49; Barbara Harff, "Bosnia and Somalia: Strategic, Legal and Moral Dimensions of Humanitarian Intervention," *Philosophy and Public Policy* 12, no. 3/4 (summer/fall 1992): 1–7; Morton Halperin, *Self-Determination and the New World Order* (Washington, D.C.: Carnegie Endowment for Peace, 1992), chap. 6.

II. NONMILITARY APPROACHES

A. Coercive Diplomatic Measures (without the use of armed force)

Diplomatic sanctions (withholding of diplomatic relations, recognition as state, or membership in multilateral organizations)
Economic sanctions
Moral sanctions (condemnations of violations of international law)
War crimes tribunals, trials

B. Noncoercive Diplomatic Measures (without armed force or coercion)

Nonjudicial

International appeals (moral suasion to conflicting parties to urge accommodation)
Propaganda (directed at violators of international principles)
Fact-finding missions, observation teams, on-site monitoring (of human rights abuses, instances of violence)
Bilateral negotiations (between opposed parties)
Third-party informal diplomatic consultations (by official entities)
Track-two diplomacy (by nonofficial, nongovernmental parties)
Conciliation
Third-party mediation
Commissions of inquiry or other international inquiries
Conciliatory gestures, concessions (unilateral or reciprocal, "tit-for-tat" gestures by the opposed parties, "GRIT")
Nonviolent strategies (by oppressed groups)
Economic assistance or political incentives (to induce parties' cooperation)

Judicial or quasi judicial

Mechanisms for peaceful settlement of disputes
Arbitration (binding decision by permanent tribunal)
Adjudication

III. DEVELOPMENT AND GOVERNANCE APPROACHES

A. Policies to Promote National Economic and Social Development

Preventive economic development aid (in conflict-prone states or areas)
Preventive private investment (in conflict-prone states or areas)
Economic trade (with conflict-prone states or areas)
Economic integration (to achieve interdependency)
Economic reforms and standards
Society-to-society, bilateral cooperative programs (in social, cultural, educational, scientific, technological, or humanitarian affairs)

B. Promulgation and Enforcement of Human Rights, Democratic, and Other Standards

Political conditionality (attached to economic aid)
International human rights standard setting
Human rights suits
Election monitoring
Military-to-military consultations (regarding military professionalism and role of military in society)

C. National Governing Structures to Promote Peaceful Conflict Resolution

Power sharing
Consociation
Federalism
Federation
Confederation
Autonomy
Partition
Secession
Trusteeships, protectorates (internationally sponsored)

APPENDIX B

●

BIBLIOGRAPHICAL ESSAY

Although no distinct and recognized literature exists on conflict prevention, a wide variety of extant sources are pertinent to the subject. To address the descriptive and analytical issues raised in this book, use was made of a large number of books and articles scattered about separate literatures—among them international relations, conflict resolution, conflict studies, multilateral organizations, ethnic conflict, and U.S. foreign policy. In addition, all chapters drew on information provided by memoranda and other unpublished sources, as well as conversations with key individuals.

In the interest of encouraging further study of this subject and fostering the sense of a distinct corpus, the most helpful sources are listed below. Their inclusion here does not implicate their authors in any errors of interpretation or fact that this book might contain. Readers should also refer to the notes.

1: BETWEEN IDEA AND POLICY

The following sources were especially helpful in understanding the historical background of preventive diplomacy, the current state of the art, and the varieties of post–Cold War conflicts.

Bellows, Michael, ed. *Asia in the Twenty-first Century: Evolving Strategic Priorities*. Washington, D.C.: National Defense University Press, 1994.

Blainey, Geoffrey. *The Causes of War*. New York: Free Press, 1973.

Bloomfield, Lincoln P. "The Premature Burial of Global Law and Order: Looking beyond the Three Cases from Hell." *Washington Quarterly* 17 (1994): 145–161.

Boudreau, Thomas. *Sheathing the Sword: The UN Secretary General and the Prevention of International Conflict*. New York: Greenwood Press, 1991.

Boutros-Ghali, Boutros. *Agenda for Peace: Preventive Diplomacy, Peacemaking, and Peace-Keeping*. A report of the secretary-general pursuant to the statement adopted by the summit meeting of the Security Council on January 31, 1992. New York: United Nations, June 17, 1992.

――. *Supplement to an Agenda for Peace: Position Paper of the Secretary-General on the Occasion of the Fiftieth Anniversary of the United Nations*. Report of the Secretary-General on the Work of the Organization. New York: United Nations, January 3, 1995.

Claude, Inis L., Jr. *Swords into Plowshares: The Problems and Progress of International Organizations*. 4th ed. New York: Random House, 1984.

Craig, Gordon, and Alexander George. *Force and Statecraft: Diplomatic Problems of Our Time*. 2d ed. Oxford: Oxford University Press, 1990.

Findlay, Trevor. "Multilateral Conflict Prevention, Management, and Resolution." In *SIPRI Yearbook*, 1994. Oxford: Oxford University Press, 1994.

Gurr, Ted Robert. *Minorities at Risk: A Global View of Ethnopolitical Conflicts*. Washington, D.C.: United States Institute of Peace Press, 1993.

Jervis, Robert. "The Future of World Politics: Will It Resemble the Past?" *International Security* 16, no. 3 (winter 1991–92).

Kanninen, Tapio. *The Future of Early Warning and Preventive Action in the United Nations*. Occasional Paper Series no. 5, Ralph Bunche Institute on the United Nations, May 1991.

Kanter, Arnold, and Linton Brooks, eds. *U.S. Intervention Policy for the Post–Cold War World: New Challenges and New Responses*. New York: W. W. Norton, 1994.

Kennedy, Robert. "Warning for National Response in the Twenty-first Century." Strategic Outreach Conference Report, Center for International Strategy, Technology, and Policy, Georgia Institute of Technology, Atlanta, August 18–19, 1993.

Kriesberg, Louis. "Preventive Conflict Resolution of Inter-Communal Conflicts." PARC Working Paper no. 29, Syracuse University, September 1993.

Larus, Joel. *From Collective Security to Preventive Diplomacy: Readings in International Organization and the Maintenance of Peace*. New York: John Wiley and Sons, 1965.

Mack, Andrew, and Pauline Kerr. "Getting It Right in the Asia-Pacific." *Washington Quarterly* 18 (winter 1995): 123–140.

Rostow, Eugene. *A Breakfast for Bonaparte: U.S. National Security Interests from the Heights of Abraham to the Nuclear Age*. Washington, D.C.: National Defense University Press, 1992.

Yankelovich, Daniel, and I. M. Destler, eds. *Beyond the Beltway: Engaging the Public in U.S. Foreign Policy*. New York: W. W. Norton, 1994.

2: CONCEPT, TOOLS, AND TARGETS

On the concepts and range of methods entailed by preventive diplomacy, the following sources were particularly illuminating.

Boutros-Ghali, Boutros. *Agenda for Peace: Preventive Diplomacy, Peacemaking, and Peace Keeping*. A report of the secretary-general pursuant to the statement adopted by the summit meeting of the Security Council on January 31, 1992. New York: United Nations, June 17, 1992.

Leatherman, Janie, and Raimo Vayrinen. "Structure, Culture, and Territory: Three Sets of Early Warning Indicators." Paper prepared for the thirty-sixth annual convention of the International Studies Association, Chicago, 1995.

United Nations. *Handbook on the Peaceful Settlement of Disputes between States*. New York: United Nations, 1992.

3: LESSONS FROM EXPERIENCE

For conflict resolution empirical theory, hypotheses about the ingredients of successful instances of preventive diplomacy, and information on recent cases, the following sources were consulted. Each case study also drew on standard sources that regularly chronicle events in various regions, such as the Radio Free Europe and Radio Liberty (RFE/RL) *Research Reports* and *Bulletin* and *Africa Confidential*.

Adelman, Howard, and Astri Suhrke. "Early Warning and Conflict Management: Genocide in Rwanda." Study 2 of the Evaluation of Emergency Assistance to Rwanda, Chr. Michelson Institute, Bergen, Norway, 1995.

Bercovitch, Jacob, and Jeffrey Langley. "The Nature of Dispute and the Effectiveness of International Mediation." *Journal of Conflict Resolution* 37, no. 4 (1993): 670–691.

Bloomfield, Lincoln, and Amelia C. Leiss. *Controlling Small Wars: A Strategy for the 1970s*. New York: Alfred A. Knopf, 1969.

Bookman, Milica Z. "War and Peace: The Divergent Breakups of Yugoslavia and Czechoslovakia." *Journal of Peace Research* 31, no. 2 (1994).

Carment, David B. "The International Dimension of Internal Conflict: Early Warning Systems, Third-Party Intervention, and the Spread and Management of Ethnic Conflict." Norman Paterson School of International Affairs, Carleton University, Ottawa, Ontario, 1995.

———. "The Ethnic Dimension in World Politics: Policy and Early Warning." *Third World Quarterly* 15, no. 4 (1994).

Centro Studi di Politica Internazionale. *Lessons of the Western Response to the Crisis in the Former Yugoslavia.* Milan: Centro Studi di Politica Internazionale, May 1995.

Clark, John F. "Elections, Leadership, and Democracy in Congo." *Africa Today* (3d quarter, 1994): 41–60.

Drohobycky, Maria, ed. *Managing Ethnic Tension in the Post-Soviet Space: The Examples of Kazakhstan and Ukraine.* Washington, D.C.: American Association for the Advancement of Science, 1995.

Fauriol, Georges A., ed. *Haitian Frustrations: Dilemmas for U.S. Policy.* Washington, D.C.: Center for Strategic and International Studies, 1995.

Fisher, Ronald, and Loraleigh Keashly. "The Potential Complementarity of Mediation and Consultation within a Contingency Model of Third-Party Intervention." *Journal of Peace Research* 28, no. 1 (1991): 29–42.

Gagnon, V. P. "Ethnic Nationalism and International Conflict: The Case of Serbia." *International Security* 19, no. 3 (winter 1994–95): 130–166.

Goodby, James. "The Logic of Peace: Priorities for Preventive Diplomacy in U.S.-European Relations." United States Institute of Peace, Washington, D.C., 1995.

Kolstø, Pål, Andrei Edemsky, and Natalya Kalashnikova. "The Dniestr Conflict: Between Irredentism and Separatism." *Europe-Asia Studies* 45 (1993): 973–1000.

Leatherman, Janie. "Primary and Secondary Dynamics of Ethnic Conflict and the CSCE's Third Party Potentialities." Reprint Series 5:PR:9, Joan B. Kroc Institute for International Peace Studies, University of Notre Dame, Notre Dame, Ind., November 1993.

Lyons, Terrence, and Ahmed I. Samatar. *Somalia: State Collapse, Multilateral Intervention, and Strategies for Political Reconstruction.* Washington, D.C.: Brookings Institution, 1995.

Maresca, John. "The International Community and the Problem of Local Conflicts." United States Institute of Peace, Washington, D.C., 1996.

McCrea, Barbara. "The Politics of Nationalism in Croatia and Slovakia." Joan B. Kroc Institute for International Peace Studies, University of Notre Dame, Notre Dame, Ind., 1995

Miall, Hugh. *The Peacemakers: Peaceful Settlement of Disputes since 1945.* New York: St. Martin's Press, 1992.

Mitchell, Christopher. *The Structure of International Conflict.* New York: St. Martins Press, 1981.

Munuera, Gabriel. "Preventing Armed Conflict in Europe: Lessons from Recent Experience." Chaillot Paper no. 15/16, Institute for Security Studies, Western European Union, Paris, 1994.

Okolicsanyi, Karoly. "Slovak-Hungarian Tension: Bratislava Diverts the Danube." *RFE/RL Research Report* 1 (1992): 49–54.

Pruitt, Dean G., and Jeffrey Z. Rubin. *Social Conflict: Escalation, Stalemate, and Settlement*. New York: McGraw-Hill, 1986.

Rogers, Katrina S. "Rivers of Discontent, Rivers of Peace: Environmental Cooperation and Integration Theory." Policy Note, *International Studies Notes* 20 (1995): 10–21.

Rupesinghe, Kumar, and Michiko Kuroda. *Early Warning and Conflict Resolution*. New York: St. Martin's Press, 1993.

Sahnoun, Mohamed. *Somalia: The Missed Opportunities*. Washington, D.C.: United States Institute of Peace Press, 1994.

Shabad, Goldie, Sharon A. Shible, and John F. Zurovchak. "When Push Comes to Shove: Simultaneous Transformations and the Breakup of the Czechoslovak State." Paper presented at the 1993 annual meeting of the American Political Science Association, Washington, D.C., September 2–5, 1993.

Shorr, David. "The Citizenship and Alien Law Controversies in Estonia and Latvia." Strengthening Democratic Institutions Project, John F. Kennedy School of Government, Harvard University, April 1994.

Simic, Predrag. "Civil War in Former Yugoslavia: From Local Conflict to European Crisis." In *Southeastern European Yearbook, 1992*. Athens, Greece: ELIAMEP Institute, 1992.

Szayna, Thomas S. *Ethnic Conflict in Central Europe and the Balkans: A Framework and U.S. Policy Options*. Santa Monica, Calif.: RAND Corporation, 1994.

Van Evera, Stephen. "Hypotheses on Nationalism and War." *International Security* 18 (1994): 5–39.

Woodward, Susan L. *Balkan Tragedy: Chaos and Dissolution after the Cold War*. Washington, D.C.: Brookings Institution, 1994.

Zametica, John. *The Yugoslav Conflict*. Adelphi Paper no. 270. London: Brassey's, 1992.

Zartman, I. William. *Collapsed States: The Disintegration and Restoration of Legitimate Authority*. Boulder, Colo.: Lynne Rienner, 1995.

———. "The Strategy of Preventive Diplomacy in Third World Conflicts." In Alexander George, ed., *Managing U.S.-Soviet Rivalry: Problems of Crisis Prevention*. Boulder, Colo.: Westview, 1983.

Zimmermann, Warren. "The Last Ambassador: A Memoir of the Collapse of Yugoslavia." *Foreign Affairs* 74, no. 2 (March/April 1995): 2–20.

4: POLICYMAKING AND IMPLEMENTATION

The following sources were consulted with regard to the operational tasks and problems involved in undertaking early warning and preventive actions, and the bureaucratic and political environment affecting them.

Binnendijk, Hans, and Patrick Clawson. "New Strategic Priorities." *Washington Quarterly* 18 (spring 1995): 109–126.

Blacker, Coit. "A Typology of Post–Cold War Conflicts." In Arnold Kanter and Linton F. Brooks, eds., *U.S. Intervention Policy for the Post–Cold War World: New Challenges and Responses*. New York: W. W. Norton, 1994.

Blackwill, Robert. "A Taxonomy for Defining U.S. National Security Interests in the 1990s." In Werner Weidenseld and Josef Janning, eds., *Europe in Global Change*, 100–119. Gutersloh: Bertelsmann Foundation, 1993.

Bloomfield, Lincoln P. *The Foreign Policy Process: A Modern Primer*. Englewood Cliffs, N.J.: Prentice-Hall, 1982.

Conflict Management Group. "Early Warning and Preventive Action in the CSCE: Defining the Role of the High Commissioner on National Minorities." Report of the CSCE Devising Session, October 19, 1992, Harvard Negotiation Project, Harvard Law School.

Damrosch, Lori Fisler, ed. *Enforcing Restraint: Collective Intervention in Internal Conflicts*. New York: Council on Foreign Relations, 1993.

Fein, Helen. "Tools and Alarms: Uses of Models for Explanation and Anticipation." *Journal of Ethno-Political Development* 4 (July 1994): 31–35.

Harff, Barbara. "A Theoretical Model of Genocides and Politicides." *Journal of Ethno-Political Development* 4 (July 1994): 25–30.

Nye, Joseph S., Jr. "Peering into the Future." *Foreign Affairs* 73, no. 4 (July/August 1994): 82–93.

Shiels, Frederick L. *Preventable Disasters: Why Governments Fail*. Savage, Md.: Rowman and Littlefield, 1991.

5: ORGANIZING PREVENTIVE DIPLOMACY

On issues concerned with the organization of a more systematic and routine international policy of preventive diplomacy, the following were particularly useful.

Evans, Gareth. *Cooperating for Peace: The Global Agenda for the 1990s and Beyond*. New York: Allen and Unwin, 1993

Peck, Connie. "Improving the UN System of Preventive Diplomacy and Conflict Resolution: Past Experiences, Current Problems, and Future Perspectives." In Winrich Kuhne, ed., *Blauhelme in einer Turbulenten Welt*, 302–304. Baden-Baden: Nomos Berlagsgesellschaft, 1993.

NOTES

1. BETWEEN IDEA AND POLICY

1. United Nations Department of Public Information, *Charter of the United Nations and Statute of the International Court of Justice* (New York: United Nations, 1990), 1–3.

2. Dag Hammarskjöld, introduction to United Nations, *Annual Report of the Secretary-General on the Work of the Organization, 16 June 1959–15 June 1960*, United Nations General Assembly, 15th sess., supplement 1A; cited in Joel Larus, ed., *From Collective Security to Preventive Diplomacy: Readings in International Organization and the Maintenance of Peace* (New York: John Wiley and Sons, 1965), 405.

3. Instructions to the secretary-general, cited in Boutros Boutros-Ghali, *Agenda for Peace* (New York: United Nations, June 17, 1992), 1.

4. "Remarks of President Bush to the United Nations General Assembly, New York, September 21, 1992," 2. Transcript provided by United Nations Publications Office, Washington, D.C.

5. The White House, *National Security Strategy of the United States* (Washington, D.C.: The White House, January 1993).

6. U.S. Senate Committee on Foreign Relations, *Nomination of Warren Christopher to Be Secretary of State*, Hearing before the Committee on Foreign Relations, United States Senate, 103d Cong., 1st. sess., January 13 and 14, 1993, 21.

7. Remarks of Anthony Lake, U.S. National Security Advisor, to the Brookings Institution Africa Forum Luncheon, May 3, 1993.

8. See "Clinton Urges New Policy toward African Nations: Constituency Must Be Built, Conference Told," *Washington Post*, June 28, 1994. Clinton speech on Bosnia quoted in RFE/RL Research Institute, *Daily Report*, no. 229 (December 6, 1994), 4.

9. See, for example, Thomas Lippmann, "Finding Theme for Foreign Policy," *Washington Post*, June 30, 1994, A10.

10. The White House, *National Security Strategy of Engagement and Enlargement* (Washington, D.C.: The White House, July 1994), 5.

11. Conference on Security and Cooperation in Europe, *Charter of Paris for a New Europe*, Meeting of the Heads of States and Governments of the Participating States, Paris, November 19–21, 1990, 6.

12. OAU Assembly, *Declaration of the Assembly of Heads of State and Government on the Establishment within the OAU of a Mechanism for Conflict Prevention, Management, and Resolution*, 29th Ordinary Session, June 28–30, 1993, Cairo, Egypt. Document AHG/Decl.3 (XXIX) Rev. 1, 7.

13. Nicole Ball et al. "World Military Expenditure," in Stockholm International Peace Research Institute, *SIPRI Yearbook, 1994* (Oxford: Oxford University Press, 1994), 389.

14. Boutros-Ghali, *Agenda for Peace*, 1.

15. Peter Wallensteen and Karin Axell, "Conflict Resolution and the End of the Cold War," *Journal of Peace Research* 31, no. 3 (1994): 334. "Armed conflicts" here means the use of armed force by governments and other entities resulting in battle fatalities ranging from 25 to more than 1,000.

16. Mark T. Clark, "The Trouble with Collective Security," *Orbis* 39, no. 2 (spring 1995): 232–258.

17. Joseph Rudolph, Jr., "Intervention in Communal Conflicts," *Orbis* 39, no. 2 (spring 1995): 259–273.

18. See, for example, Jacob Bercovitch and Jeffrey Langley, "The Nature of Dispute and the Effectiveness of International Mediation," *Journal of Conflict Resolution* 37, no. 4 (December 1993): 670–691; and the sources cited by Stephen Ryan, "Grass-roots Peacebuilding in Violent Ethnic Conflicts," in *Peaceful Settlement of Conflict: A Task for Civil Society*, ed. Jörg Calliess and Christine M. Merkel (Rehburg-Loccum: Evangelische Akademie Loccum, July 1993), 314–342.

19. Warren Zimmerman, "The Last Ambassador: A Memoir of the Collapse of Yugoslavia," *Foreign Affairs* 74, no. 2 (March/April 1995): 2–20. Speech by General Major Roméo Dallaire, Commander of UNAMIR peacekeeping force in Rwanda, 1993–94 (n.d.; draft in author's files), 6, 15.

20. Figures from *UN Commodity Trade Statistics*, cited in Michael Cranna, ed., *The True Cost of Conflict: Seven Recent Wars and Their Effects on Society* (New York: New Press, 1994), 152.

21. Ibid., 149.

22. Estimate inferred from ibid., 103.

23. Trevor Findlay, "Multilateral Conflict Prevention, Management, and Resolution," in *SIPRI Yearbook, 1994*, 26.

24. Coit Blacker, "A Typology of Post–Cold War Conflicts," in *U.S. Intervention Policy for the Post–Cold War World: New Challenges and Responses*, ed. Arnold Kanter and Linton F. Brooks (New York: W. W. Norton, 1994), 59.

25. R. William Thomas, "Armament Budgets of the Major Western Nations after the Cold War," Congressional Budget Office paper (n.d.), 1–3.

2. CONCEPT, TOOLS, AND TARGETS

1. See, for example, Stephen John Stedman, "Alchemy for a New World Order: Overselling 'Preventive Diplomacy,'" *Foreign Affairs* 73, no. 3 (May/June 1995): 14–20.

2. Hammarskjöld, *Annual Report of the Secretary-General on the Work of the Organization, 16 June 1959–15 June 1960*, 2.

3. Boutros-Ghali, *Agenda for Peace*, 11–19.

4. Ibid., 11.

5. Agency for International Development Director J. Brian Atwood is quoted as saying, "A.I.D. is the state of the art of preventive diplomacy." Andrew Meier, "Yeltsin's Next Quagmire?" *New York Times*, January 2, 1995.

6. This theme is found in remarks on the *Agenda for Peace* to the General Assembly by several representatives: Mr. Hidalgo Basulto, Cuba, A/47/PV 31, 66–71; Mr. Khalid-Ur Rehman, Pakistan, 28–30; Mrs. Zafra Rurbay, Colombia, A/47/PV 37, 63; and Mrs. Aggrey-Orleans, Ghana, A/47/PV 37, 63; all in United Nations, *Provisional Verbatim Report of the Thirty-first Meeting of the General Assembly*, 47th sess., New York, October 9, 1992.

7. Connie Peck, "Improving the UN System of Preventive Diplomacy and Conflict Resolution: Past Experiences, Current Problems, and Future Perspectives," in *Blauhelme in einer Turbulenten Welt*, ed. Winrich Kuhne (Baden-Baden: Nomos Berlagsgesellschaft, 1993), 302–304.

8. Others may prefer the terms "conflict prevention" or "crisis prevention," so as to avoid use of the word "diplomacy." But because we have made clear the wide range of actions connoted here by that word, this book follows the Hammarskjöld–Boutros-Ghali tradition in terminology.

9. Most literature and policy discourse on foreign and security policy does not acknowledge the need for this conceptual middle ground of policies operating in the medium term between ongoing, routine foreign and defense policy, on the one hand, and short-term crisis management, on the other. In some official discussions of U.S. security posture, for example, no gradations exist between "peacetime" and "crisis." Military measures are seen as appropriate only once a crisis has been reached, and diplomacy (in the conventional sense) is viewed as a means of ending wars, not avoiding them.

One reason for this conceptual gap may be that international relations thinking is still influenced by conditions and concepts that prevailed during the Cold War, when the dominant concern was massive conventional or nuclear war between states, which could erupt relatively suddenly.

10. The notion that different types of actions are appropriate and possible toward conflicts, depending on the degree of hostilities that characterizes the conflict, is widely acknowledged in the literature on war and peace. The notion underlies the sequence of increasingly coercive measures laid out in Chapters VI and VII of the UN Charter, and is found in the idea of applying proportional force in just war theory. A more elaborate treatment is found in a lecture delivered at the National War College on September 16, 1946, by George F. Kennan, "Measures Short of War (Diplomatic)"; published in Giles D. Harlow and George C. Maerz, eds., *Measures Short of War: The George F. Kennan Lectures at the National War College, 1946–47* (Washington, D.C.: National Defense University Press, 1991), 3–17.

3. LESSONS FROM EXPERIENCE

1. Geoffrey Blainey, *The Causes of War*, 3d ed. (New York: Free Press, 1973), 3.

2. Donald Kagan's *On the Origins of War and the Preservation of Peace* (New York: Doubleday, 1995), 566–571, offers a few general reflections on the need to work actively to preserve peace, but does not advance specific policy recommendations. Robert I. Rothberg's and Theodore K. Rabb's edited volume, *The Origins and Prevention of Major Wars* (Cambridge: Cambridge University Press, 1989), deals only with large interstate wars. Susan Woodward's *Balkan Tragedy: Chaos and Dissolution after the Cold War* (Washington, D.C.: Brookings Institution, 1994) is an excellent, policy-sensitive, in-depth political analysis of the sources of the wars in Yugoslavia and the reasons for the failure to prevent them. Its implicit policy advice must be gleaned, however, from the mistakes it details. Illustrative of books on ethnic conflicts is the multifaceted collection of essays in Joseph V. Montville, ed., *Conflict and Peacemaking in Multiethnic Societies* (Lexington, Mass.: Lexington Books, 1990); and a highly respected analysis of dynamics and institutional solutions is Donald Horowitz, *Ethnic Groups in Conflict* (Berkeley, Calif.: University of California Press, 1985). Ted Robert Gurr's *Minorities at Risk: A Global View of Ethnopolitical Conflicts* (Washington, D.C.: United States Institute of Peace Press, 1993) is comprehensive of potential conflicts in many regions, stressing structural and institutional solutions, rather than process interventions. Recent developments in developing early warning models are presented in *Journal of Ethno-Political Development* 4, no. 1 (1994), a special issue edited by Ted Robert Gurr and Barbara Harff. The conflict resolution literature is rife with studies of mid-conflict mediations, such as Stephen Stedman's excellent *Peacemakers in Civil War: International Mediation in Zimbabwe, 1974–1980* (Boulder, Colo.: Lynne Rienner, 1990). A useful theoretical treatment of conflict escalation is found in Dean G. Pruitt and Jeffrey Z. Rubin, *Social Conflict: Escalation, Stalemate, and Settlement* (New York: McGraw-Hill, 1986). Other such sources are cited following table 3.1.

3. The largely quantitative studies referred to are Hugh Miall, *The Peacemakers: Peaceful Settlement of Disputes since 1945* (New York: St. Martin's Press, 1992); and Bercovitch and Langley, "The Nature of Dispute." Miall briefly chronicles and analyzes several cases. The process study is Gabriel Munuera's "Preventing Armed Conflict in Europe: Lessons from Recent

Experience," Chaillot Paper no. 15/16, Institute for Security Studies, Western European Union, 1994.

4. The case-study information is drawn from the sources given in the bibliographical essay in appendix B. The conclusions drawn from the cases regarding the most important explanatory factors are at this stage of research tentative and preliminary; for scholarly purposes they should be regarded as substantially grounded working hypotheses, not definitive conclusions.

5. For example, Miall, *Peacemakers*; and Larry Diamond and Marc Plattner, eds., *Nationalism, Democracy, and Ethnic Conflict* (Baltimore and London: Johns Hopkins University Press, 1994), xviii.

6. Katrina S. Rogers, "Rivers of Discontent, Rivers of Peace: Environmental Cooperation and Integration Theory," Policy Note, *International Studies Notes* 20 (1995): 10–21.

7. It might be argued that one reason relatively little empirical analysis has been undertaken so far on the efficacy of efforts to prevent conflicts is that social scientists and scholars working in related fields have long been most interested in the causes of conflict rather than its solution. Such neglect of the causes of peace may have led to a tacit determinism in which the conflicts that have occurred are assumed to have been virtually inevitable—even though not all societies characterized by, say, profound ethnic differences have exploded into ethnic violence.

An example of this blinkered mode of analysis is Thomas S. Szayna's *Ethnic Conflict in Central Europe and the Balkans: A Framework and U.S. Policy Options* (Santa Monica, Calif.: RAND Corporation, 1994). This study draws on theory and research about critical factors that can generate ethnic conflicts, specifically the extent to which ethnic groups who are minorities in one country have ethnic kin in a neighboring country who support their cause. On the basis of positing this as a key determinant of ethnic violence, the author identifies such countries as Estonia, Hungary, and Moldova as especially susceptible to conflict. But though the author examines recent developments in these countries, he fails to look closely at what may explain the fact that the Moldovan conflict escalated to armed force whereas the other two did not.

8. Specifically, the procedure was as follows. A number of political disputes that arose after the end of the Cold War were identified, each of which was judged by informed observers to have had the potential to escalate into the use of armed force or other coercion by one or more parties, or to reach a high level of confrontation and crisis. All the cases were subject to various degrees and kinds of international or indigenous efforts to keep the disputes from escalating into violence or coercion, but while some of the disputes grew into crises and wars, others did not. Based on a survey of plausible hypotheses advanced in past studies, this study then sought to identify salient factors that are associated with one or another outcome. Each case was then examined to see if these factors were present.

9. See Bercovitch and Langley, "Nature of Dispute," 241; Miall, *Peacemakers*, 186. The widely known thesis that a "mutual hurting stalemate" is necessary for ending a violent conflict—a thesis that arose as an argument with respect to advanced civil wars—has also been used to cast doubt on the efficacy of early, previolent preventive efforts.

10. Dallaire, speech, 5.

11. Remarks at a meeting of the United States Institute of Peace Preventive Diplomacy Study Group, December 20, 1993.

12. See Goldie Shabad, Sharon A. Shible, and John F. Zurovchak, "When Push Comes to Shove: Simultaneous Transformations and the Breakup of the Czechoslovak State" (paper presented at the annual meeting of the American Political Science Association, Washington, D.C., September 2–5, 1993); and Milica Z. Bookman, "War and Peace: The Divergent Breakups of Yugoslavia and Czechoslovakia," *Journal of Peace Research* 31, no. 2 (1994): 176.

13. See Maria Drohobycky, "Ukraine and Its Ethnic Minorities: An Overview," in *Managing Ethnic Tensions in the Post-Soviet Space: The Examples of Kazakhstan and Ukraine*, ed. Maria Drohobycky (Washington, D.C.: American Association for the Advancement of Science, 1993), 15–24.

4. POLICYMAKING AND IMPLEMENTATION

1. See Joseph Nye, "Peering into the Future," *Foreign Affairs* 73, no. 4 (July/August 1994), 85. It may be noted that no one else predicted the disappearance of the Soviet Union. Besides, other events were predicted correctly, such as the attempted coup against Mikhail Gorbachev and Iraq's invasion of Kuwait. Abraham Miller and Nicholas Damask, "Thinking about Intelligence after the Fall of Communism" (paper presented at the annual meeting of the International Social Studies Association, Washington, D.C., March 12–17, 1993), 2–5.

2. Nye, "Peering into the Future," 88.

3. Another factor that complicates the interpretation of information about troubled areas' potential for conflict is that the standards defining what kinds of problems are not to be tolerated have been raised. How this shift and other post–Cold War changes have led to overly pessimistic interpretations of the prospects for peace and stability is discussed by John Mueller in "The Catastrophic Quota: Trouble after the Cold War," *Journal of Conflict Resolution* 38, no. 3 (September 1994): 355–375.

4. Strategic Studies Institute, U.S. Army War College, "Warning for National Response in the Twenty-first Century," conference report, October 1993, 9.

5. Derived from Barbara Harff, "A Theoretical Model of Genocides and Politicides," and Albert Jongman, "The PIOOM Program on Monitoring and Early Warning of Humanitarian Crises," both in "Early Warnings of

Communal Conflicts and Humanitarian Crises," a special issue of the *Journal of Ethno-Political Development* 4, no. 1 (July 1994): 25–30, 70.

6. Strategic Studies Institute, "Warning for National Response," 3.

7. Two examples of long-term structural analyses of the prospects for stability and conflict around the world are Kenneth N. Waltz, "The Emerging Structure of International Politics," *International Security* 18, no. 2 (fall 1993): 44–79; and Earl H. Tilford, "World View: The 1995 Strategic Assessment from the Strategic Studies Institute," U.S. Army War College, Strategic Studies Institute, February 1995. Other examples are listed in the bibliographical essay at the end of this book. The point is not that these analyses are not done, but that they have not been linked institutionally to the actual process of policymaking, and thus do not inform that process.

8. A process described in Lincoln Bloomfield, "Anticipating the Future: Foreign Policy Planning," in *The Foreign Policy Process: A Modern Primer* (Englewood Cliffs, N.J.: Prentice-Hall, 1987), 167–192.

9. This logic is suggested by Robert Blackwill, "A Taxonomy for Defining U.S. National Security Interests in the 1990s," in *Europe in Global Change*, ed. Werner Weidenseld and Josef Janning (Gutersloh: Bertelsmann Foundation, 1993), 400–419.

10. See Blackwill, "Taxonomy," 402ff.

11. This list of interests and threats is synthesized from three sources: Blackwill, "Taxonomy"; Hans Binnendijk and Patrick Clawson, "New Strategic Priorities," *Washington Quarterly* (spring 1995): 109–126; and Blacker, "Typology of Post-Cold War Conflicts," 42–62.

12. U.S. General Accounting Office, "Promoting Democracy: Foreign Affairs and Defense Agencies Funds and Activities, 1991 to 1993" (January 1994); and U.S. Congressional Budget Office, "Enhancing U.S. Security through Foreign Aid" (April 1994).

13. The most explicit statement of the ideas of ripeness for resolution and mutual hurting stalemate is by I. William Zartman in *Ripe for Resolution: Conflict and Intervention in Africa* (New Haven, Conn.: Yale University Press, 1992). A revised version is presented by Stedman in *Peacemakers in Civil War*.

14. See Stephen Ryan's chapter in the two-volume manuscript edited by David Carment and Patrick James, "The International Politics of Ethnic Conflict" (1995).

15. See the sources listed after table 3.1.

16. See Conflict Management Group, "Early Warning and Preventive Action in the CSCE: Defining the Role of the High Commissioner on National Minorities," 4–5, report of the CSCE Devising Session, October 19, 1992, Harvard Negotiation Project, Harvard Law School.

17. Ibid., 5.

18. For example, see Janie Leatherman and Raimo Vayrinen, "Structure, Culture, and Territory: Three Sets of Early Warning Indicators" (paper prepared for the thirty-sixth annual convention of the International Studies Association, Chicago, 1995).

19. The notion that third parties should think of the functions to be performed and the services to provide is drawn from C. R. Mitchell, *The Structure of International Conflict* (London: Macmillan, 1981), 299–313. Whereas Mitchell applies the notion to the roles that mediators should play, here it is applied to any parties seeking to prevent conflicts through whatever means.

20. Only some of these tools are easily characterized in terms of whether they are coercive or noncoercive inducements. While some could thus be called "carrots" (e.g., economic aid) or "sticks" (e.g., sanctions), other possible options are better described as "facilitators" or "services" (e.g., track-two diplomacy, policy ideas, and technical assistance).

21. For one of the few examples of such an evaluation, see a critical 1993 impacts evaluation of military-sponsored "operations other than war" programs aimed at building schools and other social and physical infrastructures in developing countries; General Accounting Office, "Department of Defense: Changes Needed to the Humanitarian and Civic Assistance Program," GAO/NSIAD-94-57, November 2, 1993.

22. See, for example, Stedman, "Alchemy for a New World Order," 20.

23. See Cranna, *True Cost of Conflict.*

24. Letter by President Clinton to newly assigned chiefs of U.S. missions abroad, quoted in "Institutional Implications of Preventive Diplomacy" (remarks by Brandon Grove at a meeting of the United States Institute of Peace Preventive Diplomacy Study Group, Washington, D.C., January 11, 1994), 3.

5. ORGANIZING PREVENTIVE DIPLOMACY

1. Gareth Evans, *Cooperating for Peace: The Global Agenda for the 1990s and Beyond* (New York: Allen and Unwin, 1993), 70–76.

2. See Peck, "Improving the UN System," 311.

3. This has been pointed out by, among others, Saadia Touval, "Why the UN Fails," *Foreign Affairs* 74, no. 5 (September/October 1994): 44–57.

4. Hammarskjöld, *Annual Report of the Secretary-General on the Work of the Organization, 16 June 1959–15 June 1960*; cited in Larus, ed., *From Collective Security to Preventive Diplomacy*, 401–403.

5. See, for example, the comparisons among North America, South America, East Asia, West Africa, and other regions in Arie Kacowicz, "Explaining Zones of Peace: Democracies as Satisfied Powers?" *Journal of Peace Research* 32, no. 3 (1995): 265–276.

6. Giandomenico Pico, "Keep the Secretary General Out of It," *Foreign Affairs* 72, no. 5 (November–December 1993): 15–25.

Michael S. Lund is senior associate, Creative Associates International, Inc., in Washington, D.C., where he is conducting research on effective approaches to conflict prevention. At the United States Institute of Peace he served as senior scholar (1994–1995) and director of the Jennings Randolph fellowship program (1987–1993), his work focusing on political development, conflict resolution, and multilateral organizations in sub-Saharan Africa and Europe.

Previously, Lund undertook research on domestic policy and policymaking at the Urban Institute in Washington, D.C., where he co-edited and contributed to *The Reagan Administration and the Governing of America* (1984) and *Beyond Privatization: The Tools of Government Action* (1988). He has taught at Cornell, UCLA, and the University of Maryland; has consulted for the U.S. Department of Health and Human Services; and was a Peace Corps volunteer in Ethiopia. He has a Ph.D. in political science from the University of Chicago and a B.D. from Yale University Divinity School.

PREVENTING VIOLENT CONFLICTS

This book is set in Veljovic; the display type is Kabel. Hasten Design Studio, Inc., designed the book's cover, and Joan Engelhardt and Day W. Dosch designed the interior. Pages were made up by Day W. Dosch. The book's editor was Nigel Quinney.